A Pilgrim Looks
at 60

A PILGRIM LOOKS AT 60

Life in the Middle of the Christian Bell Curve

James Annable

ELM HILL

A Division of
HarperCollins Christian Publishing

www.elmhillbooks.com

A Pilgrim Looks at 60
Life in the Middle of the Christian Bell Curve

Published in Nashville, Tennessee, by Elm Hill, an imprint of Thomas Nelson. Elm Hill and Thomas Nelson are registered trademarks of HarperCollins Christian Publishing, Inc.

Elm Hill titles may be purchased in bulk for educational, business, fund-raising, or sales promotional use. For information, please e-mail SpecialMarkets@ ThomasNelson.com.

Library of Congress Cataloging-in-Publication Data

Library of Congress Control Number: 2019910451

ISBN 978-1-400326396 (Paperback)
ISBN 978-1-400326402 (Hardcover)
ISBN 978-1-400326419 (eBook)

DEDICATION

Having never written a book before,
it obviously follows that I have never dedicated one either.
So I will simply say that this is for my people: the average, the often-
times invisible, and the unremarkable—those who do the mundane,
necessary things of life and church—who live out their lives in the
shadows of the exceptional.
In this, Barnabas is our patron saint.
He accepted Paul when no one else would and patiently, faithfully
labored in the shadows of Paul's giftedness. He went on to do that
again with another young man:
the future gospel writer, Mark.
My own life has been impacted by many of these "Barnabases."
What little glimmers of light may be found in these pages and in my
life, these come from rubbing shoulders with God's footmen. Salt of
the earth.
Faithful laborers.

CONTENTS: TRAVEL ITINERARY

➢ **Introduction** ~ On Being Yourself ix

1. **In the Beginning** ~ An Unlooked for Intrusion 1

2. **Japan** ~ Love Your Enemies 19

3. **Nebraska** ~ Marriage, the Trinity, and Burning the Ships ... 31

4. **Camp Upshur** ~ Discipline and Grace 47

5. **Quantico** ~ From Boom-Boom to Bitcoin 61

6. **Pensacola** ~ Sudden Change 75

7. **Okinawa** ~ Risk and Reward 85

8. **Chicago** ~ Reciprocity and Forgiveness 99

9. **Inwood, West Virginia** ~ Prone to Waver 111

10. **Tristate Bluegrass Campground** ~ Meaning and
    Emotion 125

11. **George Washington Memorial Forest** ~ Doing the Man
    Dance 137

12. **Romania** ~ Two Beatings Hurt, Not Two Meals 149

13. **Ecuador** ~ Imago Dei 167

14. **Charlotte, North Carolina** ~ Vertigo 179

15. **Kenya** ~ Showing Up 193

16. **Montana** ~ Creation and into the Wild 209

17. **LA Transcon** ~ Identity   223

18. **Good Ship Pilgrimage** ~ Friendship and Boat Therapy   233

19. **Texas** ~ Kingdom Politics   245

20. **Flight Academy DFW** ~ Words, Meaning, and Truth   255

21. **Normandy, France** ~ Enemy at the Gates   265

22. **Transformation** ~ I Shall Be Myself   275

INTRODUCTION

"Be yourself . . . everyone else is taken."

—Oscar Wilde

We're all susceptible to losing ourselves in a good story—stories with characters who will inevitably invite us to view reality from a perspective far different than our own. Stories we can connect with. When they're based on a *true* story, so much the better. Such narratives are an open invitation to dive head first into new experiences that may take us far beyond the boundaries and limitations of our own understanding and expectations. These transformational stories are the ones worth leaning into. They wield the power to transport us from the realm of ideas—from the abstract and propositional—toward a personal, but more universally relevant world of meaning we might never experience on our own.

Unfortunately, like me, the vast majority of us simply don't see our own life stories as very remarkable—and certainly not exceptional. After all, most of us consider ourselves unexceptionally average on the "bell curve" of life (a bell curve being a normal distribution resembling a bell, with the biggest portion in the middle representing what's *average*). And being *average* is something every red-blooded male spends his whole life trying not to be, then wakes up one morning discovering he's middle-aged and sore after raking the yard. So we think to ourselves, *Who wants to hear about someone whose life and story looks like our own?* Even the children of Lake Wobegon are at least "above average."

But despite being average, I began this somewhat reflective pilgrimage back into my history as a way to explain to my five children who I am and what in the world I might have been thinking at different, important points along my life journey, and in that process, discovered something (perhaps) more universal in that journey worth sharing with you as well.

Looking back, I can see my children had the benefit of growing up in a multifaceted Christian culture quite different from my own. I was raised in a time and place where the secular, worldly culture around me was central to everything I understood about how life worked. Although there were a few moral "dos" and "don'ts" sprinkled into the mix of my growing up years, religion was definitely out there somewhere on the periphery. Any religion. Maybe that part of my pilgrimage reflects a bit of your own.

Such common ground marks all of our life stories.

While reading Jimmy Buffet's memoir, *A Pirate Looks at Fifty*, for instance, I was surprised to find out how many experiences we share in common. Like Buffet, I was approaching my fiftieth birthday, and I was interested to read that he was commemorating his own five decades with a *Celebration Tour* to all the places that had impacted his life. Although few evangelical Christians would use Buffet as an inspiration for introspection, his "pirate" memoir stirred me to reflectively evaluate my own "pilgrim" path, and to take stock of where I have come from and where I am now.

Although I'm not a rock star, super rich, talented, or famous (I also can't grow decent facial hair)—and I don't currently own a Grumman Albatross, surfboard, fly rod, or Cessna Citation like Jimmy—we do (ironically) share a few things in common. We both like a good margarita, we're both called "Jimmy," and we were both blessed to make it to fifty years old in spite of our best and often misguided efforts to do otherwise.

Like me, Buffet also endured water survival school in the Navy. (Only for me, surviving the Pensacola water torture the Navy disguised as training was not quite the show and tell he got as a rock star.) As Marine pilot wannabes—and even before getting to that point where the Navy tried to drown us— prospective Marine aviators had to undergo a six-month course in infantry officer leadership indoctrination called The Basic School (TBS) in Quantico, Virginia. It was here where the Marine Corps did its best to train and shape us into some semblance of Marine rifle platoon commanders before sending all of us fit, young Marine officers to Pensacola to be corrupted by the Navy.

During TBS, we routinely hauled seventy to ninety pounds of gear on our backs for fifteen to twenty miles in Virginia's humid summer heat, and we were probably in the best shape of our twenty-something young lives. But the fact that we hard-charging guys were quaking and shaking in front of a swimming pool in Pensacola, gives you some idea of the fun and games the Navy had in store for those who wanted to saddle up their jets and break the speed of sound. I guess that's because the Navy mostly wanted us to do it all over water.

Lining those utilitarian swimming pools were multimillion dollar contraptions designed to help us survive some pretty extreme scenarios. After strapping on our harnesses, we were systematically dunked, dragged, and crashed into—and under—the water. One particularly heinous machine was called the "Helo Dunker." Six guys would be strapped into this barrel-like contraption, turned upside down, and then driven underwater head first. Of course, that water was cold and dark, a forbidding place where each guy had to egress one at a time—then do it all over again . . . *blindfolded.*

Besides enduring Navy water survival school, Jimmy B and I also seem to share a passion for surfing, flying, and scuba diving. I discovered my own enthusiasm for breathing underwater when I learned the basics of diving in the South China Sea. Instead of the usual chlorinated, concrete swimming pool, I got to acquire my scuba skills by snorkeling out to a shallow place among the coral, sharks, sea snakes, and tropical fish with my instructor, Johnny Higa. I'll never forget the afternoon a young Japanese guy on the beach convinced Mr. Higa to don his tanks and reenter the water to catch an octopus he'd spotted. Not long after, that sushi/

octopus was sliced and diced on a plate in front of us, soaking in soy sauce and looking like the remains of an alien from a sci-fi war zone.

Having grown up in Virginia Beach, I was used to being in the ocean. During my high school years, I spent every glorious, golden summer on a surfboard, patiently waiting to wring every thrilling minute from every (remotely) rideable wave. When my friends and I weren't actually surfing, we spent our days fantasizing about traveling to exotic surf destinations like the Bonsai Pipeline, Sunset Beach, Blacks Beach, and scores of other places we'd only read about in surfing magazines or seen in surfing movies. We dreamed about the day we would finally say goodbye to high school and fulfill those California fantasies, and we couldn't envision anything better. Even now, when I'm at the shore, the fresh, salty smells and rushing sound of waves and water take me back to the freedom of those careless, joyful days of my long-ago youth.

Although I didn't know it at the time, that love affair with the ocean would be my first initiation into the mysteries of Creation. It was the foundation that would anchor within me an awe of the forces of nature and an enduring love for the environment that I carry with me to this day. If you aren't aware of it already, all Christian believers are environmentalists. The first chore given to us by our Creator was to care for this remarkable creation we were placed into and entrusted with. God pronounced it *good,* and in spite of the thickets and thorns, I believe it still is. As a pilot, I never get tired of seeing the towering thunderstorms over the Rockies at night from my window at 39,000 feet, or the lights of New York City on a clear night when you can see all the way to Providence.

Such experiences always fill me with awe, wonder, and . . . *questions.* These moments inevitably spark a desire to take stock of my understanding and appreciation of God and to ask (yet again) the most profound questions of my life's experience: questions about my purpose and the meaning of my existence.

As Christian believers, the Bible tells us to examine ourselves, and I think the truths we discover are not just for our own encouragement but for others as well. I say this because the lessons I've learned traveling the road of my life are mostly communal ones. And if you look for signs of the extraordinary life God invites us into, you'll find such evidence in the lives of some pretty average bell-curve Christians who are doing some pretty remarkable things in some pretty remarkable places. I've come across quite a few Christians like that, and I'll share some of their stories too. Like your story and mine, those true accounts are all part of a larger Divine narrative—one that's shared and ongoing. Whether you know it now or not (or *feel* like it), we are all part of God's bigger narrative.

To understand this narrative, assume for a moment there are three levels of complexity in approaching an understanding of *theology* (the study of God). First, there's the *Professorial* (Seminarian) level of a particular denomination's systematic discipline, where theologians argue the finer points of whether or not an "i" belongs between the double "o" in the Greek word *Homoousian*. Secondly, there is the *Professional* level where clergy (like our pastors) train at a seminary—and through their own study and reflection of the Bible, sift that experience through the filters of their education and interpret it for us, helping us understand the larger context of *this is that* as they unfold God's plan for living well in this world we inhabit.

Finally, and most commonly, there is the *Kitchen Table* level of seeking to know and understand God. This is, of course, the level from which most of us try to make sense of how our own story fits into God's larger story and His workings in this world. And this is also where I think Jesus chose to spend most of His time (instead of hiding Himself away at rabbinical schools for the religious professionals of His day). I'm convinced He chose to spend most of His time around real kitchen tables with average folks just like you and me, with the full expectation they were capable of understanding the truth of His words and His deeds. He spent a lot of time with plain, ordinary folks, mostly asking good questions. Intentional questions.

This book you are reading now is *my* "kitchen table" perspective. It tells the story of how I've come to appreciate and understand this God who has translated Himself to me through the lives of others and the events of my own average Christian life, and how I've come to make sense of it all with a little help from some dedicated professional clergy in books and from pulpits. I've found that being a Christian is something you *are* and at the same time you spend your life *becoming*. The Bible explains this timeless journey: *We were saved . . . we are being saved . . .* and one day, *we will be saved.*

The Christian faith is full of paradox and mystery and though we may get a lot of it wrong around our kitchen tables, I think God is in that too. We *want to know*, and then we want to *know that we know*. But so much of life and faith is simply unknowable. Biblical truth points to God's character above all else and asks us to trust Him through this cloud of unknowing. It gives us just enough light to make one more step forward and enough evidence and reason to cling to the certainty of absolutes amidst a world of uncertainties. *That* I do know, and that I am convinced of, *beyond all doubt.* I want to tell you why.

I'm aware that presenting the evidence for my conclusion grows more challenging each day. In a Snapchat culture where the sum of philo-sophical thought fits into a fleeting five-second image, and opinions are relegated to a one-line electronic tweet or a car's three-by-twelve-inch bumper sticker, developing an idea or unfolding a story over many pages like this has its risks (personal revelation is always perilous). So why invite you into an admittedly average man's telling of his adventures as a Christian? Why look back with me through the historical rewind of memory? Because my personal story is part of a much larger story that's inevitably part of yours.

I hope you'll find more than you expected in the nooks and cran-nies of this account of my unfinished journey. Of course, any self-drawn history is admittedly subjective—I just happened to be an eyewitness of mine. But you may find it opens doors into unexpected places and sheds light on the path of your own pilgrimage.

CHAPTER 1

In the Beginning

"The two most important days of your life are the day
you were born and the day you find out why."

—Mark Twain

I am a commercial pilot and so it is I travel. A lot. I go from point A to point B and I do it thousands of feet above the earth and hundreds of miles an hour. Every one of my flights begins with a point of origin and ends at a destination. These journeys are a time of continuous change—from the predictable change of weather patterns and the scenery flashing by, to the unpredictability of events emerging outside of my control—sudden changes that can interrupt the journey and lead to a different destination altogether. And when those trips are over, I travel home or prepare for the next leg of my journey. In truth, we are all such travelers.

From the moment of our birth, our lives are really a pilgrimage of continuous motion into life itself, where most of us find ourselves moving rapidly through the ever-quickening stages of childhood and adult-hood—a hastening course from which there's no turning back and no way to halt our forward momentum. We find ourselves rushing *somewhere* toward *something*. There is a beginning and end to this life journey, and there are no exceptions. Most cannot escape the fact—and more importantly, the feeling—that we were built for something significant: that there is a God-directed purpose and meaning to this journey and the trajectory of this life we are living.

But it is often hard to hear the voice of God and find a firm, unshakable sense of direction and purpose amid the cacophony of competing voices tugging us this way and that. Yet direction is vastly more important than magnitude in a life. The Jewish prophet, Elijah, for example, looked in the mountains for that Voice, in the rolling thunder and the mighty wind—places where one would expect God to show up—but it wasn't in those things, and like Elijah, all I have sometimes heard is just simply wind and noise.

There is a part of understanding God that defies predictability. God rarely does what I expect, when I expect it. Still, every now and then, I've heard His unmistakable whisper of encouragement with just enough clarity to take one more step forward—to seek and find answers to one more question. Maybe to have a dying ember of faith rekindled. It is mostly a quiet, divine romancing that I find is leading me toward a promise, a place, and most importantly, a Person. One day, this whispering, wooing God will be fully known to me, and I too will be fully understood. Until that time, here I am, on this journey as are you—sorting it out the best I can.

Thankfully, we are not alone in this.

At some point on this journey, each person is confronted by some existentially important questions about themselves and the life journey they find themselves on: *Where did I come from? Why am I here? How do I live well and what should that look like? What will happen to me after I die?* Pondering these questions is vitally important because they establish the all-important foundations and cornerstones of our individual life stories and choices. Circumstances will inevitably arise that demand we confront the perils and pitfalls of life with responses grounded in our answers to these crucial questions. It is not an easy quest for any of us.

Accepting quick, expedient answers to these "reason for being" questions is always easier than giving them the thoughtfulness and seriousness they deserve. Our fast-paced, social-media driven culture has only accelerated this drift into easy answers. Drive-by truth claims are glibly tossed to us by culture mongers who expect us to find such fare meaningful, but in reality, I find this hype has more in common with Lite Beer: *Tastes great—less filling.*

Cheap and easy answers may gratify one for a brief, fleeting moment, but coming to grips with life's most essential questions and dilemmas needs the durability of essential truth, tested by time and experience. Without clarity of purpose and a passion for genuine truth, we may never reach or even identify our true destination.

What, Why, Where, and When

I am inclined (as are most people as they age) to peer into the recesses of memory in a forensic examination of the past. This is a chronicle of how one average, middle of the bell curve guy (aka myself) has attempted to fill in some of those existentially meaningless potholes and find meaning where none previously existed. I suppose at age sixty, the inevitable passage of time has provided me with some useful material to work with. Marking the years as they have unwound has afforded me the opportunity to sift these questions through the grid of some unique experiences over time. Of course, the fact that I'm six decades into the journey provokes a bit more reflection than it did at three. The bulk of my journey's behind me now, and that has prompted some self-reflection.

First of all, the notion of qualifying for the Denny's AARP special is a sobering one, and the young man I have living inside of me gets rattled thinking about this shocking truth: I am now in my sixties . . . and I sleep every night in the same bed with a grandmother. Hard to believe—and incomprehensible to imagine when I was in my twenties—but there it is. I'm sleeping with a grandma and discussing the merits of colonoscopies with my friends.

If life has taught us anything, it has taught us that the future probably holds an increasing measure of sorrow, loss, and disappointment for us. Life can be such a mixed bag of happiness and sadness. But there is so much meaning buried in that bag and so much value in an examined life—even as we prepare ourselves for the next. Living can be such a present reality.

I've realized the stock of certainties I once held onto so confidently have gradually disappeared into the dustbin of time and experience. Grace, for example, is more meaningful at sixty than it was at thirty. It has prompted me to not be so quick to judge anymore. The math of "if I do X, then Y will result" doesn't always add up like I once thought it would. As King Solomon pointed out to us, when it comes to the calculus of life, half a baby plus half a baby doesn't necessarily equal a whole baby.

I have come to appreciate that life is a lot more complicated than I once thought it could be. Parenting is harder, disappointment is more frequent—and although I'm not yet riding off into the sunset at sixty, I now know which direction the horse is facing. And there is an appreciation for the rapid passage of time and the dwindling of certain abilities I once took for granted. (I learned that lesson early in my forties when I tried to demonstrate to one of my daughters how to "skin the cat" and almost ended up in the emergency room.) Like any other old guy, I've become an amateur biophysicist as I watch the Law of Entropy assert itself on my reflection in the mirror and on the time it takes for me to roll out of bed.

Sixty years old seems like a good age to reflect back on the youth I once was, to try and see if I can remember who that guy was and what in the world he might have been thinking back in the day. The riches and depths of God seemed so entirely searchable and so much more fathomable when I was younger than they do now at sixty. Looking back over the years, I realize the importance of embracing a purposeful direction, as well as the value of the relationships, friendships, and community that helped define and make this journey meaningful. Time is becoming more precious as I get older. The things I value have changed. Even failure is more appreciated for the lessons learned.

Still, there are some lessons I never seem to learn no matter how many times I've been burned. That sucks, but I still try to step up to the plate and keep swinging for the fences. Maybe that's why my life seems like it's just getting started instead of winding down. Maybe it's a sign I've got a lot more swinging to do.

Point of Origin

I was born in Florida, and it was in Florida where I enjoyed one of the best years of my life as a young man going through Navy flight training at the Naval Air Station in Pensacola, Florida. Pensacola is called the Cradle of Naval Aviation, and it was the first stop on my quest to win the coveted Wings of Gold—the Holy Grail for all prospective knights of the air. Much of who I am now would be forged and formed then, and it was there my professional life's journey would be launched.

It was on this same base that I—as a twenty-three-year-old Marine second lieutenant and new father, married to a drop-dead gorgeous woman and living the dream—effectively heard the gospel for the first time and got the crap scared out of me. It's not as if I'd never been in a church before. And it's not like I'd never heard of Jesus or sung Christmas carols. Come to think of it, I'd probably heard the gospel before as well. But this time, it was different. Don't ask me why. It just was.

Somewhere in the Scripture it says, "The fear of the Lord is the beginning of wisdom," but in my beginning-of-wisdom moment, there was more confusion—not less—about what I'd just heard. How could I not be confused? I could not explain that *come-to-Jesus* moment at the time, but the memory of it is still with me. What I've found to be so remarkable looking back now—in all of our evangelical stories about how and when the gospel penetrates deep into our bones—is that this moment, this awakening of clarity, comes to people of all ages in so many radically different ways and situations. Such moments of revelation may be individually and personally different from mine or yours, but they mark the start of a journey that ultimately is moving us toward a common destination. We are departing from different places of origin, but we were created to arrive at this one destination. This one place. Augustine called it the

City of God, and Pilgrim called it the Celestial City. It is the Kingdom of Heaven. Described in the first two chapters of Genesis and the last two chapters of Revelation, it is a country and place where there are no more tears and no more crying. It is the place where you will be fully known and fully understood. It is a place of justice. And it is where our longings become realized fully.

The analogy used in the Bible to describe the particular event I experienced that morning so long ago is that of being *born again*. It's an interesting analogy if you stop to think about the physical process of birth or if you've ever seen a baby being delivered. Like any newborn baby unceremoniously ejected out into the world and greeted with a swat on the butt, every new Christian is introduced to a startling new reality that requires a serious sorting out process. It also requires growing up in a new environment that somehow doesn't feel as predictable or as comfortable as the old one probably did. Perhaps it shouldn't. Maybe it shouldn't *ever* feel safe or comfortable. I don't even remember exactly what the chaplain said that morning, and I would like to say it was a well-reasoned and cogent apologetic that made total sense, but it probably wasn't, and it probably didn't make sense at the time. I just knew that what I heard was true and not some fairy tale for grownups.

If someone wanted to make up an appealing religious fairy tale, they certainly wouldn't have picked the gospel account that got my attention that morning. Like an exploding truth grenade, that gospel inexplicably and unexpectedly landed right in the middle of my contented, pagan life. I remember getting up and going to work the next day wondering what had happened to me as I tried to press on and put it out of my mind. I also remember being more concerned about not washing out of flight school than I was with sorting through my emotional Sunday morning conversion experience. My "come to Jesus" moment didn't fall into the category of the near-death-by-sin stories or miraculous Damascus Road scenarios you sometimes hear about in church testimonials. At the time, life was good and things were actually looking up for me. Truth be told, life was fine by me just the way it was. I was where I wanted to be, with the person

I wanted to be with, and doing what I wanted to do. Then, out of nowhere, the gospel showed up smack dab in the center of my happy story.

An unlooked for intrusion.

Reflecting back on that experience as I've so often done, there is a bottom line I've come to realize as I've looked back and tried to make sense of that one Sunday morning—that born-again, smack-on-the-ass moment: God did not insert Himself into the world to make bad girls or bad boys into good little girls and good little boys. Nor did He come to make sad people happy or to make sick people well—things you may think should fall into God's job description and we are told too often He is supposed to be about. The fact is that He came to make dead people live. That Sunday I was spiritually smacked on the ass, took my first born-again breath (however unappreciated by me at the time), and began to live a *life*. And like any newborn creature, there is still a growing up process.

Even at sixty. Still.

Point of Departure

Being born and raised in the South, my family lived in a trailer park for many of my early years. Back in those days, living in a house trailer didn't automatically peg the social meter over to the "Southern Cracker" position like it seems to do nowadays. Like most folks in this country, we considered ourselves part of that once great American social institution called the middle class. Our mom, like all the other moms, did her wash at the trailer park laundry while we kids played in our front yards. In the summer; it was in plastic pools filled with warm, dirty water full of grass clippings, dead bugs, and who knows what else. Most moms still stayed home with their children in the late fifties, and there were plenty of birthday parties to go to and kids to play with. Like all memories, my memories from back then have been smoothed over by time and are now remembered as (mostly) pleasant ones, unmarked by any trauma save the little day-to-day experiences etched into the mind of a preschooler and elementary school student. Regardless of whether or not our house had wheels on it, Mom and Dad made it a home for us.

Snake slayer Mom reading to us kids at home.

Mom always wore a dress back in those days. So she was wearing a dress the day I remember her heroically rolling a snake to death with a broom outside the cinderblock building where she and the other women in the trailer park did the laundry. Although I'm not sure whether a person can actually roll a snake to death, that's the way I remember it. To this day, I can see Mom and her broom attacking that snake. She wielded the broom like a hockey pro, her face red and her dress flying around her as though she was performing some kind of furious hockey/Indian snake dance.

At the time, I would never have guessed (nor would my parents) that just down the road some years later, I would hungrily hunt down such snakes to eat during survival school as part of the initiation rights to naval aviation. I have always considered that year in Pensacola, Florida as one of the best years of my life, although I'm not sure my wife, Terry, would share those sentiments. At the time, our life was still pretty much all about me and my career. Besides, I figured she had our four-month-old daughter to take care of whereas I had *men's* business to attend to. I was laser-focused on getting those gold wings, and my wife was there to get along with the program. I hadn't yet figured out what constitutes the real measure of a man. That would come much later. I can tell you with assurance it isn't about me staying in my happy place. Stepping over the laundry basket and bypassing a crying baby on your way to the golf course or happy hour is not part of doing the man dance—FWIW.

My daughter, Kate, was born while I was still at the Basic School in Quantico. Among the snaky, woodsy smells and humid isolation of eastern Virginia, I learned how to be a Marine officer and what it means to act like one. This monkish place in the tick-filled wilds of eastern Virginia was where all newly minted second lieutenants were sent to learn the fundamental skills of a rifle platoon commander. It was a six-month cross we aviator wannabes had to endure on our way to the Promised Land at NAS in Pensacola, Florida.

In fact, Kate was actually born while I was on an exercise called the "Bascolex." During this training, we Marines would learn about amphibious assaults by climbing in the back of an "Amtrack" (this machine was part armored track vehicle and part submarine/boat—not the train). After we emerged from the bowels of our amphibious assault ship in the Amtrack, we'd launch off and bob our way ashore. Sitting in its dark, pitching, hot, diesel-fumed confines, we'd puke our guts out before assaulting the beach to slay an imaginary enemy with our pretend bullets. I wasn't even allowed to go to the hospital to see my wife and newborn daughter until after I had my rifle inspected. Welcome to the Corps. As the saying goes, "If they thought you needed a wife and family, they would have issued you one."

There's been a lot written about the Marine Corps, and its legendary track record is marked in broad strokes across the pages of our nation's martial history. As a young recruit, the weight of that history is deeply indoctrinated into you early on and leaves its mark as a calling of not only who you are but whose legacy you are now called to live up to. Being a Marine is not what you do for a buck, it's who you are. Oddly enough, this sense of a calling is something that has carried over almost seamlessly into my Christian walk. The idea of *being something* and being part *of a bigger something* as a Marine was my first initiation into having a sense of identity. To understand me, it's incumbent to understand that part of my life. I imagine it is true for most former Marines.

The scientist/philosopher Blaise Pascal once said, "If you want to be a believer, act like one." His thinking, I suppose, was that we grow into the thing we value the most. In other words, we become who we want to be. I often wonder why some folks find it hard to know what they want to be or what to value and end up mistakenly valuing the wrong things. The Marines taught me that there are things to value. Important things.

I was learning to be a Marine officer from the example of the men who had gone before me. The historical weight of that Marine Corps tradition presented a clearly defined set of values and an intentional road map to follow. It helped me understand who we were and what that really meant. We were Marines. It was who we already were, but it was also—at the same time—who we were in the process of becoming. I've found Christianity is a lot like that too. You are, and you are becoming. You grow into the things that you value.

For Marines, Basic School was where our transitional journey from college boys to men really began. As candidates and recruits, we learned how to use a sword properly and how to conduct an ambush. We also learned, recited, and memorized the Marine Corps history as stewards of a legacy we were not only part of but responsible to continue. That legacy was keenly felt in the halls leading to where we ate—halls lined with the pictures of the young officers who had won the Medal of Honor. Some of the buildings were even named for a few of these young men, many of whom were our age at the time. In addition to these daily reminders of history, there were memorable ceremonies and rituals that fostered our initiation into this fraternity of men.

We had a formal evening called *mess night* or *dining in* when we would gather in our dress uniforms and solemnly celebrate our inclusion into a very exclusive fraternity. In the dim candlelight of the dining hall, the beef would be paraded to the fanfare of trumpets and drum before being pronounced "fit for consumption" at the head table. Toasts were made, and finally, at the end of the meal, the "smoking lamp" would be lit, the port poured, and cigars lighted. I had never smoked a cigar before. And looking back, there is this imprint in my mind of young, flushed faces in our dress whites, seated at long tables in the formal dining setting of the great hall, taking in and soaking up the seriousness of the moment. We were all a bit unsure of how to handle all of this, but we were all vibrantly full of life and its seemingly unlimited potential. I'm sure my parents never imagined me in such a place, doing those things. I think they had very low expectations to avoid being disappointed, and in their defense, I did everything I could to meet those low expectations during high school. But life can be full of surprises. I was one of them.

A Middle Class Family

Like so many others, my parents were part of the great American middle class. Two high school graduates, my parents fit squarely within that unremarkable class of folks eking out the life of a middle-class family. I was fortunate to be born into that kind of family with a stay-at-home mom and a dad who worked two jobs to pay for the trailer that sheltered us. Here, my sister and I lived alongside our parents and a mean little dog with the benign-sounding name, *Candy*.

My memories lose their rosy hue when I think of that dog. Only three people on the planet were able to pick her up without being bitten—my mother, my father, and my grandma. Even at the end of that small, black Chihuahua's life, when it only had two teeth left in its gummy little mouth, Candy still terrorized unsuspecting strangers with a ferocity far beyond the measure of her size. At the time, I could never figure out why my mom and dad loved that dog so much. But since then, I've had a series of dogs myself, and I get it. I never came to love *that* one though. Maybe it had something to do with the fact that I often had to share the backseat of our family car with the dog and my sister, with Candy getting the honorific spot on the shelf behind the back seat, under the window.

One day, we stopped to eat a picnic lunch on the side of the road as we used to do a lot when we were traveling somewhere. Growing up, my generation never ate meals out. That was generally reserved for the very rare times when we would see grandma, and it was usually on Sundays. Back in those days, there were picnic tables along stretches of state highways, and on long trips, my mom would always pack a cooler filled with some really awful lunchmeat sandwiches to eat on the way. (If I was lucky, she'd stuff the cooler with a PB&J or two for me instead.) About thirty minutes after we'd packed up and left the picnic area that day, we noticed Candy was missing from her usual smelly perch behind our seat. Like a bad joke, every flatulent act perpetrated by that dog in the car got me in trouble, so I was all for pressing on and letting the problem take care of itself. But instead, we backtracked our previous route for the next forty minutes. We were about to give up the search when we saw some cars parked on the side of the highway with a knot of people standing around one car in particular. Sure enough, underneath the car—with her teeth bared, growling and barking for all she was worth—was our little Mexican dog, holding out beneath her four-wheeled Alamo because no one was willing to reach under the car and pull her out. But she happily jumped into Mom's arms, and off we went as if nothing had happened with Candy contentedly basking in the sun behind our heads in the backseat window. I swear that dog was smirking.

That dog would have made a great Marine.

I'm not a historian, but in *my* mind, those born in the 1930s like my parents seem to be a forgotten generation in twentieth century history. Sandwiched between the "Greatest Generation" and the "Baby Boomers," those born in the Thirties were too young to feel the full devastation of the war and the struggles of the Great Depression. Nonetheless, as that generation grew up, I'm sure they were shaped by the impact of those events in significant ways. Some of this generation would deploy to Korea or Vietnam, but all of them would come of age in the post-war shadows of a very defining time in our country's history.

My dad used to say, "The apple never falls far from the tree," so to understand who we are, I suppose we need to know what kind of tree we fell from. The hardworking, middle-class folks who were my parents are the trees I came from, and if you're my age, most of your parents were like mine too. These folks in the middle of the bell curve had no problem being unexceptional and average and probably never wasted a minute of their time to even think in those terms. They were too busy getting on with life to be looking for their twelve minutes of fame or to live vicariously through some Hollywood magazines' description of celebrity lifestyles. They possessed a certain strength of character and a sense of purpose that's absent in many of my own generation who seem to have an incessant hankering to be different and exceptional. I never saw that in my parents—there was no such yearning to *be special* or to be anything more than who they were. They were salt of the earth kind of people, and what you saw was what you actually got.

They spent their summer weekend nights dipping for Maryland blue crabs along a lighted dock with friends, then joyfully steamed and cracked those crabs while we gang of kids— sunburned and covered with mosquito bites—played outside until it was time for bed. All during my childhood, we did fun things that didn't cost a dime, and we usually did those things with friends or family. We also had to do stuff we didn't want to do as well. My parents gave praise when it was deserved and punishment when it was called for. There were no parenting "self-help" books or "how-to" experts they relied on to raise their children. Mom made dinner without worrying about carbs, GMOs, gluten free, free range, or any other sort of nutritional niceties. We ate what we had, and we had to eat everything our parents put in front of us.

"People in China are starving," they'd say. "So you'd better clean your plates!"

If we dared to ask why, we were answered with the timeless parental logic channeling the "Divine Command" theory of ethics:

Because I told you so!

My generation was, and is, quite different from that of my parents. We have scores of Christian parenting books and radio talk shows solely dedicated to telling us how to raise kids "God's way." Even the secular culture has its own secondary parenting profession as teachers and school administrators wholeheartedly insert themselves into the psychology of raising the sensitive, caring human beings they want our children to become. Everyone wants to get into the act. My kids grew up in the current culture—one in which everyone gets a participation trophy just for showing up. While they were in school, I can't tell you how many times my kids were told, "You are the most important person in the world . . . and you are special!"

What I heard growing up was quite different:

Who do you think you are, buster? You think you are something special? Well, let me tell you right now that you are not!
    You are getting way too big for your britches . . . .

If I had any doubt about my exalted place in the world, my parents were always there to remind me of life's pecking order. They never asked us what we wanted for dinner, where we wanted to go on vacation, where we wanted to live, or what room we wanted when we finally moved into a house. They valued my wisdom for exactly what it was worth.

Other aspects of my parents' generation have been lost as well: We've forgotten how to properly spank a kid, tune a car, hem a dress, and sweat a joint (plumbing). We don't remember when to harvest a watermelon, nor do we know how to prepare a turkey to roast, can food, play bridge, write a thank-you note, RSVP to an invitation, or live without a cell phone. I also think we might have lost the contentment of simply being average and unexceptional.

Do you ever wonder, as I have, what kind of legacy or inheritance was bequeathed to us? Have you ever thought about what you, in turn, will leave behind and what will endure when your strength fails and life itself is extinguished? What is it of my mom and dad's generation that will be passed on to my sons and my daughters? Although I find myself asking these questions much more frequently now that I'm in my sixties, I really don't think my parents ever thought or analyzed such things; I think they just did what they needed to do. But I'll never know for certain since Mom and Dad are gone, and all that's left of them are memories. I wish I could still ask them.

After my parents died, we sorted through Mom's and Dad's things. We not only sifted through the artifacts of their individual life stories (and mine and my sister's too), but also through the remaining fragments of a family history that will soon be forgotten. I wonder about the pictures of folks in Mom's old photo albums—folks I have no memory of. One faded photograph depicts two young men in a WWI barracks—doughboys from an almost forgotten war. Another faded print captures the youthful playfulness of a picnic under some maples with a Model A car in the background. There's also the photo of a fearsomely prophet-like old man with a white beard reaching down to his waist and the enormous woman who looms over him. Who were these people? They are long dead, and all I know is they are kin. I wonder about their stories.

Eva is in the middle of the back row, smiling up a storm.

One such photograph depicts my grandparents with their four young daughters before my dad was born. (One of my aunts died young.) Everyone in the 1920-ish picture has a stern countenance, with one exception: in the center of the photo—in the middle of the five other stoic faces—my Aunt Eva's smile is lit up like a Christmas tree, and her eleven-year-old face is uninhibitedly joyful.

What was she like to raise as a child? All I know about her is that she drove an ammo truck during the war before getting married, but died giving birth to my cousin soon after. Her sister would later marry her husband and raise her kids.

Of the few pictures I have of my Nebraska grandparents, not one of them ever showed my grandma smiling. Born in the late 1800s, she knew what life in the Plains during the Great Depression was like. If you borrowed a shovel from her, you not only cleaned it before you returned it, but oiled it as well. She never wore a dress that she did not make herself, and she tied all of her own fishing flies. (She was also a great fisherman).

Besides photographs, there were also many letters: love letters, letters of trouble and strife, letters from men at war, and letters from women at home. Some were as riveting as any soap opera. My sister became so engrossed in the unfolding drama in a series of letters my Aunt Dorothy wrote to my dad in 1952–1953; I thought she'd stop breathing right then and there when the climactic letter revealing the drama's final outcome was missing out of its envelope. There were even letters from my mom and dad to each other—private things that my mom made my sister promise not to read until after she was gone. Things like she was engaged to be married to someone else when she met my dad at the beach. There were also letters to a son and daughter from a dad at sea. It's hard to read them now, but one day I will read them all. These letters and the many, many photographs are the artifacts of people I loved—my parents.

It felt funny dismantling my parents' home after they had passed. It's interesting how the essence of a person inhabits their home, and I felt like I was saying goodbye to them all over again. Afterwards, my folks' deaths seemed permanent in a way they hadn't before. It was a sad and awkward closure. So many stories were left untold—stories I think I needed to hear as I wrestle with the important questions of life. Remember those? *Where did I come from? Why am I here? How do I live well and what should that look like? What will happen to me after I die?*

I think we all pretty much know the circumstances of our birth, but seeking to understand our life purpose once we get here can be a perilous journey filled with mishaps and missteps. But it's a journey we're all forced to make nonetheless. My journey has led me to the One who created me, and if yours doesn't lead you at some point to the One who created you, I'm not sure you can ever find a satisfactory answer to those five all-important questions, particularly the *why* question: Why am I here? The answer I've found is that every life story starts with *In the beginning . . .* and hopefully ends in *revelation.*

CHAPTER 2

JAPAN

"Love is a reciprocal torture."

—Marcel Proust

Four out of my last sixty years have been spent living in Japan, three of them as a child. Even though I was just a young lad of nine when my family first moved there in the mid-1960s, the sights, smells, and sounds of post-war Japan are something I can still conjure from memory. I remember the sweet potato guy—pushing his cart like an Asian version of the ice cream man—his rolling cart filled with sweet potatoes slowly roasting over a bed of hot coals. I recall our town being a smoky, rural place, but the idea of poor and wealthy was not yet part of my thinking about life. Looking back now through the memory of a nine-year-old, that town had the feeling of someplace from an old fairy tale—time-worn and ancient.

I was on the brink of my tenth birthday when I first experienced Japan. And like any other single-digit squirt, I had a very active imagination and very definite opinions about who the good guys and bad guys were. Of course, these images and ideas rattling around in my head were colored by Hollywood's post-World War II movies depicting Japanese soldiers as fierce and merciless enemies. As a nine-year-old, the notion of going to live in a place overrun by such enemies was a pretty worrisome one for me. (As if anyone really gave a rip about what my nine-year-old notion of a bad idea was!)

Dad had his orders, so my mom, sister, and I did as well. My father fulfilled those Navy orders to VQ-1 in Atsugi, Japan in September of 1966.

Two weeks after arriving there, we celebrated my tenth birthday in a Japanese hotel, and I was excited to get a brand-new bike to ride. But instead of getting to try it out, I spent the next month watching it sit idle in a corner as a punishment for violating some unremembered behavioral rule. My very first day of school in Japan went badly as well. In the morning, a school bus picked me up and took me to an army base with an American school staffed with some very adventuresome, young (American) teachers. But after school, I got on the wrong bus to go back to the hotel and created a crisis of sorts for Mom and Dad. (I'm sure my sister was secretly cheering for some sort of an abduction scenario.) For an hour or more, the bus driver drove me around in an empty bus as I looked out the window at houses and scenery, searching for someplace that seemed familiar. But every Japanese village looked the same to me. It was a rough start to my Japanese adventure, and I still can't recall how I made it back to the hotel that day. I just remember being driven around for a long time, wondering how much trouble I would be in when I did get back.

Still, my memories of that time in Japan are mainly good ones. During most of our years there, we were living in a house right off "Police Box" road in the small, local village of Minami Rinkan. It was a modest town having just one paved road with *benjo* ditches running down either side of it. (Benjo ditches were where folks stopped to go to the bathroom if they needed to.) And there was a cardboard factory at the end of our gravelly dirt road where we played hide-and-seek among the scrap piles with our Japanese friends. Afterward, we'd go to the corner store and buy dried squid (the Asian version of beef jerky). Despite the fact that we couldn't speak each other's language, we still managed to get along and have a great time together.

For the next three years—while Dad spent most of his time in an airplane over the skies of Vietnam dodging missiles and losing weight—I played baseball, read *Archie* comic books, and camped out in old former World War II camps with the Boy Scouts. We could actually see the crematoriums in one of the POW camps where we stayed as our scout leaders (who weren't much older than we were at the time) regaled us with bone-chilling stories describing all manner of torture and mayhem. Afterwards, we would turn in for the night and envision renegade Japanese soldiers lurking in the shadows, waiting to get even with us for losing the war. Even worse, we shivered to remember the *Tama wolf* stories we'd heard about a creature that began prowling the area after it developed a taste for human flesh, and that was forever in search of an easy meal of Boy Scout. But in all of my colorful imaginings—as I lay under the musty canvas of my tent, alert to every sound and rustle outside in the night—could I ever imagine what it must have been like to be trapped in one of those POW camps as a prisoner.

On my way to do battle with the Tama wolf.

Portland

In 1992, on a layover in Portland, Oregon, I was reading the Sunday morning paper and having a cup of coffee while waiting to be picked up for our flight. I read the newspaper's featured article about Jimmy Doolittle's WWII raid on Japan with interest, noting all the men from the Northwest who'd taken part in that raid. These men were being honored because it was the fiftieth anniversary of the day Army Lt. Col. James Doolittle led a number of air corps bombers off the *USS Hornet* for a one-way mission to bomb mainland Japan.

So much has changed during those fifty years. As World War II recedes from our memories, it is increasingly hard for us—as citizens of our globalized, tightly connected, high-tech planet—to imagine just how dire and apocalyptic the world was at that time. During the war, no one was insulated from its deprivations, and everyone had to make sacrifices. But in today's "supersized" culture, where bigger is better and even more is not enough, rationing things like chocolate and gas would be unthinkable.

Jimmy Doolittle's raid was launched in retaliation to the devastating gut punch of Pearl Harbor, after the Japanese caught the American fleet napping one beautiful, sleepy Sunday morning. In Europe, the German war machine seemed unstoppable as England was slowly being bombed into rubble, France was capitulating, and the Japanese were swallowing up the Pacific one island and one country at a time.

In in an effort to boost the morale of the American people, reeling in shock after the devastation of Pearl Harbor, Navy Captain Francis Low hatched a bold plan to send a flight of B-25 bombers on a one-way mission to strike at the Japanese mainland. Led by Army Lt. Col. James Doolittle, it was such a top secret mission even the aircrew and the president himself had few details about how and when it would take place. Some seventy-nine men took part in this mission, which due to early detection by the Japanese, was forced to launch well outside of the planned safety margin for making it to landing fields in unoccupied China. Russia was in a neutrality pact with Japan, so those fields were off limits, although one plane would eventually land there. None of the pilots had ever taken off from a carrier before, and there was no fighter escort. No one knew where they were to land. With no guns or armaments to defend themselves, eight of the aircrew were captured by the Japanese army. Of those eight, three would be summarily executed.

As I read the feature article describing these events in the Sunday morning edition of that Oregon newspaper, I looked over the accompanying pictures and bios of the seven Doolittle raid guys from the Northwest. The photo of Jacob DeShazer stood out from the rest. It depicted an emaciated skeleton of a man looking down as if lost in thought. He was one of the men who had been captured on that raid, and his story drew me into its dramatic narrative, not particularly for what he had endured—many had endured as much, or worse—but because of the unusual twist of fate born out of that experience. As I read about his capture, I wondered if he might have been held in one of the Japanese POW camps where I camped out later as a Boy Scout.

Of course, Jacob DeShazer's experience as a POW was radically different from anything I could have imagined as a young Boy Scout huddled in my tent, listening to the quiet night sounds of a post-war Japan from long ago. But what makes Jacob's story so worth remembering and retelling is the way the spiritual reality of both evil and love are so intertwined in the narrative of his suffering. I believe those experiences help remind us we should never forget that the forces of good and evil are powerful realities in this world. So powerful, in fact, that these forces shape everything we think about when it comes to religion, politics, or even relationships. In essence, life is divvied up into moral categories. Right and wrong. Good and evil. Just and unjust.

Those surviving crews from Doolittle's raid who were captured by the Japanese were taken to Japan where they were systematically beaten, starved, and placed apart in solitary confinement. Jacob himself would spend almost three years alone in such confinement. Meanwhile, three of his fellow prisoners were executed, and one man who'd become a friend was slowly starved to death. Jacob was a prisoner of the Japanese for three-and-a-half long, torturous years, and over time, the hate he felt toward his captors became unbearably consuming. Yet, how could he *not* feel that way?

No one should really be surprised that we, human beings, have such an enormous capacity and appetite for inflicting unspeakable atrocities upon one another, should they? I don't think any other creature tortures their prey like we do—most just kill and eat to survive. But humans are different, and history is rife with accounts of our cruelty. In the fairly recent genocide in Rwanda, for example, over 800,000 people were murdered—mostly by machete—simply because some were taller than others and were designated Tutsi and not Hutu. And during the Cambodian genocide of 1975 to 1979, 1.5 to 3 million people were designated "opposition" and killed at the behest of Pol Pot's Khmer Rouge. Prior to that, 6 million people died during the ethnically driven holocaust atrocities of WWII. But worst of all, soviet dissident Alexander Solzhenitsyn asserts 60 million more were killed during the political nightmare of Stalin's purges. These are just the ones we know about.

It's an uncomfortable fact that more people were killed during the twentieth century than in all other centuries combined. The scope of these murders borders on the incomprehensible. Yet all of this horrific evidence in the historical record proves humanity's ongoing capacity, and seemingly unlimited potential, to commit evil. Every day, the media competes to bring revelations of new atrocities to our attention, and it seems they never run out of material. In fact, as my friend, Mark, reminds me, if you want to know what man is capable of, just read what the Bible tells us not to do. If indeed we are evolving, I shudder to think what we are evolving into given these facts.

Apparently, the human capacity for evil is a force that knows no ethnic boundaries, does not discriminate by gender, embraces no class distinctions, and for the most part, suffers no economy of scale. As Solzhenitsyn observed while a political prisoner in the Russian Gulag, the line between good and evil runs through the heart of every man. Every person. Every heart. This tenet is central to the Christian faith and underscores the fundamental fact that no one is naturally born "good." That's a hard pill for us to swallow. Atheists choke on it. If anything, we like to see ourselves as just, fair, and good. But the human propensity for depravity comes as no surprise to parents. No one teaches a child to pull the wings off of a fly, and you don't have to teach a two year old how to lie—you have to teach them how to tell the truth.

Cut someone off in traffic and see if your self-perceived moral right to do that is appreciated. (Surely, if survival of the fittest is a viable alternative, it has to be applied to the DCA beltway during rush-hour traffic, no?) But despite our propensity for evil, there *are* well-intentioned people in this world: kind and gracious people who include those of all faiths and even those of no faith. They do their best to conform to what society promotes as "good." But they weren't born altruistic from the start. No one is. Someone, at some point, presented a moral standard for them to navigate and abide by. Moral selflessness doesn't come naturally. So that begs the question: Where *did* our universally observable moral standard come from anyway?

War and Peace

One wonders why Jacob DeShazer was questioning his debilitating hate for the Japanese in May of 1944. Such hate would be understandable and natural as a tortured prisoner of war. Yet, inexplicably, he asked one of his captors for the single Bible that was allowed to circulate in the camp. Why he would want a Bible is an easy thing to understand. Perhaps, seeing his Christian friend starve to death had something to do with it, or maybe he was just desperate for something to read. I've often wondered how a Christian Bible ended up in a Japanese POW camp in the first place. The only explanation I can think of is that, at some point in time, a Japanese soldier who was a Christian believer sought to have that Bible placed in that particular camp. (There were missionaries in Japan at one time.) In fact, I remember hearing an account from my friend, Mark, about a pastor who, when he was a soldier, became a POW of the North Vietnamese and was led to Christ by a Vietnamese soldier while hanging in a cage.

Regardless of how that Bible ended up there, reading it altered Jacob DeShazer's outlook on his situation. The torture did not stop with his conversion to Christianity, nor did it change the fact that he was slowly being starved to death. He simply stopped hating the men who were doing it to him. And even though he was still being brutalized, the short time Jacob spent with that Bible changed the trajectory of his life. After the war, he would go to a Bible school. Then he would go back to Japan.

In 1948, Jacob DeShazer returned to the country where he'd been tortured with his wife, Florence, and they spent the next twenty-five years ministering and planting churches there as missionaries to the very people he'd once hated. More than a million tracts of DeShazer's testimony, "*Why I No Longer Hate the Japanese*," were handed out in Japan as there were many in that country who wanted to read about a man who could forgive his enemies. As a matter of fact, this same man—who'd been systematically starved to death by his Japanese captors— voluntarily withheld food from himself during a forty-day fast as he prayed for the Japanese.

A few days after his fasting and praying ended, an unusual answer to his prayers turned up at his door. It was Mitsuo Fuchida, the Japanese

Mitsuo Fuchida

flight commander of the 360 airplanes that bombed Pearl Harbor. (I believe he was even the one who made that fateful radio call on that infamous day on December 7th: *Tora! Tora! Tora!*) Fuchida, an admirer of Hitler (he even wore a mustache like Hitler) and an American hater, had read one of those tracts about Jacob "who no longer hated the Japanese" and decided to go see him.

Former American hater Mitsuo would later be baptized by former Japanese hater Jacob. Who would have seen that coming? Even more amazing, Fuchida himself would later go on to become an evangelist, preaching in Japan and all over the world, traveling with Billy Graham on his crusades.

I think we can all understand Jacob DeShazer's initial response to injustice and evil in a POW camp. We've all suffered injustice and responded with anger, hate, jealousy, and bitterness. We are human after all. But it's not the fact or face of evil that elevates this historical narrative to its spiritual place of power. It is the reality of the very real love that emerged out of Jacob's spiritual change, the kind of love that transformed a man who had every reason in this world to hate a people for the inhuman acts committed against him and his mates. It is the kind of love that changed Mitsuo Fuchida as well. Seen in this light, it's not the reality of evil, but the emergence of love that makes this account so exceptional. Love does not explain the existence of evil. But it is the most powerful response to it. This is fundamental to understanding what it means to follow in the footsteps of Jesus when He said, "When you are struck on the face, offer him the other cheek." "If they take your cloak—give him your coat also." "Love your enemies." "Do good to those who hate you." Love is a response that can, in itself, be a show-stopper.

How would you define that kind of self-sacrificial love in this *eye for an eye* world we live in? What is the essence of love anyway, and where does it come from? How would something like that simply evolve? Why is this kind of love at the core of, and central to, every great poem, story, or song?

The first time the word "love" is mentioned in the Bible is when God told Abraham to sacrifice his son. That seems like a good place to start: A father sacrificing his son.

Love is a power that could not have *evolved* because it has nothing at all to do with being the *fittest*. The *fittest* eliminate enemies to make a better life for themselves. Also, it appears that to be sacrificially loved and understood is a longing in us all and a hole that is rarely filled because it is so often connected to performance. I can understand at some level how a person can take the life of another, but it is much more difficult for me to explain to someone who has not themselves experienced sacrificial love, why that person would voluntarily give up his own life for a stranger.

But Christian love is not just about giving your life up for a stranger either. Firefighters and policemen do that. Parents will do that for their children, as will soldiers for their buddies. The love of Christ demands something even more.

Every person in this world has within themselves the capacity to love, whether they're religious or not. Many of those young Marine Medal of Honor winners we would pass by in the halls of the Basic School died while sacrificing their lives for their friends, often throwing themselves on enemy hand grenades to save their brothers in arms. So what's the difference between the kind of Christian love believers are called to offer and the sacrificial love we see demonstrated in the world by believers and nonbelievers alike?

The answer to that question can be found in the final act of Christ on the cross: Christian love demands that we not just lay down our lives for our friends and family, or even for strangers, *but to lay our lives down for our **enemies***. That is the essence of the gospel. An all-powerful, God-in-the-flesh Jesus could have called down legions of angels to rescue Him from a tortuous death, but He chose to suffer and die for His enemies instead. Most people would, in the moment of need, lay down their lives for the ones they love, but not for those whom they *hate*. But that is the ethic Christians are called to, and it is the principle that lies at the heart of the gospel. *While we were yet sinners, Christ died for us . . . .* That is the story behind the story of Jacob DeShazer.

Personally, I can say it doesn't matter how many books on apologetics I've read, no one has resolved the existence of evil for me. Evil simply exists, and a good God permits it. I cannot imagine why God would allow it. So I made up my mind a long time ago to move on from what *I do not know* to what *I can know*, and the one thing *I do know* is that if there is an answer for evil, it has to be found in the remarkable power of love which stands over and against evil . . . and the freedom to choose between the two. One day in the future, Scripture assures us evil will be dealt with, but it isn't today. That's why addressing the question of love as a response to it is so essential. It is the response skeptics have no answer for and tend to ignore. But if you are walking in the footsteps of Jesus, you will understand you're called to lay your life down, not just for your friends, but *for your enemies*.

People often try to live moral lives according to an acceptable social standard. But love is something more than simply the power of preference, a sense of moral duty, or the expectation of financial reward or fame. Those things might get you started, but they will not and cannot sustain you. No one gives their life up for a preference. I think only a man empowered by a risen Savior has that kind of staying power. That is the only answer for evil that makes any sense at all to me.

Love and hate, good and evil are the competing forces that shape our existence here on earth. Reading the Bible, we discover that it wasn't meant to be this way, and that one day it will be different. That promise doesn't come from me, but from God. He designed us to live in the first two chapters of Genesis and the last two chapters of Revelation. Until that promise is fulfilled, we will perhaps always wrestle with the question: *Why do bad things happen to good people (i.e., me)?*

But C. S. Lewis would reply to us with another question instead: *If we are really and truly innately good, why would we need to make an appeal to one another to behave that way?*

Raid: Mission both dangerous, myste

LOCAL RAIDERS

Wayne M. Bissel — First lieutenant. Born Oct. 22, 1921, in Walker, Minn. Graduated from Vancouver High School, Vancouver, Wash., in 1939. Enlisted in U.S. Army after graduation and completed bombardier training. After Doolittle Raid, attended pilot training and received his wings and commission. Served as a B-25 pilot until he left the military in July 1945. Now retired in Vancouver.

Robert S. Clever — First lieutenant. Born May 22, 1914, in Portland. Graduated from Franklin High School and worked in the mailroom at The Oregonian. Attended the University of Oregon for two years, then enlisted as aviation cadet at Vancouver Barracks, Vancouver, Wash., in 1941. Commissioned as second lieutenant with bombardier rating at Pendleton Field. Injured on Doolittle Raid. Stationed at Baer Field, Ind., when he was killed in an airplane crash near Versailles, Ohio, on Nov. 20, 1942.

Dean Davenport — Colonel. Born June 29, 1918, in Spokane. Graduated from Grant High School in 1937. Studied at Northwestern School of Law until he enlisted as aviation cadet in 1941. Graduated from Advanced Flying School and commissioned as second lieutenant. Served as technical advisor for film, "Thirty Seconds Over Tokyo." After the war, commanded several jet fighter units. Flew 86 combat missions in Korean War. Now retired in Panama City, Fla.

Jacob DeShazer — Staff sergeant. Born Nov. 15, 1912, in West Stayton. Graduated from Madras High School in 1931. Enlisted in 1940 at Fort McDowell, Calif. Attended bombardier and airplane mechanics schools. Was captured by the Japanese after Doolittle Raid and spent 40 months as prisoner of war. Released in August 1945 and left the service that October. Graduated from Seattle Pacific College in 1948 and returned to Japan to become a Christian missionary, fulfilling a vision he had while a prisoner of war. Now retired in Salem.

Robert G. Emmens — Colonel. Born July 22, 1914, in Medford and graduated from Medford High School in 1931. Attended University of Oregon for three years and entered the service in 1937 at Vancouver Barracks, Vancouver, Wash. Graduated from Flying Training School with pilot's rating in 1938. Assigned to 17th Bomb Group at March Field, Calif. Joined Doolittle Raid just before boarding the carrier. After raid, interned for 13 months in the Soviet Union and wrote a book about it. After the war, served on intelligence assignments in Europe and Japan. Emmens, who retired in Medford, died earlier this month.

Everett W. "Brick" Holstrom — Brigadier general. Born May 4, 1916, in Cottage Grove. Graduated from Pleasant Hill High School in 1934 and attended Oregon State College until he enlisted at Fort Lewis, Wash., in 1939. Commissioned as second lieutenant and received pilot's rating upon graduation from Kelly Field in 1940. Sank the first Japanese submarine off the West Coast in December 1941. Remained in China-Burma-India Theater after Doolittle Raid, commanding the 11th Bomb Squadron until 1943. Now retired in Carmel, Calif.

David M. Jones — Major general. Born Dec. 18, 1913, in Marshfield. Graduated from Tucson High School, Tucson, Ariz., in 1932. Graduated University of Arizona and commissioned as second lieutenant. Enlisted in National Guard in June 1932. Earned pilot rating in June 1938 and served with 17th Bomb Group at March and McChord fields. After Doolittle Raid, served in North Africa and was shot down over Bizerte in 1942. Spent 2½ years as POW. After the war, commanded 47th Bomb Wing at Sculthorpe, England. Now retired in Indiatlantic, Fla.

THE PLANES

The following is a summary of how some of the planes did in the Doolittle Raid:

■ **Plane No. 4** (Holstrom pilot) — The plane encountered a large number of interceptor-

■ Continued from Page D1

still is considered the turning point in the Pacific war, the first major step toward Japan's surrender.

□

Pendleton Air Field, an Army base that later became Pendleton Municipal Airport, was one of the first installations to receive the new B-25s, the only bombers capable of taking off from an aircraft carrier designed for much-smaller fighter planes.

When military planners conceived the raid, they called for volunteers at Pendleton for a dangerous, unspecified mission.

"They had a short runway marked out on the field there," said the Rev. Jacob DeShazer of Salem, bombardier on Plane No. 16. "They had us practice takeoffs on that for a short while. But as soon as we got the hang of it, they shipped us off to South Carolina and Florida for more training."

Jean Shaw of Pilot Rock was a local girl who played cards and danced with the airmen at a couple of small parties held at the base.

"It seemed like they came and they went," she said. "Nobody was even supposed to know they were here. The first thing we knew, we heard they were over Tokyo."

Once on the East Coast, the men were joined by Doolittle, a former World War I aviator, test pilot and stunt flier who had rejoined the Army as a colonel. Part cheerleader and part taskmaster, Doolittle was the one who oversaw the strange modifications to the bombers — the belly guns were eliminated, the tail guns were replaced with broomsticks, the bomb load was cut down and more gasoline tanks were added, including some 5-gallon cans. The carburetors were set so lean that it was almost hard to start the planes. The sophisticated, high-altitude Norden bombsights were replaced by some five-and-dime models that would work only just above treetop level — and they did.

□

On April 2, 1942, the USS Hornet steamed out of San Francisco Bay with a strange cargo aboard. Sixteen B-25s were tied to the flight deck, while the ship's interceptors, dive bombers and torpedo planes were stowed below. Neither the Hornet's crew nor the Army airmen knew what they were in for.

"As soon as we got a ways past the Golden Gate Bridge, the Hornet's captain, Marc Mitscher, got on the loudspeaker and announced that we were going to bomb Tokyo," DeShazer said. "A great cheer went out."

The plan was laid out down to the last details in the ensuing briefings — the Hornet would be joined by the carrier USS Enterprise and cruisers, destroyers and an oiler to ship within 500 miles of Japan. If they were attacked, the Hornet's crew would have to roll the bombers into the sea so the interceptors could be brought up from below for defense.

After bombing military targets around Tokyo, the planes were to fly on to China, where they would team up with Nationalist forces fighting the Japanese occupation.

It didn't quite happen that way. The seas were miserably rough on the morning of April 18, when two Japanese patrol boats spotted the Hornet. Although the ship was 668 miles out, Adm. William Halsey decided to launch the raid. Doolittle's plane was the first one in line and faced the shortest runway. But by sailing full-speed into the wind, the ship gave him a headstart.

"Once we saw him get up, we all breathed a sigh of relief," DeShazer said. "He had only about 400 feet of runway, and we'd never gotten one up in less than 700 feet in training with a full load."

The second bomber almost landed in the drink when the pilot forgot to set his flaps properly. But he pulled out and made it. And so did the next one and the next one, until 15 planes were in the air, skimming along the wave tops toward Japan.

The last plane almost didn't get up.

"When I went down into the nose, I saw there was a big hole in the plexiglass, about a foot across," DeShazer said. "But I saw the pilot was busy so I never told him until we were already in the air."

With a jacket stuffed in the hole, Plane No. 16 joined the others, nearly an hour after the first takeoff. The Hornet and the rest of the convoy immediately reversed course and steamed toward Pearl Harbor and safety.

At noon, the first planes bombed Tokyo, Yokohama, Yokosuka and Kobe, striking factories, warehouses, gas plants, oil storage tanks, power stations, rail yards, steel mills, a tank factory and an aircraft plant. Plane No. 16 diverted slightly to bomb Nagoya.

However, getting to unoccupied China proved impossible. Because they took off earlier than they had planned, the planes were nearly out of fuel by the time they reached the Chinese coast. Some crews crashlanded. Others bailed out of their planes. One crew was captured almost immediately. Another flew to Vladivostok, Siberia, where the Soviets interned the crew for three months and kept the plane.

In all, 64 men went on to Chungking, China, three died bailing out or crash-landing and eight were taken prisoner by the Japanese. Of those, three later were executed and one starved to death.

DeShazer, who bailed out at about 3,000 feet over China, was convinced to holster his .45 by some men who said they were Chinese. But they turned out to be Japanese occupation forces, and he was thrown in prison. For the next 40 months, he and his fellow prisoners suffered through starvation, filth, malnutrition and beriberi. They were not released until the end of the war.

Meanwhile, DeShazer enjoyed a religious born-again experience and vowed to return to Japan to do Christian missionary work, a vow he soon kept. From 1948 to 1977, when he returned to Oregon, he helped to start up 23 churches in Japan.

"It really was a wonderful time there," DeShazer said. "The emperor finally told them he didn't have any more divinity than anyone else, so there was a spiritual vacuum

CHAPTER 3

NEBRASKA

"I was married by a judge. I should have asked for a jury."

—Groucho Marx

I have belatedly discovered there are two obvious challenges facing a person who writes their marriage story for others to read. First, you run the risk of your listeners' imaginations running amok and taking them to places you never, ever intended them to go. So if you're looking for something steamy, gossipy, or titillating in these next pages, be advised my editor is one of my wife's best friends. Sorry about that. Second, there's the thorny little detail of every marriage story having two sides. Yep. There is that. It also doesn't help marriage matters when I cast myself as the hero of the story. Pretty much *every* story.

Despite that, I've learned marriage is a uniquely peculiar institution in that it is both intensely personal and private, yet also public and communal at the same time. I have had a daughter married by a judge, and one by a pastor. But regardless of who officiated during the vow taking, both marriages will become lifelong spectacles lived out in front of a jury of peers, family, strangers, and coworkers. And although there are things I wish I'd known about marriage and sharing a life with someone when I was younger, such lessons can only be learned in the crucible of married life. And these hard-won lessons are costly and precious.

Maybe I should have been able to skip some of those lessons, but I didn't date much in high school. The discipline it took to be a beach bum left me no time for superficial and mundane things like dating. It also left no time for school. Underachieving can be really hard work when it's done well. Besides, at the time, a high school diploma was something meaningful to my parents, but not to me. To heck with the psychologist Maslow—I had my own hierarchy of needs. In a nutshell, my philosophy of education back then was this: *The minimum wouldn't be the minimum if it wasn't good enough.*

So at age seventeen, after barely eking out a high school degree, I packed up my surf board and left Virginia Beach with another like-minded goof ball. We headed west to California where, a month later, I found myself alone on my epic quest for the perfect wave. I also ended up registering for the draft in San Diego since the Vietnam War was still winding down in the early '70s. But as it turned out, I spent the next year and a half surfing between California, North Carolina, and Florida. It was a pretty important time in my life—as directionless and unproductive as it might have seemed at the time to anyone other than myself.

Living the Dream

When life was an endless summer.

My magic carpet was a 1966 Ford truck that burned about as much oil as it did gas, and it burned a lot of gas (but fuel was cheap back then, under fifty cents a gallon). My dad had helped me finish the inside of the cap that went over the truck bed, and we'd built a bed, a closet of sorts, and a few places to store what little stuff I had: a Coleman one-burner camp stove and lantern, some of my favorite books, a few cooking utensils, and my surfing stuff. I put those cooking utensils to good use once I found out you could buy pancake mix for nineteen cents a packet. I ate *a lot* of pancakes.

One spring, I drove from California to Florida and got stuck in a blizzard in Colorado. I simply crawled into the back of my truck (which could be heated nicely by the Coleman lantern) and waited out the storm by patiently reading in my bed, eating when I was hungry, and passing the time pleasantly enough—all the while hoping my truck would start when the weather cleared. I guess you could say I was at the forefront of the current RV revolution.

Sort of. At the time, I didn't appreciate how my dad must have felt about my plans to surf the world. My ambition to live a nomadic, semi-homeless life at the beach probably wasn't what he'd envisioned for his son's future. But he pitched in and helped me launch out to follow my dreams, however impoverished and minimalistic they may have been. I didn't realize it at the time, and maybe he didn't either, but that was a valuable lesson for me in parenting—letting your child go with a blessing, even in the face of your own unmet expectations.

As I was leaving home that summer after high school, my dad told me, "Jimmy, I can't help you at all with your plans, but if you ever decide to go to college, we might be able to lend a hand or whatever." Then he said, "Just do me a favor and call your mom collect once a month." And off I went to enjoy my unfettered freedom, living the minimum. And at the time, the minimum was good enough for me.

Until it wasn't. A year and a half later, I found myself in Nebraska where my parents had relocated so my dad could finish his education, and I set out to do what had previously been unthinkable to me—I was going to attend college. Not only that, but relocating into the heart of the great Midwest as a long-haired Southern boy was a dramatic transition. The harsh concept of *windchill factor* was totally new to me. Instead of sun and surf, I found snow and subzero temperatures, but I was determined to stay. After eighteen months of bottom feeding, I'd finally figured out there had to be a better way. In the end, the minimum wasn't quite good enough for me after all. It was just something I had to discover for myself. Attending college gave me a goal far above the minimum, and it marked a radical shift in my life path. That shift was so radical, in fact, that at the end of those four years in Nebraska, I came away with a wife, a college degree, and a commission—in that order.

Although 1970 to 1980 was a culturally and musically diverse decade (and a rich time for all kinds of great music), I think it will be forever tagged the "disco decade." This sucks for those of us who came of age during the '70s. James Taylor; Led Zeppelin; Harry Chapin; Lynyrd Skynyrd; John Prine; Crosby, Stills, Nash & Young; Willie Nelson; and a wealth of other awesome musicians are immediately forgotten when you mention "Disco Duck" or "Rubber Band Man."

What this otherwise forgettable disco music did provide, however, was a terrific opportunity for us college guys to meet girls at disco bars and college town dance venues. We all went to such places to forget about school, work, and having to get up too early for 8:00 a.m. classes. But most importantly, it gave us socially inept guys a great, ready-for-prime-time opening line: *Hey, you wanna dance?* This scenario converted the potentially stressful boy-approaches-girl overture into a fairly safe and predictable one. Even if you got shot down, it was generally pretty dark in those places, and you could easily bluff your way back to your table pretending you were just asking directions to the bathroom or something. After sitting awhile, a guy could work up his courage to charge ahead and try again.

For college kids, this disco thing was simply part of the trials and tribulations of the boy-meets-girl mating ritual of a 1970s college student. It was the forerunner of eharmony.com where you could venture out onto the dance floor, look each other over up close, ask a bunch of questions, and see if it led to a date. So far, so good. But the worst case scenario for a guy was being turned down by a girl before making it to the dance floor. It was the bone-chilling moment when you were left standing there after popping the "Do you wanna dance?" question and getting turned down—or even worse, when girls just looked at their girlfriends and simply laughed. During that nightmare scenario, you could swear everyone in the place was looking at you like you were a loser.

Trinity Math

From the day we were created as humans, the Creator Himself let us know that it is not good for people to be alone. I do not think He was necessarily commentating about sex per se, but primarily was making an observation about a much more profound communal relationship. Man was not meant to live a *life* alone. And even though we're not all destined to be married, we *were* made to be connected with other humans and live a communal *life*—a shared, meaningful life. All of us have different levels of comfort when it comes to social interactions to be sure, but there is a huge difference between being lonely, for example, and being alone. My wife, Terry, is very content in her aloneness, but she too needs and appreciates some level of social community. Whatever social interaction is comfortable for each one of us, the fact remains—we need to have *some* social contact. We were built for that.

It is why putting a person into solitary confinement is such an inhuman punishment.

Our need for social community is also part of being made in the image of God who is Himself, we are told, a unity of diversity in community. *Let **us** make man in **our** image.* God is by nature a singular community within a communal relationship within Himself. That is what the Bible tells us and intentionally leads us to believe about who God is: a Trinity of One.

Comprehending this idea of the Trinity, however, is also one of the first stumbling blocks most Christians encounter as they seek to understand the tenets of their Christian faith. It is a conceptual tangle—this notion of a Triune God who is three Persons, yet one Being. The math simply doesn't make any sense for most of us average, middle of the bell curve Christians with a kitchen table understanding of God. No matter how many analogies I have heard about this three-in-one God, they all seem a bit disappointing and insufficient. I have heard a lot of messages (sermons) on the Book of Genesis where this idea of the Trinity is first introduced, but not one satisfactory explanation going into detail on the Trinity itself. From its opening pages, however, the Bible clearly tells us of God's triune nature: He is three Persons, but one God. Still, one does not need to be an Einstein math genius to figure out 1+1+1=3, not 1. Whatever the spiritual reality of that three-in-one relationship is, I've come to appreciate some truths about the Trinity in all of its inexplicable mystery.

Implicit in all of the religions that hold to a monadic God (a singular Personage, i.e., one person = one god), there's a problem that's bigger than the *Three Person = One God* math problem. The dilemma is this—if God is an uncaused, uncreated Being who always existed before Creation, some serious questions arise: *Who was God loving before He created the universe? Who was this singular God communicating with before He created life? Did He talk to Himself or Herself? Was He or She lonely? Did He have to create in order to have someone to interact with? If He or She needed to have someone to love and communicate with, can He or She still be God?*

In response to these questions about God's eternal nature, it's important to point out that only in the Christian concept of a Triune God does love and communication exist **prior** to Creation. In all other religions, affection and communication result **from** creation. Creation in a sense reflects this triunity in how we understand and experience the world around us. Our physical reality is a triune existence consisting of time, space, and matter. Time itself is divvied up into a past, present, and future. Likewise, matter is divided up into liquids, gasses, and solids. And space, as we experience it, is three dimensional.

Nowhere, though, is the reflection of this triune nature of God more meaningful to us, and more evident, than it is in our most intimate of relationships—marriage. Love and communication are central to intimacy. A Triune God did not have to create others, because in that triune reality, there existed a loving, preexisting community of affection and communication.

Why then Creation? Maybe He brought the universe into existence because the impulse of love is creative and always seeks to reproduce itself. We all want others to experience that which we love. Love is never selfish, and by nature is reproductive. A God who is in community, enjoying life in Himself (and who wants to share that abundance), makes way more sense to me than a god living alone out there in the cosmos. Although I can't understand what (specifically) the triune relationship looks like within the godhead, I can cope with the fact that if God is God, then there will be aspects of His nature I cannot know or comprehend. At sixty, I'm okay with a little mystery. If I could fully understand God, such a god would be a pretty average and impoverished deity, joining me in the middle of the bell curve. No, Scripture makes it clear God understands Himself, and invites me to get to know Him to the extent I am able. It is an open invitation to us all. And He left us a pretty complete description of Himself to get acquainted with. Jesus said, "When you've seen me, you've seen the Father. I and the Father are one."

This is what I do know: God did not exist alone before Creation in solitary confinement.

When God said, "It is not good for man to live alone," I am thinking it was more of an invitation into the kind of life He experiences within Himself that consists of love, affection, and communication. That is also the kind of life we are invited into through marriage to one another. A unity of diversity in community. That road for me first began with a "Hey, do you wanna dance?"

Dating Games

It was a cold, windchill factor night in 1977 when I asked that all-important *do you wanna dance question*, and it changed the rest of my life. I was with a buddy at the Backlot (one of those bar/disco dance places in our 1970s college town), having a cocktail and working up the courage to ask this one particular girl to dance . . . .

Dancing is one of those interesting and bizarre quirks of human expression. All cultures have their traditional dances and ours, apparently, is no exception. But I know a lot of couples and not one of them was attracted to the other because of the shimmy and shake they saw out on the dance floor, so I am not sure what evolutionary role it supposedly serves. In the late '60s, when I was eight or so, I recall watching a rock and roll dance show on TV that featured a bunch of teenagers flailing and jerking while the band, The Troggs, played their hit song "Wild Thing." My dad and I laughed as we watched the guys thrash around, waving their arms and gyrating like they were all being electrocuted.

Now, twelve years later and sufficiently fortified by a cocktail, I approached the girl I'd been watching and somewhat confidently asked Terry's friend, Stef, that great gift of a one liner: *"Do you wanna dance?"* And I was politely turned down. Not to be defeated so easily, I immediately looked to her left and doubled down by asking Terry, who was sitting at the same table, if *she* would want to dance. To my immense, face-saving relief, she said *yes*. (Though ignorant of this at the time, Terry has this incredible gift of mercy.)

So I flailed around on the dance floor doing my best imitation of what it must look like to be electrocuted, and after sizing each other up, I thought it was safe to take the next big step and ask her for another dance. I had no way of knowing that Terry didn't really like dancing, but I'm pretty sure being a self-conscious introvert in a thrashing mob of exhibitionists had something to do with it. Even now, it's hard to get her on a dance floor. But after we got through the introductory small talk, shouted over the loud music—"What is your major? Where are you from?"—I was able to wheedle her number out of her and line up a date. Since her birthday was the following month, our first date was a birthday date. I thought I would take her out to dinner.

But taking her out to dinner meant breaking one of my codes early on: I can be a messy eater at times, and when empty plates are removed from the table after a meal, I'm usually the guy whose place is ringed with food shrapnel. It might have been a bad habit I picked up while wearing braces on my teeth as a kid, but I'm not sure. (I had the old-school metal braces complete with rubber bands and head gear.) If there were any dogs in the house, they would know to camp out under my place at the table like spectators at a baseball game, hoping to snag some fly balls. I used to avoid pizza or spaghetti because I would get so much on me, it looked like I'd been fed with a slingshot. And any kind of fat, greasy sandwiches were definitely out of the question too if I wanted to be wearing a clean shirt. *It has to be something safe,* I remember thinking, *but college-student affordable for the first date.* In the end, I decided to eat before I went out with Terry to avoid any food disasters. Even *I* understood that taking a girl out for dinner is not about the food. And this was one date I wanted to go well.

At the time, I remember thinking Terry was a pretty intimidating young woman, and I wanted to impress her in a good way. She was a beautiful, full-figured blonde who came from a large family and whose dad was a former fighter pilot. He owned his own computer billing company with an airplane only he flew, so there was a lot for me to measure up to. Her mom was Icelandic, and I thought that was kind of cool too. Terry not only spoke French (and read Sartre in French as well), but she could cook and snow ski (sort of). And she was game for just about any adventure I was up for, and had no problem riding on the back of my motorcycle or going sailing with me. Most important of all, she made me feel like I was interesting—which is what every young, red-blooded male wants to think about themselves.

After our initial date, things progressed the way I'd hoped, and we began spending a lot of time together. By the time graduation was looming just ahead, we'd been together for about a year, so it only seemed natural to ask her to come live with me in Quantico, Virginia once I was commissioned in the Marines. Apparently, I was wrong about the "only seemed natural" part of my thinking. Out of the blue, and with no warning, she pulled the pin and tossed the *commitment* grenade into my safe, happy, little world. ***"I either go as Mrs. Annable or I don't go at all."***

Burn the Ships

Commitment is something that belongs in the "too-hard box" for many people. And I've come to understand their trepidation. I was no different. Quitting when something gets too hard just seems logical. No one thinks it's smart to blow up their only escape route or opt for burning their only return-to-home ships like Cortez did when he landed in the New World. After that decision, there was no way back and no way out of danger. There was only one choice left—that of forging ahead into uncharted territory, full of unknown dangers. Commitment is like that. It means no turning back, no matter what. But like so many others, I wanted to ease into the relationship and marriage experience, primarily out of fear of making a wrong choice and losing any wiggle room. I think that's why so many more people live together nowadays before they commit to marriage. They want to practice marriage with one foot out the door to see if they're any good at it. But you can't practice commitment. You can only decide whether you're committed or whether you aren't. Then you move forward into new circumstances and unforeseen adventure.

Unlike most all other relationships, marriage is itself an intrinsic good and not an instrumental good. In other words, marriage is good in and of itself, and not good simply for what one can get out of it. It is a "burn the ships" type of commitment. Really, all relationships have, as part of their DNA, some level of commitment. It is simply a matter of degree.

I find it interesting that our relationship with God is expressed in such personal, marriage-type metaphors. As a matter of fact, God's relationship with us is so personally intimate the Bible sometimes uses sexual metaphors in describing our responses to God and His affections toward us. In one Old Testament book (Hosea), for example, He compares Israel to a spiritual prostitute saying, "You have been like a whore to me." Chapter after chapter describe His chosen people's offenses, but in the end, God can't deny His love: "How can I give you up, all my tender passions are aroused, I cannot carry out my fierce anger—for I am God and not man." The Bible is full of such passages. It's no secret that both the

Old and New Testaments use marriage analogies to describe our truest relationship with God. He uses bride and groom references instead of employee and employer language to illustrate the nature of that relationship. He speaks of a marriage feast, of a wedded couple, of faithfulness or infidelity, and commitment versus betrayal. We are invited to the great marriage feast of the Lamb, and He goes before us to prepare a place for us so we can be where He is.

The Song of Solomon is a whole book of Scripture describing this human and divine romance in the most intimate of terms. And that sacred romance is rooted in trust, faithfulness, and commitment. Knowing this, it should come as no surprise that commitment is as significant and central to the Christian faith as it is to marriage. (Ask any Christian living in the Muslim world about that.) We, the Church, are the bride of Christ after all. As with all commitments, it is way easier to half step our Christian faith than "burn the ships" and go all in. That's because commitment is not a popular word, especially in today's Western, so-called Christian culture. It smacks too much of servitude and sacrifice, and who really wants to be a slave?

We all know slavery is a bad thing and freedom is a good thing, right? Ask any American in the "land of the free." God is full of grace anyway, right? We want to be free to do what we want, even if that means we might not do what we know to be right. Anyway, grace is there to take care of any tab we might ring up in the process, right? Besides, doesn't the whole New Testament go to great lengths to let us know we are not under any law? Isn't there freedom in Christ? Isn't that the point of the gospel? If salvation is a gift, then why can't I live my life with no strings attached, particularly since God is full of grace and full of mercy? But I've found we really mean something else when we use the word "freedom" like this. It's not really freedom we're seeking but autonomy. And they are not the same thing. Autonomy is derived from two words: *auto=self* and *nomos-=law*. We want to be a law unto ourselves.

If we look at commitment as a way to earn God's saving favor, then commitment is an illegitimate means to that end. As Christians, we *already have* a relationship and are *already in* a relationship. It is now just a matter of how much we are willing to invest in it. It is a matter of degree. It is a matter of intentions, and thus a matter of commitment.

Jubilee

In the Old Testament, we are told that God, in His grace and wisdom, made a provision for a "do over" when it came to financial troubles and failures. It was called jubilee, and it still impacts us today. Chapter 11 of the United States Bankruptcy Code originated in this very practice. Our own laws recognize we sometimes need a fresh start, or reset, in life. Such laws are a reflection of our nation's Christian heritage, and I think we are the only country on earth that applies this law to forgive financial debt so a person, or a company, can reorganize and start over. And like the biblical principle of jubilee in ancient Israel, modern bankruptcy laws generally allow the forgiveness of debts after seven years. But jubilee in ancient Israel wasn't just about debt forgiveness. It transformed everyone and everything.

Every seven years, Israel's year of jubilee meant the land itself would be given a rest. (After seven years of use, leaving land fallow for one year turns out to be a good farming practice.) Slaves would be given their freedom, and there would be a restoration and reset of the entire society. Not only would the slaves be set free, but their previous masters would give them the best of the flocks and best wine to take with them. There was an exception, though.

If a slave loved his master, and didn't want to leave his service after seven years, he could *choose* to stay as a *doulos* or bond servant. The master would use an awl to pierce his ear as he stood against the door-post. It was a sign of commitment to his master and his household, and it indicated he'd chosen to remain a slave for the rest of his life. With no more chance of jubilee, it was an *all-in* kind of commitment—one that embraced servitude and rejected autonomy to retain relationship with a beloved master. Paul, the apostle, described himself as such a slave when he joyfully referred to himself as a *slave to Christ*. Paul was showing us it's better to be the slave of a good master than be free to serve ourselves.

Such commitment is hard to appreciate in the *land of the free* and the *home of the brave* where Nike exhorts us to "just do it." But there are greater things and higher purposes in life than mere freedom to do whatever we want. Navy lieutenant John McCain was offered his freedom from the torturous captivity he endured in the Hanoi Hilton as a POW in Vietnam because of his dad's position as an admiral of the Pacific fleet. Lieutenant McCain refused that freedom because of the obligation he felt to a higher call of duty. Only after many long years and damaged health would he finally regain that freedom.

I have gone in and out of the Master's house many times, but I have generally enjoyed that relationship mostly on my terms, not God's. I loved having all of life's big, eternal questions answered. But eventually, I realized that I had never really "nailed my ear to the door," and was always holding something back—and thinking about it as I write this—I probably still do. When the disciples were first called by Jesus, they left their nets and followed Him, but later went back to those same nets. It was only when they finally understood who He truly was and what they were being called to that they finally left everything and followed Him. I still go back to my nets every once in a while. (God knew full well the quality of our commitments and promises when, in making a covenant with Abraham, He alone walked through the parts of a severed beastie.)

There are many scholars who believe Jesus came in the year of jubilee, and that many of His conversations with folks used jubilee language: *Forgive us our debts as we forgive our debtors*. Jesus asked them (and us) *not to worry about what they will eat or what they will wear* knowing that was a legitimate concern for those being asked to refrain from planting or harvesting fallow land for an entire year. Previously, he'd stopped in the middle of reading a jubilee passage to announce, "Today this has been fulfilled . . . ." Some of His parables were jubilee parables, like the ones about masters forgiving debts. But the most important part of this jubilee principle is that He came to set the captives free to choose Him . . . or not.

We can choose to serve ourselves, or we can let Him nail our ear to His doorpost once and for all. Such commitment is a door that leads to a life you can't experience unless you choose to walk through it. Something fundamental happens to a relationship when the decision is made to go all in.

Marriage is like that too. After thirty-eight years, there are some things I have discovered about marriage and about why God would choose that relationship to illustrate the one He desires to have with us. Commitment and self-sacrifice are merely the means to a greater end, because these things are not ends in and of themselves. Terry already loved and accepted me before we were married. Marriage is a sacred metaphor, which is why the Christian community is so protective of how the culture treats it. Marriage is a picture of the nature of God—a loving unity of diversity, in sacrificial community. To be married is an invitation into the life of God as He is within Himself.

There is not much I can add to all of the marriage literature out there other than to say that in thirty-eight years, we have experienced the good, the bad, and the mediocre. It has been a remarkable journey in some ways and a very painful one in others. We have had kids and conflict, feast days and fasting days, and experiencing it all has gradually helped me make sense of myself and my purpose in the world. I sometimes wish I knew back when we were first married what I know now, but then I realize that there are some lessons best learned the hard way through trials.

In one of Jesus's longest prayer, he prays for unity that we may be one as God is One . . . so that others may believe. Everyone in the world knows Christians sometimes have a hard time getting along with one another. We get divorced. Churches split (which is a kind of divorce). But when a separate man and woman become a unified one in a marriage, then that in itself becomes a powerful apologetic for a Triune God and a relationship worth committing to—once you've made the decision to accept the truth that marriage is good and sacred, then go all in.

I cannot explain the Trinity. Some things about God are just beyond our capacity as humans to understand. It is like trying to define the boundaries of infinity, or a toddler trying to understand a calculus proof. There are depths there that are totally unsearchable and incomprehensible. God is God and we are not, and it is best to leave it at that. Anything else is to invite Him down off of His throne onto the middle of the bell curve.

But I think I can give the world a little picture of what a "unity in diversity" might look like. It is found in the reflection of my marriage relationship with my wife, as we two strive to present one unified flesh to the world: affection and communication in relational harmony. We share and portray a unity of diversity in loving community.

The jury is still out on *our* marriage, and it is on trial for all to see. My advice? ***Burn the ships.***

CHAPTER 4

CAMP UPSHUR

"If we don't discipline ourselves, the world will do it for us."

—William Feather

One of my old commanding officers was fond of saying, "If you don't know where you are going, any road will take you there." I was the poster boy for that adage. Like so many young men my age, life just happened for me, and then it happened *to* me. I lurched from one weekend to another with just enough gas left in my energy tank to grind out one more stupid assignment for school or cram for one more exam, always seeking to take the path of least resistance. Even if there were a few ditches along those *anywhere roads*—as far as I was concerned—they were still good enough for me.

Two things happened during my sophomore year of college to change that *anywhere road* trajectory: I met the girl who is now my wife, and a Marine recruiter visited the college's student union building one fall afternoon. Impressive in his dress blues, the Marine gunnery sergeant stood in the midst of the student union chaos like a Presbyterian preacher at a Halloween party. The table in front of him was loaded with neatly stacked brochures and a recruiting video played on a screen behind him. The video showed a military pilot standing on a runway with a pair of F-4 fighter jets flying in formation behind him. The young, blond-haired guy with a helmet under his arm was explaining how a "cat shot" takeoff from the bow of a big gray boat was better than sex . . . whoa! I was a young, blond-haired guy . . . !

One thing led to another, and before I knew it, I was calling my dad to tell him I'd been invited to Omaha to take a physical for this Marine program I'd heard about at school. My dad, who had experience in these things, tried to advise me.

"Jimmy, whatever you do, do not raise your hand or sign anything until you talk to me first."

But life was something that still just simply *happened* to me—and it just so *happened* that while I was there, I ended up raising my hand and signing a bunch of papers. Predictable.

Once Dad found out what happened in Omaha, he said something very significant (and fundamentally true) to me. After eyeing all of the stickers and tee shirts I was sporting when I got home, he told me the military was made for average people. And by and large it is. I think life is too. Because average, by definition, is where most of us live.

Of course, the military has had its shining stars, including astronauts and presidents. It's also had its share of knuckleheads like Lee Harvey Oswald and Gomer Pyle. But on the whole, the military machine grinds its gears and runs its wheels on the strength and efforts of average guys like me. After recruitment, we're no longer free agents acting as individuals. Instead, we're molded into a group wearing the same uniform and acting as a unit. We are given orders, and those orders are relentlessly reinforced. We're only told what we need to know and shown what (and how) we need to do it.

This seemed to be Jesus' approach also—when He selected fishermen to be the foundational leaders of the church and when He said, "Follow Me." He told them what to do, then led by example, and showed them how to do it.

Wake-up Call

That first summer of OCS, it was ninety degrees and humid when we college boys stepped off the buses at Camp Upshur. It was an isolated, somewhat monkish retreat carved out of the Virginia woods on the sprawling Marine base at Quantico. The drill sergeant who was waiting for us was a broad-shouldered, square-jawed man right out of central casting for the *Sands of Iwo Jima*. He sported three purple hearts among a bunch of other ribbons, and he had a diagonal scar that ran down from the corner of his left eye to the corner of his mouth. Not once, in the six weeks he was with us, did I ever see him smile. Maybe the fact that any enlisted Marine over the age of twenty-six and any officer over the age of twenty-nine was a Vietnam vet had something to do with it.

He ordered us to line up and stand in painted footprints on a small asphalt parking lot lined with rows of rusty, corrugated metal Quonset huts. Overwhelmed, I did my best to hide my shock and dismay. *What the heck have I gotten myself into?* I thought. When he pointed to the painted feet I was to stand on, I politely thanked him.

He just looked at me for a moment before he said, "I get a fitness report every six months, and I'm paid every once in a while, and that is all the thanks I need . . . *candidate*."

Next, we were given a physical (where we prayed to God they would find something wrong with us that wasn't life-threatening but disqualifying), before being herded off to the barbershop for a twenty-second military haircut and our "issue." When we came out with shaved heads and green clothes, no one recognized anyone else. We all looked the same. That was the point—we had to learn to stand at attention and march everywhere as a group instead of as individuals.

One of the funniest things you will ever see is about forty college guys, some ready to graduate and some scholarship athletes, trying to learn how to march in unison. I wish I had a video of those first days of learning how to put one foot forward at the same time. But learn we did. And as we stood at attention in our *sateen* utilities with starched covers, our drill sergeants began to mold us young, immature college boys into something that might one day resemble Marines. It was the beginning of my introduction to the largest fraternity in the world.

1978 Marine Candidate–a long way from school.

I have accomplished a lot in my lifetime, both in my personal life and in my career, but when I look back into the past and examine the young man I once was, the thing that I am most proud of is that I was a Marine. In many significant ways, it marked me for life, and it was a turning point at precisely the time I needed one.

When I came back from that first summer—after the two six-week courses in Quantico I had to attend—I noticed something different about myself and my approach to life. I did better in school, and I was more respectful of others and things. But the biggest change—looming before me like the pot of gold at the end of a rainbow—was that I had a vision of what I wanted to do and who I wanted to be. The Bible says that without a vision, young men perish, and though I may not have been perishing prior to this major course correction in my life, the *anywhere* road I was on at the time was leading nowhere. Now I knew where I was going. And my new direction and purpose lay before me like the yellow brick road to Oz.

Sports teaches you discipline, and I appreciate the opportunity and ability to have participated in sports. But the Marine Corps took such discipline to a new level, and I think the discipline I was introduced to in the USMC played a very large role in any success I have ever had thereafter. Self-discipline doesn't come naturally to most of us, and it surely didn't for me. To those who say, "It must be easy for you, but not for me," that is simply not true. If it seems easier for some, it's not because they were born standing at attention. It's probably been a way of life for them for a long time.

Like commitment, discipline isn't a *goal* or an *end* in and of itself. We aren't disciplined just to be disciplined—that's kind of like practicing to bleed. No, discipline is always a means to a greater end and goal. If we lose sight of that goal and focus on the *means* rather than the *ends* of why we are doing a thing, it's hard to be disciplined. Acquiring discipline requires having a vision of where we want to end up and what we want to accomplish. After that, we just need to keep putting one foot in front of the other.

Zero Dark Thirty

Our mornings at Camp Upshur began at 0400 hours (zero dark thirty, we called it) with an inspection and a formation followed by a march to the chow hall. We only had thirty minutes for the company to line up (150 or so of us), file through the food line, and actually eat. If you were the last squad at the end of the company, you only got the dry cereal and white bread that was left, and you only had about thirty seconds to wolf it down. Afterwards, we marched back to our Quonset huts, quickly changed into our PT (physical training) gear, and formed up for PT. All PT began with the Marine Corps Daily Seven, a group of calisthenics that loosened you up for the nightmare morning that was to follow.

The day began early and ended in utter exhaustion. I had never run in boots before, and I'd never run with full canteens on a web belt while holding a rifle. After finishing that first three-mile run in boots, I was bending over and trying to catch my breath with big sucking gasps.

The drill sergeant came up to me and asked, "What are you doing, candidate?"

"I don't know, Sgt. Instructor!" *I am dying, Sgt. Instructor!*

"If you want to be a leader in *my* Marine Corps, you better have some bearing and not look like some tired college boy sucking wind."

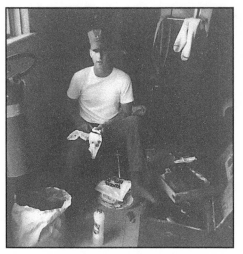

Brass, boots, and buckles.
Just a few of a candidate's housekeeping chores.

(Which is precisely what I was—a college boy sucking wind.) "Aye, aye, Sgt. Instructor!"

"**Stand up straight!** You better watch your **bearing!** I don't give a crap if you're tired, you better not **look** tired."

"Aye, aye, **Sgt. Instructor!**"

I wanted to quit. Bad. I think we all did. *What in the world was I doing here?* I thought. And who was I kidding anyway? I should have been rolling *into* bed at 4:00 a.m., not getting up at 4:00 a.m. for a day of physical and mental abuse. But all fifty of the other guys in my unit were enduring the same things and thinking the same thoughts. To quit meant I couldn't hack it, and they could. And who wants to be called a quitter, right? If I quit, I'd have to go home and tell everyone what I was doing back so early. I'd have to explain that I'd quit because it was too hard, and I didn't want to do that. Besides, I'd started to make some friends, and we'd become a community bound by shared suffering. I didn't want to let them down either.

If we'd gone through it all by ourselves, the majority of us would have said, "*Are you kidding me? I am **not** putting myself through this crap anymore . . . .*" But that's the point. Our drill sergeants were doing their best to get us to quit. But we didn't, and we learned the value of simply doing the next thing—then the next thing after that. Putting one foot in front of the other taught us a valuable lesson in perseverance. There was the peer pressure, to be sure, but more than that, you had to reach deep down into your gut and tell yourself, *I am not going to give up yet. I can do it one more day.* The fear of failure is a legitimate motivator.

From the very beginning (although we did not know it at the time), everything we did was focused toward the welfare of who we were to lead. We were taught to handle stress and model confidence before others who might need to see it in someone else. When we set off on grueling fifteen-mile hikes with seventy-pound packs, every fifty minutes, we would stop and get off our feet—but not the platoon leaders who they were training us to be. They kept walking up and down the lines, checking the feet of their men and making sure no one had any symptoms of heat stroke.

During that summer, I learned that cutting corners or half stepping a responsibility could get people killed. I learned that no matter what you think you can do—you are always capable of much, much more. This philosophy of training for mental toughness is reflected in the thoughts of the biblical prophet Jeremiah when he reminded his people, "If you have run with the footmen and they have tired you out, how then can you compete with the horses, and if you fall down in the land of peace, what will you do in the thickets of Jordan?"

Leadership

Leadership is a popular theme prevalent throughout industry, churches, politics, family, and communities. You can't swing a dead cat and not hit a "leadership conference" somewhere in an airport hotel conference room. Schools push the notion that "every student is a leader." And churches seems to be constantly searching for the perfect "leadership development" program. Sometimes I wonder what these programs and conferences even mean when they use the word "leadership." And I wonder how they'd actually describe a leader guy or leader gal. What *is* a leader? It was the Marine Corps that first peeled back the curtain on the concept of leadership for me. They even had a definition for it that I remember to this day: "To influence men and women in such a way as to accomplish the mission." That kind of influence usually involves sacrifice.

While flying on a trip for my airline, I heard an account describing that kind of sacrificial leadership from a fellow Marine I was flying with. He told me about his uncle who'd been interred as a POW during WWII in one of the cruelest POW camps in Europe. Apparently, that uncle didn't talk much about the war, but he was prodded out of his usual reticence when his newly commissioned nephew was being grilled by family members about when he'd get out of the Marines, use his education, and get on with his life. The former POW uncle stepped in and said, "Leave him alone. He is a Marine. Not only that, he is an officer." He went on to add, "Now let me tell you what an officer is . . ."

He explained how the POWs at the camp where he had been imprisoned would muster early every morning. Despite their desperate needs, they gathered in the rain, or in the freezing cold, or in the sweltering heat. Every day. Every morning. Some of the men were sick and needed medicine, some had no shoes, and all of them were hungry. But without fail, each morning before the muster, the officers who were POWs drew straws to see who would step out of formation and request the things their men needed. Even as prisoners in a German stalag, they were still responsible for their men. The officer who drew the short straw would step out of formation, make his requests on behalf of his men, then have the living crap beaten out of him for making those requests. Sometimes the punishment was worse than simply a brutal beating. But the officers would draw straws again the next morning anyway, and each morning afterward. They modeled sacrificial leadership to their men at a very difficult time, in a very difficult place. These officers conveyed a powerful message: *If we can endure this—so can you. Stay the course. I can do this—so you can do this too.*

I'm not sure many "leadership seminars" or "leadership development programs" emphasize the cost of being an influential leader. This aspect of leadership is rarely mentioned or discussed. But there's a price to be paid for stepping out of the formation. Leadership always has a cost. What's more, an impressive title or a corner office doesn't make you a leader if there's no one following you. What's most important is to step out in front at a difficult time, in a difficult place.

If we couldn't hack a hike in the Virginia woods when no one was shooting at us, how could we handle things when it really mattered and people were bleeding in the "thickets of Jordan?" At Camp Upshur, I learned most obstacles standing in our way are mental obstacles, not physical ones. All discipline starts in the mind where all life-giving habit patterns actually begin. The Marines first taught me that principle, but biblical truth and my own experience has reinforced it over and over again. Scripture tells us to *"take every thought captive."* Either we control our thoughts or our thoughts control us. How I *choose* to think about something determines how I tend to respond physically. And this cause and effect sequence creates the habit patterns and moral boundary markers that shape my life experience. If I begin to think about my many irritations and problems at work, for example, I find myself disgruntled with my job and lose motivation. But intentional positive thoughts are just as powerful; if I mentally determine to think really great thoughts about my wife, for example, my feelings of affection for her follow. The Bible is correct when it says, "As a man thinks in his heart—so is he. Transform your thinking . . . renew your mind . . . Think about these things that are good, right . . . ."

The Discipline of Grace

I was like many other contented, happy-thinking pagans when the Lord showed up in my life. Prior to that, I hadn't really thought about God at all, and I certainly wasn't interested in doing anything to earn His favor. There wasn't much I wanted to change about my life and circumstances. I was okay with where I was and what I was doing. I simply didn't know any better. And I'm in good company. Originally a theist, C. S. Lewis said he got in the car one day to go somewhere, and when he got out of the car, he was a Christian. He suddenly and spontaneously understood and believed the same gospel he'd heard all his life. Same here. Before coming to faith, I wasn't trying to be good, and I wasn't trying to keep any laws or earn any favors. I did not desire God or seek any sort of Christian life. Fear of judgement got my attention initially, but even that emotion didn't sustain me for very long. It was simply the prelude to something more profound.

Once I became a Christian, it didn't take me long to understand there was a division and tension between two political parties called *law* and *grace*. As church congregations moved out of denominational buildings with steeples and into shopping malls, theaters, and schools, there arose a new enemy of the faith, and that enemy was labeled **legalism.** Churches were **grace-filled** and not **under the law.** It appeared that evangelical equations went something like this: **Freedom = Grace, Obedience = Legalism.** From the pulpit, I heard the message that Christianity isn't a religion but a *relationship* with Jesus. And so it is. But like marriage, it's not a one-sided kind of relationship. Those don't work. I've been in one-sided relationships and they suck. (I actually tried that approach early in my marriage, and it didn't work out too well there either.)

Law and grace are two concepts that need sorting out when a person first becomes a follower of Christ. Truth be told, I'm still sorting them out. Our God is, in fact, a law-giving God. No question about that. But there's also no question He is a God of grace as well, and it seems to me I've spent much of my life leaning into one or the other of those two realities. I've tried to strike a balance between law and grace, just as other Christians have been doing for nearly two thousand years. Paul wrote a letter to the Galatians because they were too legalistic, and he wrote another one to the Corinthians because they weren't legalistic enough. Both law and grace are equally important principles of, and to, our faith. Law defines the nature of the holiness a Holy God requires of His family, but grace is His acknowledgement of our inability to achieve that holiness. But we still have to run the race with endurance, and that takes a strong degree of perseverance and discipline.

As a Marine recruit, I learned the discipline of "showing up" at Camp Upshur, whether I felt like it or not. It didn't matter that our days began early and ended late; that we got up at "oh dark thirty" before dawn (if indeed we slept at all after being given Sisyphean tasks we spent all night trying to accomplish under the glare of bathroom lights) because we had to march to chow, complete PT, march back, shower, march to chow again, and then—at the worst possible time of day since we were already exhausted—sit for classes in hot rooms with big fans running in the back. In those classes, we learned the basics of small unit tactics and other such martial material along with Marine Corps history. Our minds were being introduced to *who we were* and we began to see our place in something bigger and more storied than our own individual narratives and comforts.

When the Apostle Paul writes to Christ followers, he uses a lot of martial themes to describe this arduous Christian journey of ours. He tells us we are engaged in a war with an enemy—and that we have armor we need to put on to fight that war successfully. Like any soldier in any army at any time, there are disciplines and rules of engagement to follow. But in some quarters of the evangelical community, the need for these *spiritual disciplines* is met with indifference or labeled with the thinly veiled accusation of *self-effort*. It is not. I am not sure what it is other than simply effort. It is Paul, the apostle, who calls us to exercise ourselves unto godliness. Believe it or not, that takes effort.

The criticisms of self-effort are legitimate when spiritual disciplines are seen as an *end* in themselves rather than a *means* to a greater end. No amount of work can climb and surmount the hurdle of sin. The goal of discipline is not to earn God's favor, or PT your way into heaven. We can't accomplish that by following the law. The law simply shows us how God defines holiness—a holiness we can't humanly achieve. But a disciplined Christian life enables us to live the way disciples are called to live as Christ's emissaries, saved by grace. Discipline equips us to fulfill the Great Commission and join God in His redemptive work to save a battle-torn world.

We *are* in a war after all.

The Will of God

Jesus once told a parable of two sons who were told by their father to plow a field. One son enthusiastically agreed to do it, but he never actually did the job. The other son initially refused, but gritted his teeth and finally did the work anyway. Jesus asked the question, *"Who then did the will of My Father?"*

Thomas Aquinas once said there were two ways in which we can conform to the will of God: One way is to simply do what He asks us to do—feed the hungry and take care of the poor. But the second and more profound way we conform to the will of God is when we do those things for the same reason God desires us to do them—because our hearts break for the widow and the orphan in their distress. We should grieve over those who are hungry, and then do something about it. But many times, we can't align our hearts with God's heart for a situation until we first submit to being obedient to what God would have us do, whether we feel like it or not. Understanding often comes afterwards, and we comprehend the heart of God a bit better than before.

I can't imagine Abraham being excited about sacrificing his only son, and I doubt he slept at all the night before. He must have agonized over the awful, incomprehensible thing God was asking him to do. He certainly didn't decide to obey and do that horrific thing because he felt like it. But he trusted God was good even when he didn't understand. Now, thousands of years later, we know what Abraham did not—that God Himself would provide *His* only Son as the sacrifice. Because we're made in His image and likeness, He asks us to be like Himself in inexplicable ways—just as He asked Abraham to do the thing He would later complete on a Roman cross at Golgotha.

There are a lot of things I simply can't do anymore (it's just a matter of physics) that I was able to do as a young Marine candidate so many years ago. Yet I didn't believe I could do them back then either. Some of the things we were asked to do were silly, and they seemed to have no connection to anything significant or purposeful. We were just told to pay attention to detail even though we had no clue how these little things fit into a bigger picture and a larger story. It was only later that our task assignments made sense. Obedience to God is like that also. It's a hard thing to obey orders when you don't feel like it, or when those orders don't make sense. The Bible is littered with stories of Jesus asking people to do odd and seemingly ridiculous things (like lowering a net on the other side of the boat, or to leave a boat and walk on water).

Many of the things God asks us to do may seem unreasonable or impossible. They require belief in His power and a faith in His goodness. You and I can trust and have faith in what we are being asked to do because we have confidence in Who it is that's asking us to do it.

Semper fidelis is the Marine Corps motto. ***Always faithful.*** It is how they trained us.

God can use that in His disciples too.

CHAPTER 5

QUANTICO

"A cynic knows the price of everything but the value of nothing."

—Oscar Wilde

E very now and again, I am reminded of my Olympic-level impulsiveness to do something really, *really* stupid financially. I find this is something I can't seem to grow out of, but like an alcoholic, I've tried to learn over time to tame and conquer the beast. As a brand new second lieutenant who'd just graduated from college, for example, I was intrigued when the United States Marine Corps (in its infinite wisdom) allowed a car dealer to come chat with us fresh-out-of-college-guys about buying a car. So after one of our many classes at The Basic School, we were treated to a visit from a retired Marine Major: Boom-Boom. He sold sports cars.

That night when I got home, I loaded up my confused, seven months pregnant wife into our roomy, 1974 olive-green sedan so we could zip down to "Boom-Boom's" sports car dealership. While looking at all the colorful RX-7s, MGBs, and Spiders sitting there so beautifully displayed and shiny with their rag tops and chrome grilles calling to me like a siren calling a sailor to the rocks, I also happened to recognize some other like-minded guys from my company doing exactly what I was doing. *I think*

I like the dark yellow RX-7, I decided. Meanwhile, Terry was thinking . . . *Why are we here?*

After she pointed out the obvious to me, "We will soon be three and there are only two seats in these things!" My mind still refused to comprehend the impracticality of buying a sports car. I desperately tried to think how we might be able to stuff a car seat behind and *under* the folding convertible top of that RX-7.

The lust for shiny, sporty things can cause you to lose your mind. Really.

The One that Got Away

As an American, part of our philosophical heritage as a citizen of this Great Republic is the credo, "To have is to be." Anyone born in this country comes into it as a consumer who will grow, live, and die as one too. Consumerism is what drives our politics, business, entertainment, and religion, and it's how we Americans calibrate our "happy-to-be-alive meter." I'm no different, I suppose, and neither are you. All of us would probably agree that, given the choice, we would rather have more rather than less.

This is why storytellers so often use the "rags to riches" storyline seen in the classic Cinderella tale and Jane Austen's romance novels—in which the most important component of the main story is that a poor person becomes a rich one. Usually through a romance. Of course, we are teased and pleased with how the romantic nature of true love finally wins the day as a wealthy Mr. Darcy or Prince Charming falls for the poor, pretty girl and lives happily ever after. We believe that's how all stories should end. Truth be told, we want to see *ourselves* as that Prince Charming or Cinderella. (We also want to be wealthy and live happily ever after.)

Rarely is there a story about a rich person giving everything up to live happily ever after in poverty. (Mother Theresa is the gold standard there.) At some point—whether love is involved or not—money, riches, wealth, and possessions are at the core of every popular tale in some form or fashion. In our particular romance story, my wife's challenge has always been about hanging on to what we have before her own prince charming fritters it away on the latest gadget, geegaw, chainsaw, farm implement, or sports car. She keeps a grip on our checkbook like a momma grizzly with a freshly caught salmon preparing for hibernation.

Yet in the strange calculus of humanness, our lives are not really defined so much by what we have or acquire, but by what we have lost or will one day lose. In other words, it's not what we acquire but what *we fail to acquire* or what we lost that often haunts us.

Ask any fisherman about the one that got away and you'll understand how I felt about that sports car I wanted so badly in 1980. "Losing it" dialed back my fun meter in a big way, and I'll never know the temporary joy of owning it. I say *temporary* joy because it would have grown old and rusty as all material *things* do over time. But had we ever lost our infant daughter, Kate, we would have been devastated for the rest of our lives.

I've owned many cars since that day in 1980 when that pretty yellow RX-7 slipped through my grasp. I even owned a sports car years later. Still, it was that pretty, little yellow RX-7 I still think about and remember the most. Only now do I realize that it never would have, nor could have, met all of my lustful expectations. I have often wondered why a man as blessed as I've been seems to be so easily distracted by the siren's call of new stuff.

I don't think I'm unusual in this tendency to value what I *don't* have rather than gratefully value the things that I *do*. Even my health. As the years have taken their toll physically and I've begun to lose abilities I once so thoughtlessly took for granted, I think most about those things I can never do again instead of what I can still do *now*. I've found that learning to be grateful for what I have *today* is the key to contentment. A meaningful life and a contented life are somehow intertwined in the fabric of a *good* life.

More Is Never Enough

We keep our boat at a small little marina off the South River below Annapolis, Maryland. As you walk down the rickety, unkempt dock to our boat, you pass a small house sitting on a barge-like structure surrounded by the odds and ends of a tinkerer and the hand-me-down artifacts of living. Lawn chairs on the grass across the bulkhead, a small grill on the "porch-deck," and pots of flowers sprinkled around their small two-story floating home. A rowing scull sits on the back, and various lines and hoses are randomly peeking out of the structure like a patient recovering from something serious in a hospital ICU. A tomato plant balances on a piling, courageously spreading its leaves, trying to live life in this alien world of boats and crabs. Yesterday, as I was passing by on the way to our boat, I saw John—who was the captain and master of that floating home—sitting in his lawn chair under a big shade tree reading Ayn Rand's *Atlas Shrugged*. John can talk knowledgeably on just about any topic you might broach with him in the course of a conversation, anything from bee keeping to celestial navigation to apparently now being able to answer the question of *"Who is John Gault?"* Most conversations that involve rabbit trails off the main topic can be frustrating and time-consuming, but with John, they turn into delightful little adventures to unexpected and interesting places. John and his wife—who is a master of all things fiber from knitting to quilting to sewing and has the machinery to back it up—live very simply, pay no taxes, and are the envy of every boat owner who walks by them sitting in the shade, enjoying their morning coffee or afternoon cocktail. It is what we all aspire to do—nothing if it and when it suits us.

While we were sitting in a couple of lawn chairs one Saturday afternoon, discussing the plight of our health care system, one of our boat neighbors walked up with some bacon-wrapped scallops, some grilling tools, several bottles of wine for his guests, and offered us a scallop while he put his steaks on the grill. Now there is not a food group on this planet that bacon does not make better and certainly those scallops were no exception. As John and I were going over all of the food we liked with bacon and that our moms used to cook in bacon grease, John made an interesting comment seeing how it was coming from one whose sole income is social security and whose home is no bigger than most garages when he said in all seriousness, *"I wonder how the poor folks live."* Indeed.

I come from a family of very modest means. Having an air conditioner for our trailer in the South was a big deal when I was small. So was finally getting my own bedroom when we finally moved into a real house that didn't have wheels. My wife, Terry, whose home was small and whose family was large, had to sleep in the same bed with her sister when she was growing up until her sister, Kris, graduated from high school and left home. One bathroom for four girls and one boy. My own family, of which I am now the chief bread winner, has experienced both the rise and fall of income deficiencies and income bounty. In both cases, it seemed our standard of living swelled or shrunk to whatever we had coming in. I have no problem spending money in either case. The odd fact is, if you have $10.00 in your pocket and no debt, you are wealthier than one quarter of all Americans. Yet statistical polling shows that no matter what your income level is, everyone polled from four- and five-figure income earners to six-figure income earners all said they would be more content if they had X amount more of income coming in. Evidently, more is not enough. Of course our government is the insatiable super-hero in that regard when it comes to more. I think there is a governmental department which sole job is to make up new words for large amounts of money it owes and says it needs.

What is it that we really value that drives us as consumers? We certainly know the price of things. In junior high and high school, we knew (with all of our adolescent wisdom) we needed to acquire certain things so our peers would value us. We had to wear our jeans in a certain way, drive a certain kind of car, or show we had certain stupid gadgets we wore or toyed around with. As we got older, this kind of thinking didn't seem to change much—just the price of the stuff we "needed" to acquire to gain other people's respect.

Although Terry and I own a boat, it isn't a *must have* we bought to impress anyone. Plus, we're outliers in the boating world in that we've owned and operated this same boat for over seventeen years. When the novelty wears off and the thrill wanes (or the bilge pump fails one too many times), most folks feel the need to get a bigger, better, newer boat. I get that. But that's not on my list of *must-haves.* Looking at other parts of the world, we sometimes scratch our heads at the *must-haves* of other cultures because these things don't seem like *must-haves* to us. It may be a particular bird feather for a feathery coat, or it might be small feet (so they bind them up), or it could be a certain number of cows. Some *must-haves* may even cause folks to drill holes in their earlobes and stretch them out to the size of a half dollar. That one's certainly not on my list. (Tattoos aren't either, but they may be on yours.) But whatever the motivation, most folks have something in common: They figure they *must have* a bigger and better—or simply different—*something* to be happy. It is interesting the prophet Haggai would refer to this universal "must-have" impulse thousands of years ago: "Think carefully about what you are doing. You have planted much but have harvested little. You put on clothes but are not warm. Those who earn wages put their money in pockets with holes in them . . . ."

I would guess most buying impulses are generally emotional in nature, and it's questionable what kind of return we actually get from them in the end. Too many times, I've heard different preachers prey on their congregation by appealing to their innate *"I'd be happier with more"* emotion and exhorting them to *give* more (generally to their church), so they can *get* more from God . . . if they just have enough faith, etc.

In many cases, that easy enrichment is actually a curse and not the life-transforming blessing some preachers promise. Some of the unhappiest people on the planet are also the wealthiest. I was reminded of this when I found a *yachting* magazine left in the cockpit of one of the airplanes we were taking out of Miami. It listed 100 of the world's largest or most expensive yachts. One guy had *two* multimillion-dollar boats on that list. *Why would he own two yachts?* I wondered. Just because he could, I guess. Still, I can't believe he is any happier on his palatial yacht than I am on my boat. I know that's true as I remember the many evenings we've sat outside on our flybridge, drinking $10.00 Costco wine with old friends, enjoying the delightful quiet of creation and the comfortable fellowship of one another's company. Sometimes we sit long into the evening because we just don't want it to end. These happy hours, I'm convinced, have been a little foretaste of heaven. Regardless, whatever heaven will be like for us, it most certainly won't have anything to do with owning the latest iPhone so many of us are looking forward to, but the reuniting of old friends and family. It's sad so many people don't recognize the value of those relationships until long after they're gone.

It is why I say that it is not what we have at the moment that is most meaningfully lasting to us, but that which we've lost.

Lost

We went to visit my sister and her husband, John, in Nebraska last summer to try out the new crossbow I'd gotten for Christmas. The crossbow had been sort of a half-serious, half-joke item since the day I walked into the Bass Pro Shops in Grapevine, Texas and saw it hanging on a rack, fully armed with all of the lethal possibilities one could possibly imagine. The store (in all of its marketing wisdom) had even rigged up a mannequin to look like it had just speared a very large fish with the lethal arrow still connected to the crossbow by a line—just to help unimaginative customers like me envision all of the weapon's awesome potential. I suddenly realized I didn't know how I'd managed to live so long without a crossbow and told my wife, Terry, how every man ought to have one of those things. I would have had better luck snatching a salmon from the mouth of a hungry grizzly than expect her to relinquish the several hundred dollars one of those things cost. But my boys (being males) seemed to understand my fascination with that crossbow and the manly virtue of owning such a thing (and probably hoped for a chance to shoot it). So they went in together and bought me one for Christmas. I was so thrilled

I drove all the way from our apartment in Euless, Texas to my sister's place in Nebraska just to shoot that thing.

When we got there, it turned out that my brother-in-law, John, had just had all of his teeth taken out, which was a bit of a surprise to us. I knew he must have had a good reason for it, but I couldn't really understand what he was saying when he tried to explain (the best he could) with no teeth. But John was a practical guy, and he always had a good reason for stuff he did (except when we were in college), but still—no teeth. Here was a man who was as carnivorous and as epicurean in his appreciation of a good steak as any man I know. In addition, John is a great cook and griller of all things that swim, walk, or fly, and when he's the one cooking a meal, there are two things you can count on: it will be some sort of protein (something he probably shot or fished out of the local trout pond), and it will be creatively marinated, sautéed, and seasoned with something unusual. John was finally fitted with new teeth, but I will go out on a limb here and say they're not as good as his old ones. The point is, we take teeth for granted, and their loss defines us more than any of the new appliances we have to store that $90 tenderloin we bought at the butchers to eat in a brand new home on the golf course.

Most of the time, we only see the value in something after it's gone. I suppose it's the same with people too. But that's not something new to those of us living a consumer life in the twentieth century.

It was certainly no surprise to Jesus. I think there had to be a mighty good reason the Incarnation was born into a carpenter's family (How much work does a carpenter get in a desert community?) in a backwards area of the world, in an animal shed. It's also interesting that news came first to the shepherds, who were the lowest in the socioeconomic order of the time. When Jesus spoke to His disciples about the underlying impulses and desires behind the lust for wealth, He was telegraphing the fact that this desire to acquire leads us to so many unhappy places. He would spend a lot of His time reminding us that our lives are not defined by what we have. Almost half of the parables He would teach had something to do with money, as did one out of every ten verses in the Gospels. Why?

Money cuts across all religions and all cultures as a universal form of value that's used to tangibly express our desires. When our inner Midas directs our affections to prioritize objects over people, Jesus has something to say we probably ought to pay attention to. He communicated some of those things in a story about a rich man and a leper.

Most of us are familiar with Jesus' parable of the rich man and Lazarus. When the rich man left his home every day, he had to step around a poverty-stricken fellow covered with sores. We know this man was wealthy because the Bible takes great pains to describe his clothes, which were made of fine purple linen—the garments of someone with wealth and status. But it wasn't a crime to be wealthy since his wealth would have been a sign of God's favor. And the Bible doesn't say he was a bad guy or mean or irreligious. It doesn't say he neglected to tithe, or failed to keep the law regarding adultery or swindling, or that he was a bad Jew. The bottom line is that we are never told that the rich man was an immoral person. Instead, we are told that he thought about his brothers even as he himself was suffering. In fact, later on, when this rich man is in a state of obvious torment, he isn't thinking about himself but about his brothers and how to spare them from suffering the same fate.

The rich man's crime was the fact that every day, he passed by a fellow human being and had the means to alleviate his suffering but did not. As a poor beggar with no status, Lazarus was essentially *invisible* to him. We don't know the name of this rich man, but Lazarus is the *only* person in *any* of the parables Jesus honors by identifying him by his name. In so doing, He turns the world's value system upside down. It was not the rich man's wealth that appears to be an issue in this story, but the moral failure of his indifference. The opposite of love is not hate—it is indifference or apathy.

One day, my daughter, Victoria, was driving with my wife and they saw a man by an intersection with a sign that read, *"Homeless, hungry, need food!"* Victoria said to her mom, "We have some cash and money, why don't you stop and give it to him?" Good question. Why *don't* we stop and share what we have with those who don't?

Later on, I told my daughter that I do sometimes give money to folks like the one she saw with the sign, but sometimes I don't. And I don't usually have a good reason for choosing why I will help one and not the other, but here is the thing: the minute you lose that inner tension and struggle between deciding "*should I*" or "*shouldn't I*," then I think you have a problem. The poor, and even the appearance of the poor, should grab our attention—not because of their poverty per se, but because of the suffering it often brings.

Then I told her the story of Mary D.

A friend of mine was at a hotel during a layover (in Denver, I think) when he looked out the window facing the rear of the hotel and saw a man rooting in the dumpster several floors below his window. Thinking he ought to go down and give this man the means to get a proper meal, and with the full intention of doing so, he first went to shower before taking on the day. But by the time he got to the dumpster, the man was gone and my friend thought he'd lost an opportunity to bless someone less fortunate. He went back inside and ate a big breakfast, then decided to see the city. As he walked out of the hotel lobby, an old woman was standing there, holding a sign we all see too often these days: "Hungry, homeless, and penniless."

So my friend walked up to the woman and told her he wouldn't give her any money, but he *would* take her into the hotel and buy her breakfast or lunch—an offer she enthusiastically agreed to accept. As she ate, he got to know her name and learned a little about her. When he went to pay, he introduced Mary to the waitress but the waitress refused to let him cover the cost of Mary D's meal.

"I know what you are doing," she said. "You were in here before, and I am paying for this woman's meal!"

My friend gave the waitress his card and said, "Okay, but if you see her again and she needs anything, call me."

Months later, he received a letter from the waitress which went something like this:

Dear Mr. M,

I want to update you on Mary D, and I wanted to thank you for bringing her into my life. After I lost my mother, I had been wanting someone to take care of. Mary is now blind and lives with me.

Money $$$

Money itself is not a bad thing, nor is spending it to suit our fancy when we are fortunate enough to have some. When I have the money, I will choose rib eye over minute steak every single time. But you cannot have a quality give-and-take relationship with money. You can certainly feel affection toward the things it buys, but in the end, it's an illegitimate one-way emotion wasted on things instead of people. Money and things don't last forever. They aren't eternal. But people are. And you are too.

A five dollar bill is just a piece of paper, and a penny is a just a bit of metal (that ironically takes two and a half cents to make). Each of these things has no value in itself, so what gives that piece of paper or piece of silver, copper, or gold its value? The government makes money, decides its value, and then backs this assertion with its own "full faith and trust" that it will make good on its promise that the sawbuck or nickel is worth what it claims. Most times, the nation that prints these otherwise worthless pieces of paper not only declares their worth but also imprints the image of their king, queen, dictator, or president on its face before telling the world this money is worth something: *This currency or coin has "X" amount of value because we, the Government, declare it to be so, and we back that claim up with our word and the image we've put on the currency makes it official.*

As we all know, the issue of value isn't settled so easily, though, since the currency of a country can become worthless no matter what the government says it's worth. What gives money its value is the communal understanding that it has an agreed upon worth by all of us who use it. At any one time, there are a number of countries whose currency is so devalued that its money is worthless. We can probably all agree that it doesn't really matter what a government says (think Weimar Republic here) about the worth of its currency. Ultimately, the value of money is decided by those who use it.

The reason Jesus spent so much time talking about money is that He was communicating to us what He really considers precious. He not only created us and stamped *His* image on us and declared us valuable, but He also backed that claim up by His words and the sacrifice of His own perfect life. When He tells us we are treasured image bearers of the King, we can truly believe we have value—the very thing every human being longs for most keenly. Like currency and coins, though, there has to be a communal understanding of a human being's value. And we find that defined in the words and deeds of Jesus in His teaching about money and His imperative to not only love God, but love other people as much as we love ourselves. These commands serve to underscore the value of loving people, if only for the sole reason of the One whose image we bear. We all have a deep longing to be loved and valued, but God also longs for us to value one another as He values us.

I think that's why paper, wood, metal (even gold) do not cut it as true treasure worth our blood, sweat, and tears. They represent a means to an end (helping people), not an end in themselves. God was pissed when the Israelites tried to make images of wood and gold to worship because, at the end of the day, these idols were really just inanimate hunks of wood and cold chunks of metal that bore no resemblance to the Creator God who asks us to value what He values—living people made in His image. "Be like your Father in heaven," Jesus said, "who causes the sun and the rain to fall on the evil and the good alike." Treasure *people*. In spite of this command, our affections tend to gravitate toward the hard currency that helps us maintain the illusion of control over our lives and circumstances.

I am in the twilight of my career as an airline pilot now and have a mandatory retirement age looming in the not-so-distant future. The answer to the question, "When do I retire?" has always been, "When you have enough . . . and when you've had enough." But how much is enough?

I guess I should ask my wife. I still can't trust myself with that answer.

There is a new cyber currency on the world scene that may one day replace the paper and metal we use now to quantify the worth of material things. It is money you can't see and can't touch, and it exists only in the digital world of the Internet. (Ironically, so many dismiss the idea of God as someone you can't see and can't touch . . . but everyone considers cyber currency real enough to trade online for stuff.) I think I'm too old to live in this new world of Internet bitcoins and crypto currencies. It's hard to know what they're really worth.

But God has already told *us* what we're worth: We are worth dying for.

CHAPTER 6

PENSACOLA

"There is nothing permanent except change."

—Heraclitus

Managing expectations and disappointments is something I have struggled with over the years, and I am sure I am not alone in this. What I have come to belatedly discover, is that my biggest issue with that problem of managing expectations can be summed up it two words: *sudden change*.

When used in a sports context, "sudden change" refers to a team on the move—on the offense. The team is rolling along and then disaster strikes. An interception. A fumble. Instead of moving forward with confident optimism, the team reverts to defensive maneuvers, just trying to avert disaster. It's an unfortunate reversal of fortunes. Our lives are like that too. They can be marked by sudden change that disrupts our most carefully laid plans without warning. Such change can be positive or negative. It might be a lottery win, a pregnancy, a job loss (or gain), or a diagnosis. Sudden change. Stuff happens. Whatever form this happens to take, when a sudden change occurs, life is not the same as it was just a minute before.

I can recall a phone conversation with a friend whose toddler daughter was not progressing the way normal toddlers do at that stage in their development. He took her in to the doctor and then called me later in tears. His daughter was diagnosed with a particularly devastating disease attacking her nervous system and her life expectancy would be diminished and she would be debilitated and confined to a breathing apparatus and wheelchair at some point soon. He told me, "Jim, I will remember this day and the exact time we received this awful news, and remember it for the rest of my life."

Maybe you too can recall such news and how it felt at the time—how it is burned into your soul like a branding iron burns and scars and marks a thing for life.

All of our life journeys are marked by such changes somewhere along the way.

My poor wife of thirty-eight years experienced such a change in the days following our marriage. Back then, weddings weren't such a big production as they seem to be now. At least ours wasn't. It was a fairly modest affair with the reception held at our small town's local Lions Club. The affair was so modest, in fact, my two best men and I had to share a hotel room with only one bed in the room. So this is how guys deal with that: one guy gets the bed, one guy gets the blankets and bedding and sleeps on the floor, and one guy gets the pillow and sleeps on the floor. (No way were three college guys going to sleep in the same bed together.) Through the unfortunate circumstance of me losing the rock/paper/scissors decision-making process, I ended up on the floor with a pillow the night before my wedding. It was also the night before the Nebraska–Oklahoma football game.

Through a scheduling glitch on Terry's part, the wedding was scheduled the same day as the annual Nebraska–Oklahoma rivalry football game. It wasn't really her fault though, as I had pretty much tuned out of the whole wedding planning process due to the pressure of being a full-time college student who had just spent the previous summer in Marine OCS. In fact, my dad was the one who picked out the tuxedoes we were to wear for the ceremony. When we realized "our" mistake, Terry and I actually had to change the time of the wedding because Terry did not want to have "Folks in my wedding with AM radio earpieces listening to the game when I get married." That was probably a good thing since Nebraska lost the game in typical, heartbreaking fashion.

So we got married and "left" for our honeymoon—which was a night spent at the Red Roof Inn in Omaha (both sick from the cold/flu, stress, and lack of sleep)—then got up early the next morning and went to the mall where we saw two movies in a row before going back home. I had class and work the next day. Oh, and did I mention we moved into the apartment with my roommate who was still living there?

All of this definitely qualified as "sudden change" for the poor, brand spanking new Mrs. Annable. She had taken the whole week off from work (probably hoping for a very different honeymoon), but resignedly decided to go back the next day to work as well. The honeymoon, such as it was, was definitely over.

For me, the harsh reality of sudden change was really brought home when we finally got orders for flight training. When I first checked into Pensacola Naval Station, I was "fresh meat" for the duty roster and assigned the "duty." The "duty" is mostly an onerous all-night phone watch, delegated to newbies who are supposed to stay on the alert to put out any fires that might pop up in the night. I was really just there to be "blame fodder" if something did indeed go wrong, since no one actually wanted those newcomers on "duty" putting out any fires. Junior officers are the ones who get tagged for this duty—usually once a month—and it's typically uneventful. But not always. My first time at the duty desk, the phone rang and I was told there had been an "incident" involving an aircraft in one of the training squadrons and that, in fact, it might have crashed. Since the last thing they wanted was to have a young, fresh-out-of-college person making any important decisions, there was always a list (usually taped to the desk) of people to call when something actually happened. So I consulted my list, and saw the first item was "DO NOT TALK TO THE MEDIA."

This incident was a perfect example of "sudden change." One moment,

I was bored—a minute later, I was scrambling to respond as required wondering if there was anything that was to roll downhill, and if there was, if it would roll on top of me.

Reporting for flight training to VT-3 Red Knights.

I found out later what had happened during the "incident." An instructor had been out conducting what was called a FAM syllabus ride with a new student—a student with maybe four or five flights under his belt— in one of the practice areas. Whiting Field had three such training areas at the time, and the instructor and student had been in training area two, which was up toward the border of rural Alabama. It was a good day to fly, and since the student was a capable one, the flight was expected to go as most all flights do with a skillful student and competent instructor.

Until a turkey buzzard showed up and collided with the plane.

Sudden change.

Because the airplane was going at such a high speed, the big bird came shattering through the canopy into the student. Instantly blasted with blood and buzzard guts, the instructor in the back couldn't communicate with his student who was slumped over the control stick in the seat up front. He thought the student was dead, but continually tried to communicate with him anyway until he was forced to make a decision—to keep trying or to get out before he, too, became a casualty. So the instructor reluctantly bailed out and parachuted to safety. Fortunately, the student woke up and when he did, he awoke to a sudden-change reality in which he found himself alone in an aircraft with no canopy—one in which he had never landed solely by himself—with a dislocated shoulder, a damaged arm, and no instructor in the back. Rising to the challenge, he managed to make an uneventful landing in one of the outlying practice fields and eventually was awarded an air medal for the feat.

His instructor wasn't so fortunate. Having bailed out, he found himself in the unfortunate circumstance of having bailed out . . . over an *alligator* farm. Yep, sudden change. Surviving that, I think, deserves some kind of medal of its own.

There are myriads of stories like these we can look back on and see how things were going along just fine, thank you very much—until they weren't. For me, the predictability of life has value. I get irritated when someone moves a thing out of its place from where I know it should be, and it's missing when I impatiently need it. When I go to work and fly somewhere, the best thing that could ever happen is . . . nothing. It's like seeing your daughter go out on a date—every dad knows the best thing that could happen is, again—nothing.

But if experience has taught me anything, it's taught me that life will throw us all curve balls.

Vanity of Vanities

One of my favorite books of the Bible (maybe because it addresses this idea of managing expectations), is the Book of Ecclesiastes. It is an honest book, and when you read, it you can't help but connect with its raw, unfiltered perspective of life. Theologians categorize it as part of what they call "wisdom" literature, and I think that's a truly apt description for what it offers. There is a lot of wisdom buried in that book as it talks about seasons of life and expectations—words that ring true for me as I enter my autumn season with a few unmet expectations under my belt. Due to those sudden changes I've been talking about, the flight path I mapped out for my life hasn't always gone the way I planned. But Ecclesiastes offers a healthy perspective on what really matters and what doesn't.

No one really knows who wrote Ecclesiastes. For a long time, it was assumed that Solomon did, but many who study such things now believe that's not the case. As a matter of fact, Solomon is never mentioned by name, and any seeming references to life similarities with that king (who is known for his wisdom) are gone by the middle of the second chapter. It's as if the book's actual author wants to credentialize what he writes by connecting himself to the Wisdom of Solomon (whose life ended badly, by the way). The mystery writer(s) also criticizes and catalogues the injustices of Israel's ruler of his time (which, presumably, would have been Solomon). But most of all, the writing and the spirit of the book itself leads one to believe that it was written not long after the return of Israel to the promised land following their long exile, and has a lot in common with the Book of Malachi. Certainly, the topics addressed have more relevance for the time of Malachi than to that of Solomon's time.

In Malachi, the accusation leveled against God was that He did not love them. They see themselves as victims of injustice rather than the bride of the promise. In contrast, the writer of Ecclesiastes is writing to a people who seem to have a deep disappointment with God and where their circumstances have now placed them. Withholding his identity, the writer merely calls himself the "Preacher" or "Teacher."

Like sifting through tea leaves in the bottom of a cup, the Teacher in Ecclesiastes is asking us to examine the criteria we are using to judge our circumstances during any "sudden change" in our lives. He questions the wisdom we use to exegete providence and forces us to step back from the moment of sudden change to get a clearer view of the big picture. The book seems to examine for us the difference between God's perspective and our own. It contrasts the vantage point of God, who never changes, with the way we ourselves are so changeable in response to God and His goodness. We sometimes look for love and happiness in all the wrong places, perhaps in the midst of (and because of) our vulnerability to the destabilizing effect of sudden change.

In Malachi, the Israelites challenge God by saying that all who do evil seem to prosper, so the wicked must be good in the sight of the Lord since God has blessed them. Where is the justice of God in that? In fact, Malachi begins by saying, "I have loved you saith the Lord, yet you say how has thou loved us?" God is responding to a people saying, "Our circumstances suck and you are responsible."

While flying with another pilot a few years ago, the topic of Christianity came up during the flight. As we talked, he revealed his grievance with my worldview:

"Jim," he said. "My mother left me and my brothers to follow after Jim and Tammy Faye Bakker and their 'ministry' and left our family at a time when we really needed her. I have a lifetime membership to some Christian resort in South Carolina, but I didn't have a mom when I needed one."

He went on to add, "So you bet I have an axe to grind with Christianity!"

Many do. But in spite of terrible cases of fraud and parental neglect, there are countless authentic Christians who are good ambassadors for the cause of Christ. Joni Eareckson Tada is one such representative. Despite the fact that she suffered a paralyzing diving accident that left her a quadriplegic at sixteen, her life has been one of encouragement and faithfulness to God through her books and ministries to help the most helpless. She is one who moves victoriously from the understandable "Why me?" to the harder question of "What now?" I mention Mrs. Tada because hers is a very public testimony and one my generation has connected with.

I don't know if she found comfort in Ecclesiastes, but it certainly has helped me to navigate the certain, inevitable realities of life. Bad things happen. Sudden unfortunate things happen "under the sun." Humanly speaking, how does one ascend from the pit of hopelessness to gain perspective, and then in turn find a path to rise above the circumstantial? The Teacher tells his audience that power may belong to conquerors (in this case, the Persians), but wisdom rests in the prerogative of God's people to know Him, and wisdom tells us that this is the better part.

Life Under the Sun

Life is indeed fleeting, and though there are things God has given us to enjoy "under the sun," the real gift of joy comes from knowing God Himself—not *because* of our circumstances, but *in spite of* our circumstances.

The central issue examined in Ecclesiastes seems to me to be that of trying to discover how we can tell if God is actually for us or against us. How do we interpret "sudden change" in light of this? Can we really know that we stand in the light of God's favor if there are no discernible signs that we can see? How do we who live "under the sun" see past our own efforts to see a more divine perspective and reality?

The Teacher/Preacher begins the book with his conclusion that "Stuff happens under the sun" and unfolds his argument that "God is in control" throughout the rest of the book. "Vanity of vanities . . ." he will conclude. He offers us two versions of how people conduct their lives—one positive and one negative—and he will ask rhetorical questions like, "What good does it do if a man . . . ." But in the end, he will offer us this conclusion: God's character is rooted in absolute, perfect goodness. We can bank on that.

Augustine believed that the only two things you should love are God and the soul because these things never change. I disagree with Augustine on love, but one thing is clear to anyone who has ever read the Bible—God never changes. He is good. Always. We may not feel it in the emotion and turmoil of the moment, but His goodness is our portion. It may be doled out in increments we wish were larger or more consistent, but "portion" is a word used many times in the Book of Ecclesiastes to testify that His goodness is real and tangible, even in the face of death.

Death is a stark reality, yes, but regardless of our circumstances, be they good or bad, Christ invites us to know that death can be vanquished. There is promise and hope in the cross—not in our present circumstances.

In the end, the Teacher urges us to enjoy life. It is a gift. Although we don't know the hour we will leave this present world, we can find enjoyment in simple pleasures if we can rise above the noisy cacophony of our culture, telling us what the good life should look like. One of my favorite verses on marriage for example comes from this book, "Enjoy the woman you love all the days of your fleeting life, for she is your reward in life."

Manna

Of course, sudden change also happens in good ways. It may take the form of an unexpected check in the mail or good news about a job or a relationship. The interesting thing about a sudden change for the good is that our response is often uncannily similar to that of a sudden turn for the worse. Airline pilots, I have found, are the poster children for that strange phenomenon.

There's a joke we tell that goes like this: A newly hired class gets furloughed (laid off), something which happens from time to time. So the CEO comes in a room where the class is all gathered and tells them he knows these pilots have left good jobs or the military to come work for the airline, so what the company's going to do is to pay them a year's salary so they have time to find other employment, or until they get recalled. Every Thursday, they would be issued these checks, and all they had to do was to come collect them. The CEO asked, "Any questions?"

One guy raises his hand and asks, "Can't you just mail them to us?"

Indeed. Some folks are never satisfied.

There is always something better out there for us, we presume. I think we have all heard the saying that, "He/she doesn't handle success very well," or, "So and so is never satisfied." There is a lot of truth in that.

When Moses led the Israelites out of Egypt and out of slavery, they came to a point where after all the miracles, after all the promises, they were hungry. So they did what we all do when discontented—they grumbled. They grumbled against the leadership, against Moses, and even went so far as to say they were actually better off in slavery than where they were.

So God did a strange thing. He tested them by blessing them. Manna to eat. Clothes that did not fall apart and wear out. He told Moses that when they grumbled, they were really grumbling against God.

Change is inevitable. The seasons illustrate that. There is a time for everything under the sun (humanly speaking). I think part of the answer to the question, "*How do I live well?*" needs to be held in an overall perspective that the Teacher in concluding Ecclesiastes offers us: "Don't let the excitement of youth cause you to forget your Creator. Honor him in your youth before you grow old and say, "Life is not pleasant anymore." Remember him before the light of the sun, moon, and stars is dim to your old eyes, and rain clouds continually darken your sky.

"Remember him before your legs—the guards of your house—start to tremble; and before your shoulders—the strong men—stoop. Remember him before your teeth—your few remaining servants—stop grinding; and before your eyes—the women looking through the windows—see dimly.

"Remember him before the door to life's opportunities is closed and the sound of work fades. Now you rise at the first chirping of the birds, but then all their sounds will grow faint.

"Remember him before you become fearful of falling and worry about danger in the streets; before your hair turns white like an almond tree in bloom, and you drag along without energy like a dying grasshopper, and the caper berry no longer inspires sexual desire.

"Remember him before you near the grave, your everlasting home, when the mourners will weep at your funeral.

"Yes, remember your Creator now while you are young, before the silver cord of life snaps and the golden bowl is broken. Don't wait until the water jar is smashed at the spring and the pulley is broken at the well. For then the dust will return to the earth, and the spirit will return to God who gave it . . . ."

That's the whole story. "Here now is my final conclusion: Fear God and obey his commands, for this is everyone's duty. God will judge us for everything we do, including every secret thing, whether good or bad."

CHAPTER 7

OKINAWA

"Every man is a . . . fool for at least five minutes every
day; wisdom consists in not exceeding the limit."

—Elbert Hubbard

Sometime in late 1982, the XO (Executive Officer) of the VMAQ-2
(an electronic EA-6 intruder squadron) plowed into the back of my
1953 Chevy station wagon, and with the insurance claim money from
that accident, I bought my wife a one-way ticket to Okinawa, Japan. Terry
was seven months pregnant at the time, and the plan was for her to travel
halfway around the world with a two-and-a-half-year-old (including an
eight-hour stopover in Tokyo) to join up with me during my unaccompanied tour in WestPac. In short, I asked her to get on an airplane with her
bags (no wheels back then) and a toddler, and meet me on some island
halfway around the world I had never even been to myself.

When I was in the Marines, most FMF (Fleet Marine Force) units
were on what we called a deployment cycle. That meant six out of every
eighteen months, you were deployed either on a ship with the Navy,
or with the 1st Marine Division in Okinawa, Japan, or the 1st Marine
Aircraft Wing in Okinawa or Iwakuni, Japan. We called it WestPac (the
Western Pacific region covering Hawaii and all of the Pacific island chains

down to, and including, the Philippines). Back in the early eighties, with the Cold War still icy hot, the US military would periodically conduct a lot of what they called "exercises" in places like Korea and the Philippines. Once they'd immortalized these military exercises with random names like "Team Spirit" or "Cope Thunder" (probably named after some general's marital status at the time), we would all gather our gear and launch out to burn the American taxpayers' hard-earned dollars, training to fight yesterday's wars as rowdy and often unwelcome guests descending on some poor Asian locale. Having a base there in the Pacific made it easy to do that.

As I was deciding what to write about this unusually bizarre time in my life, I found myself wondering where to begin—or if I should even say anything at all. (Anyone who's been deployed to WestPac knows what I mean, and right now they're thinking, uh oh . . . .) My greatest successes from that year in WestPac (I did my two six-month deployments back to back.) were that I made it out alive in one piece—still faithful to my wife, not an alcoholic, and not ending up in a smoking hole on the side of some South Korean mountain. Not everyone was so fortunate.

I say this time was bizarre because some of the things that went on there would strain the credulity of those who have never faced stressful circumstances far from home. We were young men in our mid-twenties, living and working in a place that was very foreign—not just geographically, but culturally as well. For a certain segment of the junior officers in the squadron, weekend nights could turn into something like the bar scene from Star Wars. Raucous and alien. It was a strange concoction of testosterone, alcohol, and naive arrogance alternately wrapped in a stress sandwich or long bouts of boredom. What made it worse was that we were all generally the same age. "It seemed like a good idea at the time" was about as reflective as it got when surveying the aftermath of any particular weekend adventure in WestPac. Many years later, a friend of ours who'd raised four boys told us all we needed to know about young males: Get two of them together and their collective IQs halve. Add another and it halves again. Now get a whole group together and add alcohol and things get strange fast. Even bizarre.

My wife, Terry, is a gamer, and she made a remarkable sacrifice going over unaccompanied to spend that time with me instead of going to stay with her mother. Looking back, I cannot say enough about how grateful I was that my family was there with me. I was at a time in my life when I was easily influenced and far too impressionable, and her being there definitely had a restraining effect on how big of an idiot I might have been if left to my own devices.

After hearing Terry was coming overseas to stay with me, another friend of mine, J, decided to have his wife come over as well. They had a little boy Kate's age, and she and Christopher became fast friends. We both ended up living out in town in a four-story apartment building called the "Kishaba Mansion," which is probably Japanese for "roach-infested, two-room, prison-like dormitory." One of those two rooms was the bedroom/bathroom area and the other was the kitchenette/living space where we kept our dishes and eating utensils—exactly four plates, four cups, and four sets of cutlery. The apartment was 500 square feet total, if that.

We lived on the fourth floor, which is important in this respect: Ten days after Terry had a C-section delivery of our son, Alex, I took off for a two-week detachment to Hawaii. She was left alone with an infant and

a two-and-a-half-year-old, a standard transmission car with no seatbelts and the steering wheel on the wrong side, and two days' worth of groceries. I came back with a tan and a mustache to find Terry had learned how to schlep groceries up four flights of stairs juggling a baby, a toddler, and a bag of vittles.

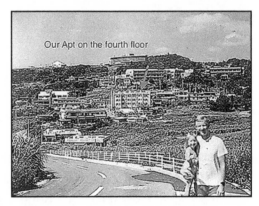

Kate and I near our apartment in Okinawa.

The wife of one of our friends came overseas as well and, interestingly enough, was led to Christ by another military spouse in that same building. But her husband—a no-nonsense "it's black-or-white" Marine—politely declined to have anything to do with this new religion. He was a man of integrity and refused to pretend to be something he was not. I always admired that about him.

And although he courteously put up with going to church with his family, he kept his distance from Christianity for many years—even after he was out of the Marines and back in civilian life. Undaunted, his wife faithfully attended church and BSF (Bible Study Fellowship) as she continued to homeschool their kids. Still, it wasn't until twenty-five years later that we got their annual Christmas card with the news that he had finally come to faith in Christ. One of the first things he did as a new believer was to get on an airplane and fly to where his parents still lived to share the gospel with them.

Terry and I getting ready to dive.

Like I said, he was always a man of integrity.

Not all of the time in Okinawa was a hardship for us. While our kids played in the Kadena Air Force Base officer's nursery, Terry and I went diving in the South China Sea. We rented scuba gear from special services for ten bucks, then snorkeled out to the reef to explore a wonderful world of neon-colored fish and fauna. Holding hands, we explored an underwater world exploding with color and beauty. A naturalist once told me that most fish are color blind, and I wonder if God designed their colorful variety of shapes and hues simply for our enjoyment.

We ate out in town at least two or three times a week, the yen at that time having a very favorable exchange rate. Many times, the Japanese waitresses would grab our little tow-headed kids and whisk them off to show their colleagues and fuss over them while we ate. Although small, Okinawa was full of historical significance. During World War II, the population infamously and tragically jumped to their deaths off suicide cliffs rather than endure the American occupation. Even though our troops pleaded and begged them to stop, many Japanese believed what they'd been told about the horrors we would subject them to as occupiers and chose death instead. I'm sure footage of that awful historical event is available at the Library of Congress.

Alex with our waitress.

On Sundays, we would go to the Air Force base for an impressive brunch, or in the evenings, go get an hour-long massage followed by a coffee at Pianissimos. It was a delightful little place that served finger foods and coffee against a musical backdrop of movie themes, amplified in all of their full-throated glory from a wall of giant speakers, so good I swear you could hear the breathing of the musicians as they played.

Because I was officially "unaccompanied," I had a BOQ (bachelor officer quarters) room in what we affectionately called the "Low Rise." These were living quarters in which each bedroom was connected to another bedroom by a bathroom, and it was awful. It was where the lieutenants lived, and it was not to be confused with "Menopause Manor" where the captains and field grade officers were quartered. Each of us had a "mama san" who came once a week to pick up our laundry, and so on Fridays, I would take our laundry to my BOQ room and have it washed and folded. Because I was living out in town, my room was the one that shared a bathroom next to the "BVI." The BVI was a room that was set aside as a squadron bar, and it had been there for a very long time (since the early

89

days of Vietnam) and one wall was nothing but *Playboy* pinups. You could peel back layers and find Miss So-and-So from twenty years ago.

I used to take Kate with me—she would have been three and a half at the time—when I would pick up and drop off my laundry, and I'd sometimes stay and have a beer with whoever was there. (There was always someone in the BVI.) When we got back to the apartment, Kate would tell Terry she'd seen my "sisters." Since Terry put pictures of our extended family on the refrigerator in our apartment (she had three sisters and I had one), Kate thought the girls in the BVI pinups were my "sisters."

There were some epic parties at the BVI, and it was not unusual to drop off my laundry Saturday morning and see broken glass and bodies passed out in various places on the floor like a hit scene from a mafia gangland slaying. Truth be told, had I not lived out in town, I most likely might have taken part in the frenzied, unfettered frat parties that took place at the BVI. Maybe not. Our squadron CO (commanding officer) generally turned a blind eye to what went on there, most likely because he remembered what it was like to be a JO (junior officer) himself far from home in a foreign place. Or maybe he thought professed ignorance would be his safest option and the better part of valor.

I wasn't entirely above reproach as, on more than one occasion, I participated in a lengthy "happy hour" with some of my squadron mates—a habit kept in check by the embarrassment I felt having to face the disappointment of my wife. Thankfully, I never stuck around for some of the hijinks that would inevitably come later. Although I was already an evangelical at the time, I wasn't a very knowledgeable one. Nor had I ever been discipled by an older, more mature believer. That was before I really understood that my Christian faith was more than merely a set of propositions I found agreeable, but a life in which I inhabit. So I have to conclude that the Holy Spirit protected me from a lot of foolish mistakes that could have caused some real and lasting damage to my soul, if not my health.

Reign of Folly

That is precisely the dilemma faced by King Rehoboam as he suc-
ceeded to the throne of his father, Solomon: to live wisely or choose folly.
Like many a young man, he was following in the footsteps of a flawed,
partially wise father. And like so many others, he had his "posse" of young
men he ran with and emulated. Like me, he was influenced by peer pressure and foolishness. Only he was a king, and his choices affected a nation
instead of a single family. That story is recounted in both the biblical
books of Chronicles and Kings—narratives that tell the story of a young
man (in his forties) who was given wise counsel by his elders but aban-
doned it for the immature, foolish voices of his youthful friends.

Now, I'm not one to give advice about how to raise kids because I am
just an average parent who happens to be married to a woman who is an
exceptional mother—and that's made all the difference. But here is a bit of
parenting advice for what it is worth—the two best things you can ever do
for you kids are these: (1) have a good marriage and, (2) make sure they
have good friends. Both of those you can control.

I find it interesting that Rehoboam was such a fool because his father,
Solomon, wrote many, many proverbs explaining to his son the perils
and pitfalls of abandoning wisdom for the seductive, flattering voices of
the foolish and foolhardy. Perhaps it's because Solomon himself chose
the path of disobedience to pursue his own passions, marrying women
who worshipped other gods and ultimately succumbing to their flattering
voices to worship them too. In doing so, he betrayed the highest truth he
knew of worshipping the one true God.

In the Book of Deuteronomy, for example, the Lord had given specific instructions to the kings of Israel to not gather a multitude of wives,
amass horses, or accumulate gold and silver. Yet he would choose to do
all of those things, and as his life unfolded, the dire consequences of those
actions inevitably followed. The Bible says that even when Solomon was
doing the things that he knew he should not do, his wisdom never left
him. From this, I have to believe that wisdom is more than simply knowing right from wrong—more than discerning the difference between the

"oughts" and the "ought nots." It is actually applying that knowledge by allowing it to govern your actions. Wisdom is listening to the right voices and doing what you know to be correct in spite of your feelings.

Solomon's son, Rehoboam, obviously witnessed some hypocrisy in his father's life and may have devalued his father's proverbs and sayings when Solomon's actions did not marry with his teaching. Who knows? There is definitely a lesson in there for dads. But what the Bible clearly does say is that Rehoboam deliberately chose to listen to the young nobles he grew up with instead of the wise voices of his father's elders. As war and rebellion ensued, God's people were fragmented and divided for millennia. It wasn't until the restoration of modern Israel in 1948 that a single nation existed again. It's a sobering reminder that the power of a single man's folly can change the fate of an entire nation.

The Bible is full of exhortations for us to impart "generational value." Older women are told to teach younger women, and in the same way, Paul called his younger disciples like Timothy and Titus to imitate him. Life is not meant to be age segregated as much as it is today in our modern culture. There is a certain amount of wisdom that comes when a man or woman is "full of days."

When I read about Rehoboam's youthful folly, it is far too easy for me to distance myself from his narrative when, in fact, I once had far more in common with Rehoboam than I would like to admit. My saving grace over the years is to have had mentors as stubborn as I am, who refused to let me be less of a man than God has intended for me to be. They didn't just tell me—they showed me.

WestPac Warrior

As I conjure the memories of my year over in WestPac, the memories slip through my mind like an out of focus slideshow, evoking some sadness, some excitement, and large helping of shock. The disconnected soup bones of events and images floating randomly in my broth of memory. One such image is of Olongapo. This city lay on the other side of a bridge over a waterway where carcasses, trash, and sewage drained into the bay and where boys in their sampans would dive for the pesos thrown off into the water. Along the waterfront itself, a dirty street lined with bars and shops catered to whatever ship happened to be in port. For a dollar, you could get a haircut or a manicure or the shine put back on your boots. I saw J get a shave so close it drew blood.

My visit to Wake Island is a happier recollection. Used as a mid-Pacific refueling stop for military aircraft, the island is just a small coral atoll in the western Pacific Ocean. I brought my fishing poles along hoping to catch a shark as the tide rolled into the lagoon in the evening. But the only action we experienced was when we hooked a great, massive moray eel instead. Not hooked really, but hanging onto the flounder we had gigged just hours before. It refused to let go, and the moray's jaws were fixed in such a viselike grip on its prey that even as its weight hung free, it took two of us to pull it up and land it over the rails onto the bridge. The next day, we wandered over to the bird sanctuary on the seaward side of the island hoping to try our luck in the surf with our remaining flounder/bait.

One of the guys with us, B, was a big guy who was six-foot five and every bit of 250 pounds. After glancing up at the curious sea birds hovering closely above us, he whacked one out of the sky with his fishing pole, then hooked it up as bait and tossed it into the water. What happened next is the stuff of fishing legend . . .

This is just the head: the rest of the body is dragging on the floor!

Not thirty seconds after that bird bait hit the water, a strike nearly tore the rod out of his hands. Since I had planned to catch Jaws, the mother of all sharks, the line was stout and didn't break. Adrenalin coursing, we took turns on that rod, each of us trying not to be dragged into the breakers, and finally, after what seemed like forever, we saw a massive body rolling and thrashing around in the surf. Without thinking, B sprinted for the surf and dove in to grab it. After what rivaled an epic WWE match, an exhausted B grappled the monster fish out of the surf so it was half in and half out, and the rest of us charged in to help wrestle it ashore. Not to be outdone, the rest of us were soon knocking birds out of the sky, hooking them up, and tossing them into the surf hoping to replicate that heroic fish/man battle. We did catch some ugly looking fish, but not another one like B had landed. Conceding defeat, we took a piece of rebar from one of the gun emplacements and carried B's monster fish dangling between us like two Sherpas on an Everest portage.

Another time, I recall chasing two A-4 Skyhawks into Iwo Jima—a sacred place to us Marines—and I have images of us climbing through the

A view of Iwo Jima from my plane.

island's catacomb of caves that had lain undisturbed since WWII. Live ammunition still lined the walls of those caves, and the cave floors were littered with gas masks and piles of empty sake bottles. Out of the 21,000 Japanese soldiers who defended that island, only 800 would survive. The battle for Iwo Jima was a thirty-day nightmare, one of many such in the Pacific Island campaigns of WWII. As we walked through the silence of the tunnels and the refuse of war, the weight of history descended like a thick blanket of fog, leaving us alone with our thoughts in that tomb of a place. There was a Coast Guard Loran station there back then, and the four "Coasties" who came to pick us up and show us around must have had their own stories on what they had done to deserve that particular posting, literally in the middle of nowhere.

During our time in Okinawa, I participated in more than a few exercises in Korea, a place very much in the news as I write this, and I remember it as a place that was on a constant war footing. Long stretches of highways had runway markings, and it was not unusual to see machine gun emplacements in the middle of towns. North Korean infiltrators were constantly being shot or discovered. And when we would fly, the North Koreans would try to sucker us into flying into their airspace. Even our own troops along the DMZ were suffering casualties over the years, quietly unreported in a forgotten place of a forgotten war.

While in Korea, I remember going to Taegu, Pohang, Yechon, Seoul, Kunsan, and Osan, but most of what we did there, I've long since forgotten. I just remember Korea as a mysterious, mountainous, and rural country that was entrepreneurially energetic. When we had time to shop in Korean markets, I bought eel skin purses, knockoff sunglasses, and brass lamps made from the shell casings leftover from the Korean War thirty years prior. The eel skin purses lasted a long time and were Terry's favorites. And I still have some of those shell casing lamps in my basement.

I also recall a trip to the Philippines when I had to take a cab from the Naval Air Station at Cubi Point to go see one of my troops who had been thrown in the brig at Subic. Located on the island of Luzon, the naval station on Subic Bay is where the Air Wing stayed when carriers were deploying there or when squadrons on various exercises would base out of, or over to, Subic Bay where the ships were ported and docked. As I was talking to the cab driver on my way down the hill, I learned that he was a guerrilla during the Japanese occupation and had spent four years in the jungle fighting and surviving. I ended up paying him to drive me around so I could hear his story, and I never did get down to check up on my Marine.

I remember that year in WestPac as mostly a good one and one of the best years Terry and I had while we were in the Marines. Our lives were simple and full, and for a couple of young kids in their twenties, it was quite an adventure. We spent a typhoon in our apartment with half a dozen other women, for example, and attended a fight between a *habu* (a very poisonous snake) and a mongoose. Not wanting to miss anything, we spent as much time as possible out in town trying to soak up as much of the culture as we could.

Yes, it was a risk to venture out like this—especially risky for a pregnant wife to travel alone with her toddler to a foreign place she knew little about, with no idea who her doctor would be, or where she would live. It was risky for me too, as some of the guys pushed back at the idea of me bringing my spouse over, and my own XO suggested that I should not do it. But I could only afford a one way ticket, and even that was only due to the poor driving skills of a fellow pilot. Despite all that—and even though we lived in a roach-infested, two-room, rundown tenement—we shared the adventure of a lifetime we will always look back on as a golden year. Although not without its challenges, that year was a time lived outside our comfort zone, and we were the richer for it.

Risk is like that. And every time I have rolled the dice in favor of the better story, albeit the harder and riskier path, our own stories have been enriched. That has remained true whether it meant taking my wife and thirteen-year-old daughter to an Iron Curtain country like Romania

Terry shopping with Kate in Okinawa.

without having met the people we'd stay with or even knowing how to contact them, to buying Terry a one way ticket to Okinawa.

Thinking back now as I write this, I am reminded once again of the biblical Book of Ecclesiastes and the lessons it gives about youth and the fleeting nature of the days of our lives. If I were to sit down with that young man who was me so very long ago in Okinawa, there would be some things I would want to share with him. I would want to remind him to enjoy those golden days God has given us "under the sun," when all things seemed possible and we were full of strength and the vigor of youth, and to remember the better part of what it means to live well.

I would remind him that there is nothing better than to rejoice and to do good in one's lifetime, and that sometimes it is better to go into a house of mourning than one of feasting. It is often a more honest place. I would want him to understand that wisdom is better than strength and that the words of the wise are better than the loud clamoring of fools. I would suggest that "It seemed like a good idea at the time" is simply a recognition that most of the tribal, youthful ideas concocted in wine or jest are preludes to "This will not end well." Most of all, I would encourage him to rejoice during his days of young manhood, knowing that the days of the prime of life are fleeting, and we will soon stand before God in judgement.

I would tell him, "Fear God, and keep His commandments."

I would also add by way of encouragement: if you have a choice in life between two roads to take, then take the one "less traveled"—in spite of the risks—if it is brimming with the potential of a really great life story.

Lieutenant Shogun and his lady.

CHAPTER 8

CHICAGO

"To be a Christian means to forgive the inexcusable
because God has forgiven the inexcusable in you."

—C. S. Lewis

B ack in the mid-eighties, when I first got hired by the airlines and
was doing my probationary year as a pilot in the metropolitan Wild
West city of Chicago, I flew with a captain who was raised on a farm up
the road in rural Wisconsin. Since he was raising his own family in the
Chicago suburbs, he decided to take his kids to a livestock auction to let
them get a taste of some of the sights and smells of his own years of growing up on a farm. That was the plan anyway. What was *not* part of his plan
was going home with a baby lamb. As somewhat of a justification, he told
me he'd always thought taking care of animals instilled a sense responsibility in a kid. At first, the lamb was easy to bottle feed and take care
of and they can be domesticated to a degree, but as the lamb grew older,
they were faced with a dilemma: What do you do with a farm animal in
the suburbs? Their solution was to take it for walks or to baseball games,
and people would always ask what kind of dog it was and comment on the
strange way that "dog" sounded.

"Doesn't it have an unusual bark?"

That trip with my farm-raised captain left a big impression on me, and I was determined to get some acreage and raise sheep when we moved back to Virginia. In the back of my mind was the idea of teaching my own kids how to handle responsibilities through livestock chores. At a minimum, they'd at least know the difference between a sheep and a dog. Unbeknownst to me was that "kid's chores" have a nasty habit of falling back on the chore giver, or what is worse, the poor wife who wasn't sure about the whole thing to begin with.

So, armed with a book called *Raising Sheep the Modern Way*, we purchased two pregnant Hampshire ewes and an old turn-of-the-century, non-air-conditioned farmhouse on a few acres of land. *How hard could it be to take care of a few sheep?* I thought. But when we became shepherds, my wife learned what she'd *really* signed up for when she'd promised "for better or for worse" the day we got married. Before long, one of our ewes got mastitis, and I had to tell my seven-month pregnant wife, "Here is what we have to do: insert this paste up the ewe's nipples into her udders and give her a shot three times a day. I have to go on a three-day trip, and I can't do it, so you will have to do it."

Terry must have hoped she'd heard me wrong and asked, "How long did you say I have to do all this?"

"Just three days," I told her.

Needless to say, we both learned a lot about sheep. The main thing we found out was that sheep are really nothing more than big, fluffy, stupid prey animals—somewhere on the bottom third of the food chain, if not the very bottom. They will freak out and simply die on the spot if they are too frightened, or just lie down and not be able to get back up again. If you let them, they will overeat until they bloat (which basically means they will eat themselves to death.) They will do the stupidest things you can think of and some you never imagined possible. I'm not exaggerating when I say they are a high-maintenance, suspicious, needy, easily preyed upon critter. But oddly enough, sheep are the very creatures God compares us to.

Sheep and Shepherds

The Bible's favorite analogy for the Christian Church describes a community made up of sheep and shepherds. When God is pissed at poor church leadership, for example, he calls them out as careless shepherds, and when He talks about the rest of us, He calls us sheep because we are so, well . . . *sheep-like*. And not in a good way. Just like sheep, it seems our natural inclination is paving our own way to self-destruction.

Raising sheep and knowing shepherds has helped me make some sense of the Church and why God decided to use that particular analogy in describing the nature of things. Churches are made up groups of people (think "herd") who are a melting pot of diverse personalities with different ideas about how "true religion" is supposed to be expressed and experienced during services; how sacred music is supposed to sound and how others are supposed to act in a sacred setting. In other words, everyone has a different opinion on just about everything related to church gatherings. This chaos is held in check by leaders (shepherds) who are usually seminary graduates who have spent three years learning to read "dead" languages (Latin, Greek, and Hebrew) in ancient biblical manuscripts and then interpret prophetic imagery depicting the spiritual things that they think God wants us to understand. But despite all of their exhaustive preparation as shepherds, leading sheep is hard. That's why churches often seem like an unruly, organizationally dysfunctional collection of people—they're acting like a bunch of sheep all trying to run off in different directions to places that are not healthy for them.

To follow the analogy further, the Bible says some of those sheep aren't real sheep at all but wolves in sheep's clothing.

Reformation and Reformer

As I write this, it is the 500th anniversary of the Reformation, that seminal event in history which changed the forward course of the Christian Church forever. Like all historical events, trying to fully understand the various strands of political, spiritual, and ecclesiastical complexity that shaped the Reformation is akin to piecing together a coherent reflection from a shattered glass that is refracting in all directions. It was as though Martin Luther plucked the theological dandelion out of the ground and blew its seeds to the four winds. These seeds landed in all sorts of places and began taking root and slowly began changing the world. One thing we know for sure: the Church has never been the same since. Even the Catholic Church would undergo its own reforms not long after.

For my generation of Bible church baby boomers, Martin Luther looms over the faith like both sunlight and shadow, leaving a complicated legacy that is both inspiring and—when you peel back some of his own peccadilloes—disturbing. He instigated an upheaval that not only freed Christians from ecclesiastical oppression and ignorance, but from the ecclesiastical chaos of institutionalized religious traditions. The Reformation came at just the right time during the growing competition between two definitely distinct cultures. It provided a bastion for biblical truth in Northern Europe that stood in stark contrast to the more worldly values of the Renaissance gaining steam in the south. Of the two revolutionary movements, unfortunately, it seems the naturalism/humanism of the Renaissance has left a far more lasting footprint on Western Europe than the spiritual illumination of the Reformation.

Although the Reformation burned so brightly throughout the Western European countries where it originated, the light of that religious fervor has now been largely extinguished. (But thankfully not completely.) Now centuries later, only the cold ashes of indifference remain in some of the very places it once flourished. (I am reminded that the seven churches Christ addressed in Revelation would all be gone a few generations after the Lord's ascension.) As for myself, I used to find the black-and-white Calvinist doctrines of the Protestant reformer a sort of refuge in the early years of my faith. It seemed a systematic, intellectually satisfying approach to understanding the intricacies of the gospel and it helped divide those who had a "strong" doctrinal stance from those who had "weak" ones. Age has brought with it a little more balanced perspective on things, hopefully, and I am not as certain about certain things as I once was. I think it a good thing. As Oscar Wilde once said, "I am not young enough to know everything," and into my sixth decade, I now know what I don't know. The gospel is too big, too mysterious to be put in some of these doctrinal boxes.

In small groups, for example, Calvinism's hard edge led to heated discussions over "*who's in*" and "*who's out*" concerning the question of salvation and spawned debates over the question, "*Are babies saved or not?*" (As if the fate of eternity rested upon our answers.) But I've found there is far more mystery and depth to the Christian faith than simply tying it up and putting it in a systematic doctrinal box—and it's in those very places of mystery God seems to move and work most miraculously—in ways that lead perhaps to more questions than answers. Yet God is at work just as much in these difficult questions as He is in their life-changing answers. How can we even receive such answers when we don't first ask the difficult questions? I am not a Calvinist now. I am not sure what I am to be honest with you.

Jesus Stories

I was confronted with a few of those questions while flying with a pilot who also happened to be a Mormon a few years ago. It was a beautiful afternoon on a transcontinental flight to the LAX in Los Angeles—a trip I've always enjoyed because I get to fly over some of the most beautiful and challenging terrain on the planet. Spread out below, we saw the Cumberland Plateau, then the great farming regions of the Midwest, the high crags of the Rockies, and finally the barren desert areas that marked our approach to the West Coast. The scenery was breathtaking, but when you're cooped up in the cockpit with the same guy for hours on end, there's a conversational ritual that goes something like this:

"What did you fly before you came here?"

"Where do you live?"

"Where did you go to school?"

"You married? Got kids?" etc. . . . (Now that many of us are in our fifties and sixties, we also ask, "Have you had your colonoscopy yet?")

As usual, I was trying to pace myself conversationally to prevent "peaking" too early and running out of things to talk about; a scenario that either forced me to repeat myself or sit in an uncomfortable silence for the next couple days. (Besides, you can only laugh at the same jokes so many times. . . .) Although I don't always connect with the other pilot I'm flying with and may just end up staring out the window, which I am okay with, I enjoy hearing people's stories. But that wasn't the case on this flight. On this particular morning, my Mormon copilot told me a personal story about his family and his relationship to a brother who had wronged him grievously. As he shared the details of the story, there were tears in his eyes, and it was clear that what had happened was patently unfair. But what he said next surprised me.

"Jim do you know what happened? God told me this, 'I have forgiven you so much, why can't you forgive your brother?' You know what? I love my brother more now than I ever have. That was two years ago."

This seemed like the kind of a story Jesus would tell, and the lesson for me was clear.

You need to forgive like that man forgives, so that even after two years, it would still bring tears to your eyes.

But when I shared this remarkable story of forgiveness in my small group from church, the first reaction I got was: "Well . . . he is a Mormon and isn't even saved!"

Really? I remember thinking, *Are you sure about that? And you know that how?*

I once heard that if you easily reject a culture or a religion, it is because you really do not understand it. Then as now, it's easier to reject people than it is to try and understand where they're coming from and why they believe the things they do. Fortunately, we have Jesus' example to follow. When Jesus was laboring in His earthly ministry, for example, there were many competing forces at work in Israel both politically and religiously— just as there are now in modern nations. The Samaritans were one group that was particularly scorned by Jewish religious leaders even though the Samaritans were also Jews.

When Solomon died, the Kingdom of Israel had become divided into two separate regions: Judah occupied the south with its capitol in Jerusalem, and Israel ruled the north from its capital city of Samaria. Each one thought they were the true religion of the ancient Israelites, and the Samaritans even had their own Pentateuch which, of course, they believed was the authentic one. Although the two groups came from the same family tree, they were in fact bitter enemies. Each region held to its own form of Judaism, and the religious leaders on both sides taught their followers to avoid all contact with each other and to even avoid setting foot on one another's territory. Despite these prohibitions, there was periodic fighting—the Palestinian version of the feud between the Hatfields and the McCoys.

Then along came Jesus, and He did something that was shocking to Jews—He praised a Samaritan!

As a matter of fact, the Samaritans are mentioned in the gospels six times—and in all of these instances (but one), Samaritans are referred to favorably, with the exception being when the disciples were concerned that Jesus had gone over to the Samaritans. Most of us have heard His parable about the "Good Samaritan" who shows compassion on an injured traveler while a religiously conservative Levitical priest hurries by instead, on his way to some religious function perhaps . . . .

Likewise, many of us are familiar with the biblical account of Jesus approaching the Samaritan woman at a well where she's drawing water by herself. During their interaction, I find it interesting she reminds Jesus that, "Our fathers worshiped in this mountain, and your people say that in Jerusalem, that is the place to worship."

It was a perfect opportunity for Jesus to set the record straight and settle the divisive question once and for all, of whose Jewish doctrine was the authorized godly system of worship for the people of Israel. Instead, He unexpectedly told her to stop looking to worship God in some specific place—that truth and life was standing right in front of her—and that He alone was the only acceptable "place" of worship as the Messiah they'd been waiting for. It appears most Jews didn't understand that. She evidently did, even though she was a despised Samaritan. It makes me think of that Mormon pilot who'd forgiven his brother's wrong and loved him anyway. I'm also reminded of the Lord's Prayer that teaches us to forgive others (because we've been forgiven by God).

The Law of Reciprocity and Imitation

Although Jesus consistently taught His followers to "love your neighbor as yourself," it's just contrary to human nature. Even His twelve apostles struggled to get along with each other. According to the Gospels, they periodically argued about which one of them was greater. But it's really not surprising that there would be tension among them. I'm not sure if we can appreciate from this distance of two thousand years how culturally unsuited they were for each other's company: There was a Greek boy named Phillip, whose Hellenized name suggests a background as a Sadducee; and a Maccabean boy named Simon, perhaps from the pharisaical religious tradition (as was probably Christ). Another apostle was a zealot who opposed the Roman government of the time and yet another who was an instrument of that same government, like Matthew, who was a Roman tax collector. All of these competing ideologies came together under the tutelage of a poor, not very handsome rabbi from the boonies.

And it wasn't just Jesus' inner circle that made for strange bedfellows. There was the Pharisee Nicodemus and a Samaritan woman. Other disciples included a woman caught in the very act of adultery and a blind beggar who stood up for Jesus against the Jewish ruling hierarchy after Jesus restored his vision. Another was a Roman centurion. Children and church leaders. Women who financially supported Him. This motley group probably looked a lot like the church you and I may be attending now. A diverse community called to unity.

Every gospel account but John's describes the events of the upper room and the Passover meal He ate with His disciples, after which He used a cup of wine to announce "This cup is the new covenant in My blood, which is shed for you" (Luke 22:23 NKJV). The synoptic Gospels each detail this important event: "This is My body, broken for you . . . This is my blood . . . ." The interesting thing for me is that John's gospel leaves out this very significant description. Instead, John's account takes us right to the foot washing part of that Passover meal. In Luke's gospel, immediately after Jesus shares His New Covenant, we read that "an argument broke out among the disciples as to which was the greatest . . ." (Luke 9:46 GNT). Apparently, they just couldn't help themselves. In response, Jesus shocked them all when He broke down His wardrobe and got down on His knees and started washing their feet (something no slave was even required to do). He explained, "You call Me Teacher and Lord, and you say well, for so I am. If I then, your Lord and Teacher, have washed your feet, you also ought to wash one another's feet" (John 13:13–17 NLT). It was an unforgettable lesson in humility—as if He was saying, "*Since I did that for you, you do that for one another. Stop arguing. Allow yourself to be defrauded. Forgive like I forgive.*"

That is what following Jesus looks like in the Kingdom of God.

I've found there is a law of reciprocity that wends its way through the Bible. God says those who bless true Israel, He will bless, but those who curse Israel, He will curse. Likewise, He says, "If you are merciful, I will be merciful to you . . . I will forgive you your debts as you forgive your debtors." Coupled with those biblical promises are biblical instructions on how to actually become merciful and forgiving. These are expressed in the principle of *imitation*. In the New Testament, we are called to imitate Christ, Paul, or authentic people of faith. It appears that it's what we actually *do* that matters, not what we think or feel about someone or something. Jesus illustrated this point by telling a parable about two brothers and their father's request they get a field plowed. One seemed eager to please and enthusiastic about doing what his father asked, but in the end, he never went to plow. The other brother resented the idea of doing this chore, and apparently did not feel like plowing anything, but in the end, he did as his father requested. Jesus asked, "Which one did the will of the father?"

Churches are made up of individual people who are meant to actually do what Jesus asked us to do—to relate to each other in a new, unified way that represents life in the Kingdom of Heaven. As in a marriage, there are hierarchal principles of headship and submission meant to create the peace and order necessary for a church (or marriage) to be effective in its mission of multiplying God's love through the family of God. So when reading the Apostle Paul's biblical passages concerning roles in marriage, it shouldn't come as much of a surprise when he immediately switches gears, saying he's not just talking about the relationship between husbands and wives but also about the mysterious, sacred relationship between Christ and His Church. Unfortunately, that union is troubled by unruly sheep and imperfect shepherds.

Even though the Reformation ushered in a spiritual enlightenment that moved the Church from the Dark Ages of human religious tradition into the light of accessible biblical truth, it also ushered in its own forms of oppression, hypocrisy, and theocracy. These would further splinter the Church into factions much like the Samaritans and Pharisees had done centuries before when they, too, were fighting over who was "doing it right." Perhaps this is why Jesus' longest recorded prayer was for unity—so that others could believe the gospel. We Protestants forget that for about 1500 years, we were all Catholics. In our differences, it's all too easy to forget what we have in common. A common mission, a common enemy, and a common Lord.

New Beginnings

While living in Chicago, Terry and I began going to church consistently again. We ended up attending an old United Church of Christ sanctuary in the main downtown area, and we went for no other reason than because we thought we should. We were some of the youngest folks there, feeling out of place in the sparsely attended, white- and gray-headed congregation. But the youth pastor and his wife were our age, and we soon got to know them and began to attend a Navigator's 2:7 study. That's when we really began to seriously examine and learn about the faith we had embraced. A Navigator's study is not a bad place to start a pilgrimage with. It was also the place we first encountered church division.

The youth pastor convinced the senior pastor to have an "open door" service on Sunday mornings for any younger folks or simply folks off the street, and that effort soon paid off. It became a very well-attended group of younger folks who were in much the same place where Terry and I were spiritually. Eventually, though, for reasons unknown to us, that service full of young folks somehow became a contentious issue within the larger church, and the contention boiled to a head during a congregational meeting. Since the United Church of Christ was a congregational-run organization, the open door service had its open door closed by a simple raising of hands.

I just remember feeling sad about the whole thing.

It's just really hard for Christians to get along sometimes, probably because Christ's teachings can be difficult to accept and apply in their entirety. When Jesus says to cut off the hand that causes us to sin, most would insist He couldn't possibly have meant us to *actually do that!* Another famous passage that's seemingly ignored is the one in which Jesus exhorts a rich, young ruler to give away his assets to the poor in order to actually follow Him. Jesus' teachings convey an "all or nothing" kind of finality that most people just can't obey if it takes them outside their comfort zone. (Then those who do, like monks, we criticize.) Most of us professing Christians are like the son in Jesus' parable who said "yes" to his father's command to plow the field but never actually did it. It's much easier to *look* Christian than to actually obey Christ.

We also have an enemy who knows how to use the "wolves in sheep's clothing" and our "old man" sin natures to best advantage to wreak havoc in churches. Most churches have communion once a month, and for the most part it is a sacrament everyone can agree on—except that they can't. Some churches insist on using wine and dipping bread out of a communal cup, or using grape juice and taking it individually instead of waiting and partaking as a group. Luther and Calvin vehemently disagreed with one another about communion, as they did about other matters. Many denominations still testify to the church-splintering impact of those disagreements.

Maybe we should just wash each other's feet more. Although foot washing isn't considered a "sacrament," perhaps it should be for the sake of church unity. I've only experienced it twice in my life, but both times were a powerful experience.

I found out it's hard to hold a grudge against a person who is washing your feet while praying for you.

CHAPTER 9

INWOOD, WEST VIRGINIA

"Faith in the sense as I am using the word, is the
art of holding on to things your reason has once
accepted, in spite of your changing moods."

—C. S. Lewis

All of us really live two lives: the embodied reality we show the world
and the internal realm of our thoughts, fears, moods, and imagination. We talk to ourselves constantly and tell ourselves all sorts of weird
things and we think all sorts of random, often disconnected thoughts.
This jungle of a thought life is part of who we are, who we want to be,
and who we wish we were not. Our self-talk can be positive or negative,
empowering or paralyzing. It can be a safe place and a refuge, or a not-
so-safe place that misleads and confuses. Here, within this private inner
realm of ours, God seeks to meet us and transform us with the truth
about Himself—a truth that changes our minds and the embodied reality
we present as *us* before the world. But doubt and faith both find their
audience in the thoughts and feelings of this hidden chaotic place.

Knowing something, believing something, and having faith are not
the same things. I can know about God and *believe* all the things my particular religious tradition tells me about His nature and attributes, but

having *faith* in that knowledge is what affirms to my spirit that these things are indeed meaningful. It is God Himself, we are told, who activates this faith in us. Who initiates that process? Why some experience life-transforming faith and others don't is a mystery of God-imparted free will and God's all-encompassing sovereignty. It is a mystery and hard for me to fully comprehend, and so it is as we are told by the Apostle Paul that, "The depths and wisdom of God are unsearchable" (Romans 11:33, author's paraphrase).

That seemingly fundamental process of faith, faithfulness, belief and trusting hasn't always been so clear to me. Perhaps it still isn't. My lack of surety was painfully evident one evening during a church retreat I attended in the mid-1990s. Sitting amiably in a small group at a Catholic conference center in West Virginia, I had no clue I was about to embarrass myself. But things started to go wrong right away when the leader innocently lobbed a theological icebreaker to the group. Anyone who's been in a small group, or has led a small group, knows these "icebreakers" are meant to be a safe, harmless sort of warm-up activity. They usually consist of questions designed to loosen everyone up and prime the pump for the main "sharing" event. The question our leader posed seemed easy enough: *"What is one thing you know for sure?"*

Since I was going to be the last one in the circle to answer, I thought I had plenty of time to come up with a really good response that would sound pretty good to everyone else too. Church is a lot of things, and one of the things it happens to be is a social institution with its own set of accepted norms, language, and communal boundaries. We all want to fit in and at least look and sound like we belong. Playing outside the church-yard rules or moving the accepted communal boundaries is generally not well received nor appreciated I've discovered over the years.

So one by one, the folks around me answered the leader's question by sharing the one thing they knew for sure:

"Jesus loves me," said one.

"I know for sure I'm going to heaven when I die," replied another.

"I know that I'm saved," others said, or "That God exists . . ." etc.

Meanwhile, I was furiously processing the question in a bit of existential panic: *What do I know **for sure**? What do I know **for certain**?* At that moment—as the group's attention slowly made its way around the circle to me—the only thing I knew *for sure* was that the question seemed a spiritual minefield, and it wasn't safe at all. I remember blurting out something totally incomprehensible that had absolutely nothing to do with religion, church, God, or West Virginia, then sitting there feeling like a cross between a politician and a moron.

Why was that question so troubling for me? There are definitely things I can know with certainty, and things I know *for sure*. I consider myself a man of faith who's a committed believer in God, heaven, and Jesus, and I'm confident that when the role is called up yonder, I'll be there. But rightly or wrongly, I get stuck on the word and idea of *certainty*. Why would we call it *faith* if it was a *certainty*? I may overestimate a lot about myself—how good I am at ping-pong, my ability to play the fiddle, my parenting skills, or how funny my jokes are—but I can honestly say that I do not overestimate my faith. I've stubbed my toes too many times for that. A struggle from the beginning, my faith journey has been a constant challenge for me. Maybe that is something you can relate to as well. I've never enjoyed a consistent, confident feeling of certainty 100% of the time in my journey. It's not that I'm lukewarm. I just have to periodically take the time to examine my faith, and review what I logically believe to be true about the nature of God and the universe. Depending on what sort of issue I'm looking into—or what season of life I'm in—my "faith grade" generally fluctuates from a D+ to an A− and back again. Is fifty-one percent confidence in something good enough? Eighty percent? Ninety-nine percent?

Doubt

Doubt and this constant reexamination of my faith used to bother me until I discovered that I wasn't alone in this particular struggle. The Bible itself shares the stories of some guys way more impressive than me in this regard. John the Baptizer actually heard the audible voice of God saying Jesus was His Son, yet toward the end of John's life, he sent some of his followers to ask Jesus if He *really was* the Son of God. I guess even hearing God Himself speak doesn't silence all doubt. And Gideon didn't just throw out one fleece, but two. I suppose the Bible wouldn't spend so much time telling us to be faithful if it wasn't such an issue for some of us. It must have been an issue for the Hebrews too, since there's a whole chapter in that book devoted to providing great examples of "faith under fire" for us to follow.

We are told in the Bible that some people have a gift of faith. I know a few of those people. But whether or not you see yourself having that particular gift, we're all commanded to be faithful, and we are all charged to build up whatever faith we already have. It works that way with all the spiritual gifts. Just as some might have a gift of hospitality (which means some don't), like it or not, we're all instructed to be hospitable even if it's not one of our strengths. Subconsciously, I think we all expect others to operate in our own individual strengths or gifts, but that's not how God designed the church to function. When I need help in areas of giftedness where I'm weak, I've found it's encouraging to lean on others who are strong in those areas—as they, in turn, have leaned on my strengths. It's humbling the way our weaknesses compel us to develop our faith (and other spiritual gifts) in the context of relationships. There is a marked difference between unity and uniformity. We all have different gifts and strengths in certain (different) areas, and we all have weaknesses in others.

Welcome to the body of Christ.

So what do I know for certain—know **for sure**? I know the difference between *faith* and *credulity*. Faith doesn't offer God the blind trust of credulity, and it doesn't believe without evidence. Rather, faith is an intelligent decision based on reason and observation. We Christians are not gullible people, though we may come across like that to a superficial culture with no time for lengthy, thoughtful answers. Abraham went up to sacrifice his son, Isaac, because he *reasoned* God would raise him from the dead, based on what he knew of God's nature and His track record of miracles in Abraham's own life.

In the same way, "Doubting Thomas" (the go-to disciple whenever questions of faith pop up) was not asked to believe without evidence. Thomas wasn't there to experience firsthand what the other disciples had, so Jesus gave him the evidence he needed to believe. Likewise, the Bible tells us Jesus went on to do more miraculous things, and *they are written that you may believe.* He also never criticized doubters and I think there is even a blessing for those who are poor in spirit, which doubt sometimes leads to. Jesus simply met them where they were—where He meets all of us. He gave John's disciples a list of evidences showing why John should have faith in His claim to be the Son of God and actually went on to praise John despite the baptizer's doubts. Like John, we can find reassurance in the fact that our faith in Christ rests on some pretty good evidence, and something this important *should* rest on good evidence. It's also good to know so many books have been written to examine the proofs provided by the New Testament itself, having verified its authenticity using secular textual criticism and so forth. The evidence is there if you choose to examine it. Scripture tells us God allows Himself to be found when we seek Him honestly and with a heart for truth.

Truth

At the very core of faith is the issue of truth and how to find it. In a world rife with competing truth claims just like ours, Pontius Pilate asked Jesus, "What is truth?" I've asked that same thing, as we all have. Dr. Ravi Zacharias helped me answer that question by encouraging me to examine truth claim with three essential questions:

Is it logically consistent? Does it makes sense and conform to the rules of reason?

Is it empirically adequate? Is there actual evidence that bolsters a truth claim? What's in the historical, geological, physical, and archeological record?

Is it experientially relevant? We don't live in the world of propositions. How does it relate to the embodied life of real people with real issues, concerns, fears, and hopes?

Not only should faith be *experientially relevant,* but it must manifest that relevance in our life experience in order to increase our faith and give encouragement to the part of our inner self that talks a lot.

My "know for sure" and "certainty" issues only arise in a more meaningful sense when I'm confronted with actually having to act on my faith. I've found it is one thing to *say* I have faith, but it's quite another to act upon it. In that sense, I've discovered faith is like a muscle that has to be exercised to grow, and to my chagrin, such exercise usually involves something a wee bit outside of my comfort zone. Yet the more I exercise faith—and I'm talking about the *"Well, I'm not sure about this, because it doesn't make much sense to me, but the Bible tells me I need to do this thing"* kind of faithfulness—the more I see the evidence of faith revealed. When I step out in that kind of "here goes" faith, I've found my willingness to step out over bigger things becomes much easier. From what I understand about the Hebrews, they didn't really have the word "faith." Their word was actually *faithfulness.* When Habakkuk wrote, "The just shall live by faith," he was actually saying the just shall live by *faithfulness.* Faithfulness was, and still is, an action word. It's the same word used to describe the hook we hang a coat on, or an exhausted Moses having to have his arms held up during a battle by the faithful men who supported him on either side.

A Dark Night of the Soul

When my wife, Terry, gave birth to our twin daughters, I quickly discovered someone else would have to step up to the plate and cook if the older kids and I wanted to eat. That someone was me. I started out just buying the precooked Costco frozen lasagna kind of meals that were easy and simple, but they got sort of old after a while, so I graduated to trying my hand at the "mix and make" kind of stuff. Although every guy genetically knows how to grill, and the older three kids and I could have happily lived on hamburgers, my exhausted wife (who keeps the checkbook) said we couldn't afford it. I actually kind of enjoy cooking now—mostly because I like to eat—and being a picky eater, I can make the stuff *I* like to eat if I don't mind shopping for the ingredients. But that time was my introduction to the kitchen and its own language of tools and measures.

That's how I found myself in Martin's grocery store one afternoon, waiting in line to check out. Glancing at the magazine rack by the checkout counter, I saw a *Life Magazine* special edition on Mother Theresa, looking out of place amid *People Magazine* and various freak show gossip rags. I've always admired Mother Theresa—for living in a place I could never live and sacrificing her life in a way I never could—so I bought the magazine and took it home to read. I already knew she was a remarkable woman of faith and a living illustration of self-sacrifice and compassion. Ironically, she'd died on the same day as Princess Diana, one woman celebrated for *who she was* and the other celebrated *for what she had done*. Of course I know Princess Di did some very philanthropic things for the poor in some awful parts of the world, but very few have gone *all in* as Mother Theresa did, going to live and die among the impoverished like Jesus.

As I read about Mother Theresa's life, I also learned things I'd never known about her. For example, like John the Baptizer, she too had heard the audible voice of God while riding on a train. She was told, *Go to the poorest of the poor.* Then again, she heard Him speak those words a second time: *Go to the poorest of the poor.* So she did, not sure how to begin or where she was supposed to go. But knowing Calcutta was full of the desperately poor, she started there, and when she saw a man dying on the side of the road, she picked him up and carried him home. That in itself is a miracle considering this woman might have weighed ninety pounds soaking wet. Her answer to God's call began by carrying a dying man home. Thus began a ministry that would redefine sacrifice and compassion.

Hearing God's voice changed her life and impacted her destiny for the rest of her days—as she did her best to embody and fulfill the command she'd been given. As a result, the entire world was introduced to a living saint. Like John, she also struggled with a season of doubt despite her obedient self-sacrificial life. A dark night of the soul. Letters revealing her personal struggles from that time were actually presented as evidence for her canonization. Surprisingly, they were used to *support* her qualification as a Catholic saint. The reason given was this: like John of the Cross, only someone who so intimately knew the fellowship of the Lord would so clearly long for that intimacy when it was diminished or missing for a time or a season. When David cried out in his psalm, "My God, I cry out by day, but You do not answer me . . ." (Psalm 22:22 NIV), it was a prophetic precursor to Christ's own plea from the cross. Only someone who has known God's presence—in a remarkably intimate way outside our normal human experiences—can know what it's like when it is diminished. The simple fact is that we are all prone to waver in times of trouble when God seems absent or uncaring. But we are told in Hebrews 10:23 KJV, "Let us hold fast . . . without wavering . . . ."

From my perspective, the uncertainties of my faith don't bother me the way they once did—or maybe the way they *should*. I've also arrived at that age where I don't care as much about whether or not I fit in, or if I have things totally figured out. Habakkuk himself had trouble reconciling his faith to the evil of his own time. He looked around and was puzzled by the reality of so much wickedness on the earth. Like us, he would ask, "If there is a God in heaven, then why are things like this?" But we also read that he exercised patience, standing on the watchtower and waiting for the answer he believed would one day come.

My issues with faith are sometimes like those of Habakkuk: *Why are things the way they are?* At other times, I'm more like the man in the Book of Mark who said, "Lord I believe . . . now help me in my unbelief." I don't want to be like the atheist who refuses to believe in something that there may be good evidence for, simply because it doesn't fit into his or her own comfortable narrative. There is a difference between being ignorant and being *willfully* ignorant. Even Christians sometimes jettison their faith during times of trial and uncertainty (the two seem to go together) and rush into the willful mine field of unbelief. But in times of uncertainty and doubt, I've learned the best approach is to try to exercise humility and patience—to find solid footing by reasoning from what I already know to be true, instead of forming conclusions about things I don't understand.

It Is Written

Probably what bothers me more about myself than these questions of doubt and certainty is that even when I do know what I ought to do, I either don't do it at all or I do something I know I shouldn't. Of course, that's not just my issue, but a problem for all human beings from the very beginning. When Eve was tempted with something forbidden and was asked, "Did God really say . . . ?" she—knowing very well what He had said—still went ahead and did the only thing she knew for a fact she was not supposed to do. She famously had no help at all from Adam who was supposed to speak up. I'm convinced that's why Jesus countered each one of His temptations in the wilderness with God's very words saying, "It is written, it is written, it is written . . ."

Like Eve, many Christians know what God has said, but connecting the dots to obey and doing something about it is another problem altogether. Knowledge versus doubt is rarely the issue when living a Christian life. There are multiple books on just about every aspect of that life, and what you don't want to buy, you can Google. Attend any church and you'll be offered a smorgasbord of Bible studies, Sunday schools, small groups, men's studies, women's studies, and one-on-one discipleship. I know some folks who spend all their time going from one Bible study to the next. The more they study, the more certain they are of things concerning how the world will end, who is going to make it into heaven, and which system of theology Jesus embraced. It is a good thing for a man or woman to be inspired by the Bible—but when the rubber meets the road, what does it actually inspire you to do? How does it change you? In some cases, knowledge actually leads to pride, we are told, while love (which is an action word) edifies. It illustrates.

At sixty, I am okay with a little mystery when it comes to God and life. I know I should live with my wife *in an understanding way* and guard my words so I don't blurt out hurtful stuff that I end up spending the rest of the time trying to unsay. Despite all the good "how to live" information I've collected over the years, I find myself more interested now in being practically shown what that information looks like. I want to see it lived out in an average Christian life like my own. It's essential we be able to move from the merely propositional to the personally practical embodied world we inhabit. What good is change for example, if you can't see it? If there's no visible change, is there really any change at all?

There is a lot of mystery and paradox in our Christian faith. Fair enough. But we also know science has its own share of paradox and mystery as well. Jesus is both fully human and fully God—light is both a particle and a wave. We believe there is a spiritual dimension to reality, and similarly, science has long believed there are at least ten other dimensions. Like the law of gravity, we can't see the Holy Spirit, but we can see His effects. Science and Christianity are not competitors for truth. There is so much both belief systems do not know, and even the *scientific method* begins with a hypothesis or a guess about something you observe or something you *believe* to be true and need to experiment.

I've discovered that everyone believes in something. Everyone has a construct on why things are the way they are. Even atheists. One major difference in being a Christian believer, however, is that you also have to be a disbeliever at the same time, dismantling some of the contradictory constructs others accept. That's because truth, by its very nature, is exclusive. It can't be more than one thing at a time in a buffet line of opposites. Believing what the Bible tells us about ourselves and the world is often at odds with what we have been raised to believe or long held to be true. In this way, truth and faith are intertwined. Therein lies the rub.

I consistently tell myself all kinds of stuff. You do too. It's called self-talk. This inner life—where I tell myself all sorts of things—is primarily governed by my emotions, primarily fear. The antidote to that, I've found, is that I need to speak truth to myself. But that's a challenge when I really want to just compromise and roll with whatever makes me look good to myself, whatever is more comfortable to believe, or however I may be feeling at the time. No one wants to tell themselves they're a thief or a liar. Sometimes I know what the right thing to do is, but I talk myself out of it because it's too hard, too inconvenient, or too sacrificial. This is where I manufacture my own doubt about doing the right thing—kind of along the lines of *Did God reeaallly say . . . ?* In those situations, I tend to give myself the benefit of my own doubt. Convenient.

Faith breaks into that self-talk and says, *I know you think you have all the answers here, but you aren't even asking the right questions*—like when God crashes Job's party and reels off around thirty questions about who He is and who Job is. So it's not a question of knowing the right thing to do, just a matter of doing it, and who you are willing to trust: myself or the One who created me.

"Did God really say . . . ?" is a good place to start. When the hard thing to do is also the right thing to do, actually doing it only increases your faith. It also makes for the best story.

There is a whole chapter in the Book of Hebrews that celebrates all of the men and women who were biblical examples of faithfulness through the millennia: Sara, who laughed in disbelief when God told her she would get pregnant at ninety; Abraham, Isaac, and Jacob who all lied at some point because they were afraid they'd be killed (since they were married to attractive wives) or lose a blessing; Moses, who was chastised by his wife for not doing what he knew every Hebrew boy, including his own son, was supposed to have done (circumcision) according to God's command; and Gideon who tested God with the fleeces—twice—and whose life ended badly. These were all imperfect people who questioned God and hedged their bets by trusting what their own voices told them to do.

Sound familiar? Yet these folks are the very ones touted as faithful in Hebrews 11.

If we lived in a black-and-white world, living by faith would be a whole lot easier for us all. But we're forced to live out our lives in the murky shadows of the grays and uncertainties of our present, fallen-world circumstances, and the way forward—even if we want to do what is right—is often disturbingly unclear. Rightly or wrongly, I find myself throwing out more "fleeces" than I used to. *If this happens, then I will do that.* It's not easy, but I'm learning to be okay with uncertainty.

I've come to the point where I realize God does not owe me any explanation, nor is He under any obligation to answer all or any of my questions. A quick reading of the Book of Job should make that clear. But I've also realized God doesn't hold those questions against me or consider it a sin to wrestle with doubt. I'm convinced, in fact, that God is as interested in such questions as He is in any of the answers I might be seeking. During these moments of search and struggle, a deeper understanding of Him emerges.

C. S. Lewis would agree. He says, "If ours is an examined faith, we should be unafraid to doubt. If doubt is eventually justified, we were believing what clearly was not worth believing. But if doubt is answered, our faith has grown stronger. It knows God more certainly and it can enjoy God more deeply."

Flannery O'Connor was one of the great southern writers of the last century whose stories revolved around disturbing, distasteful characters in the process of transformation and encounters with grace. Her writings were also informed by her Catholic faith and how the world was invested with the reality of God, and she had this to say in her book, *Habit of Being*:

"I think there is no suffering greater than what is caused by the doubts of those who want to believe. I know what torment this is, but I can only see it, in myself anyway, as the process by which faith is deepened. A faith that just accepts is a child's faith and all right for children, but eventually you have to grow religiously as every other way, though some never do.

"What people don't realize is how much religion costs. They think faith is an electric blanket, when of course it is a cross. It is much harder to believe than to not believe. If you feel you can't believe, you must at least do this; keep an open mind. Keep it open toward faith, keep wanting it, keep asking for it, and leave the rest to God.

"When we get our spiritual house in order, we'll be dead. This goes on. You arrive at enough certainty to be able to make your way, but it is making it in darkness. Don't expect faith to clear things up for you. It is trust, not certainty."[1]

---

[1] O'Connor, Flannery. The Habit of Being. New York: Farrar, Straus and Giroux, 1988.

CHAPTER 10

TRISTATE BLUEGRASS
CAMPGROUND

"I love to sing, and I love to drink scotch.
Most people would rather hear me drink scotch."

—George Burns

As life unfolds, one of the big questions that emerges from whatever goals you have set for yourself (if any), in my mind, is the question of meaning. *What makes life meaningful?* Is what we are doing worth all of this striving and suffering? The question itself seems to be an analytical one that would call for a true/false factual response. It is more complicated than that, though, isn't it? If life is deemed "good" by all the metrics and goals I set for myself, does happiness now surface and take over? The answer to that question, I have discovered in my own six decades of life's journey, isn't generally found in our stock of truth statements and accomplishments, but it is buried in our emotions where the heart is connected to the head, and so a more holistic answer to these existential "meaning" questions begin to emerge. In other words, where do truth and meaning collide, or at what point does truth and life experience become meaningful? Does it have to be?

I've discovered one way that emotions are connected with meaning, at least for me, is through music. I play the fiddle . . . sort of. When I was in my late twenties, I went into a pawn shop in Havelock, North Carolina (for reasons I can't even remember now) and completely in character and in keeping, impulsively bought a used violin. Although I'd messed around with a guitar when I was a teenager—trying my best to imitate some of my favorite singer/songwriters, who so effortlessly seemed able to pick and pluck, making wonderful sense of the language of music—none of those guys I enjoyed listening to played the fiddle (that I am aware of). I don't know what I was thinking at the time. I had no idea how to play the

Victoria plays her violin at a wedding.

danged thing. (This is the burden my poor wife lives with.)

When we moved to Winchester, I seriously took to learning how to scratch out something on the fiddle, which sounded a little like something that I enjoyed. I took lessons from our good friend, Cathy Nelson, a wonderful musician who plays in the Maryland Symphony and who taught music at Shenandoah University. Later on, she would spend years teaching my twin girls, Victoria and Jenna, the violin and viola, then conduct their practices and performances for the Youth Orchestra at Shenandoah University.

I worked with Cathy for about six months until I could read a bit of music and know the general geography of where to put my fingers on the fingerboard. After that, I bought "how-to" cassette tapes from various fiddle players and began learning the songs I wanted to play, sometimes taking my fiddle on trips with me to practice on my layovers, much to the horror of those hapless souls whose rooms adjoined mine.

It was a good start, I think.

By first learning the structure of the fiddle and what each of the particular strings were called from my music teacher, Cathy, I was able to fill in the blanks and bridge what I heard on the cassettes to the stringed wooden box resting on my shoulder. Still, when I was learning how to play a new song, it was often a long, laborious, and repetitive process. But once I learned the thing, I was able to start putting my own personality into it, adding a little bit of this and a little bit of that to kind of make it my own. That's why no two fiddle players will play the same tune in exactly the same way, and probably why my songs were a bit hurried and sounded somewhat disorganized to begin with. To hear the chaos that is sometimes my fiddle playing is to probably understand me I suppose.

My learning the fiddle was hard on my wife and anyone in the house. You can only listen to "Forked Deer" or "Soldier's Joy" so many times before you want to start rummaging around the liquor cabinet for the cooking sherry. The kids fared better since they were already used to chaotic noise. But as I was getting a little better at playing, I was able to get together and make music with a couple guys on Tuesday nights. The group included Mike, a very fine banjo player and bass fisherman who knew every rill and ripple in the Shenandoah River; Mark, my mechanic friend (whose truck I crushed), a decent twenty-something bass player who acted and sounded exactly like my dad; and Brad, a guitar player who was probably the best of the bunch. We gathered at Mike's house in the evening after work where we'd play some songs together, visit for a while, then play some more.

Sometimes, we'd drive over the Virginia line into West Virginia and head to the Tri-State Bluegrass Campground where bluegrass aficionados from Western Maryland, Virginia, and West Virginia would gather every other weekend during the summer to play. We'd sit or stand around smoky half lit campfires, playing bluegrass music late into the evening hours. The mostly elderly campers would park themselves nearby in lawn chairs, tapping their feet to the tunes or periodically singing a favorite song in the dim, smoky half light of the fire's glow. It was a great place to learn new tunes and hone my skills playing with others, while also semi-hiding in the dark along the edges of the firelight.

Musicians, or at least bluegrass players, are a very accommodating and helpful community. That's probably because most of the tunes they play were passed down to them by others—at least that's the way it was where I come from. I find that significant. Although not many folks would use learning to play a bluegrass tune as a metaphor for life, I've found much of what we desire to be and do is passed down to us and primarily modeled for us. Like a fiddle tune, it may seem pretty rough when we first try it, but with repetition and practice, we will get pretty good at playing out our dreams and aspirations one day. Like a bluegrass tune, we put our own personality into it, and no two of us play life's pilgrimage out exactly the same way.

You may have noticed by now that I'm partial to bluegrass music. In particular, the old Appalachian tunes (where the fiddle itself is sometimes cross tuned) which songs reach back through time—songs that have been memorialized and passed on through the years by succeeding generations of fiddle players. These were the songs played at dances, centuries before there were stereos and iPods, and played when folks were too poor to have electricity in their homes. There is a certain honesty about that acoustic music that sprang from the Great Depression and other equally hard times and hard places in our history.

Such music represents a sort of shared human experience that's been memorialized and set to music. I prefer these old tunes to the present things we hear, much like I prefer the older hymns to the present contemporary Christian praise and worship songs. To me, many of the old Appalachian fiddle songs are honest in the way funerals are more honest than weddings.

Songs are our stories put to music.

Isn't it interesting how music can move us and change our moods and feelings so powerfully? This is why the Scots marched into battle to the sound of the pipers and drummers. It's also why kings and commoners alike rise to their feet in response to the climax of the "*Hallelujah*" chorus from Handel's *Messiah*. Anyone who's seen a movie can understand the way a film's musical score conveys meaning in a way mere visual images on a screen cannot. The music helps us connect to what we are seeing in a far more visceral way.

We've all felt the stirring impact of songs such as "The National Anthem," "Taps," "Danny Boy," "Battle Hymn of the Republic," "Dixie," and "Amazing Grace." Played at just about every funeral or memorial service I've ever attended, "Amazing Grace" has a poignant tune and lyrics that are truly appropriate at such a time. Yet, it is also a song that fits in with the old Appalachian/bluegrass music just as well as it does in any hymn book. Even when I play it on my fiddle, it still sounds good, which says more about that tune than it does about my fiddle playing. "Amazing Grace" is relevant for both living and dying.

Such songs have the ability to strengthen us for the work of living because they grant us the motivation of a deeper sense of purpose. Jim, my fellow "boat therapy" shipmate, is always half singing, half muttering old hymns under his breath when we actually do get around to doing some work on the boat. It's as if he is talking to himself when he does that. I don't mind since he's just "Speaking to himself in psalms and hymns and spiritual songs, singing and making melody in your heart to the Lord."

Whistlers do the same thing, but in a more irritating way.

Art and Meaning

For all professional clergy and lay ministers, I suppose the challenge is always how to make abstract truth meaningful. That's because we're forced to use analogical language or metaphors to describe what something is *like* when it comes to describing things we cannot touch or see. Jesus did that by telling parables. Central to the Book of Matthew, both geographically and to its message, are these stories about the *Kingdom of God*. In trying to describe the unimaginable concept of this Kingdom, Jesus could only tell us what it is *like*: It is like a pearl of great price that a man sold everything to buy . . . .

When confronting David with his sin of adultery and murder, Nathan did not come right out and accuse him of those things. Instead, he chose to tell David a story about an unjust man who stole a lamb. If you remember, David was infuriated by the unjust man's callous behavior, and then Nathan told him, *"David . . . you are that man!"*

Why would Nathan choose to confront David's calculated crime of passion by firing him up with a story? I think he did it because our emotions are part of the fuel our brain uses to power the locomotive of intellect that drives our actions. By shifting the situation from the propositional (truth) to the personal, Nathan made David's sin *meaningful* to him and enabled him to access the truth—the terrible emotional and physical impact of his actions on those he'd taken advantage of. Sometimes we need to have God's heart perspective before we can truly understand our own sin.

My friend, Don, is part of the professional clergy. Like many people, both Christian and non-Christian alike, he has suffered on and off with depression. He keeps a painting behind the desk in his office of a man collapsed in the arms of a risen Jesus. That picture is very meaningful to him, and when his thoughts wander off toward self-condemning places, he will look at the painting to help reorient his thoughts and feelings to the healthy place of truth. For him, that picture is like a bridge across troubled waters.

John is another friend whose wonderfully gifted daughter was attending Virginia Tech during the time a man senselessly opened fire in some classrooms, killing students and teachers. Knowing one of the students, and being understandably upset and distraught, I found John's advice to her interesting. His daughter was a very accomplished violinist and he simply told her to take her instrument and begin playing it. There is something in music and art that allows us to communicate emotions in ways words alone cannot. Her music gave voice and expression to her grief.

Something else about music and art is that it reaches us not simply on an emotional level and connects us with truth, but surfaces spiritual realities for us as well. Henri Nouwen must have read the Parable of the Prodigal Son hundreds of times as a theology professor, but it wasn't until he sat in front of Rembrandt's painting, *The Return of the Prodigal Son,* that the story of his own life became meaningfully understood by him as he stared at the prodigal brother.

Art and Worship

As I've read through the Bible, I've noticed a common phenomenon: whenever something really, *really* significant takes place in the life of a person or a group, they break out in song. Randomly embedded within the narrative of biblical accounts—in both the Old Testament and the New Testament—we see such spontaneous singing from Moses and Miriam, Hannah and Elizabeth, and from men like John the Baptizer's dad, Zechariah, and Jesus' mother, Mary. We see this singing from young girls and old men. There is even a whole book of the Bible that's nothing but psalms (songs). Although we don't have the notes to those tunes anymore, we know they were songs people actually sang, and we still have all the glorious words of the Psalms to inspire worship. Many have put those words—those Scriptures—to music through the millennia. Such songs are so important that Scripture assures us that all Christians will be singing a *new* song in heaven one day. For those of us who don't sing, I wonder what that will sound like, but it's promised as a reward we should all be looking forward to, so I'll find out one of these days. Solomon even wrote one whole book of the Bible, the Song of Songs (or Song of Solomon), that is actually a love song, but it is still one of the books that is sometimes referred to as part of the Bible's wisdom literature that also includes Job, Psalms, Proverbs, and Ecclesiastes.

Why would those we read about in the Bible sing praises to God at key moments instead of just shouting out a truth statement about how they are feeling, or roaring their approval the way we do at football games? Why do we sing in church and not just chant truth statements together or cheer? What is the difference between music and mere noise? What drove me to take the time to not just listen to my favorite music on the radio or stereo, but to actually want to imitate these things myself on an instrument I had never played before? Why is music such a necessary part of us, and not just to us humans but also to the birds, whales, coyotes, and all other things in creation? (We are told that even the stars were singing during the Creation.) Why is it that a whole bunch of people singing together sounds really good and makes you want to join in? Why do people sometimes move around and sway when they sing? It almost seems as though we were hardwired to appreciate and communicate through music.

Perhaps it is because God Himself is a singer and makes music. Not only that, but the Bible tells us that *He* sings over *us*. If we are indeed made in His image, that would make sense, would it not? This is part of our identity and legacy as divine image bearers. It is because we are made in His image that music plays such an important role in our lives.

So why would it matter if God sings and makes music or not?

In some significant way, music reflects some of the activity of God within Himself as a triune community; we know He communicates within Himself, just as we know He communicates with His Creation. This is why worship is so central to a church service and why it is every bit as meaningful as a sermon. It is also why participation in the Christian community through worship is so important. Yet most men I see—at least in the churches I've been a part of—do not sing or worship. On one level, I get why singing love songs to another guy is problematic, but not all songs we sing in worship are like that. I think most of the old hymns have some great lyrics a guy could get into singing: "Onward, Christian Soldiers," "On the Solid Rock, I Stand," "Amazing Grace," "When I Survey the Wondrous Cross," and "Shall We Gather at the River" are just a few such hymns. There is something essential about community participation in worship—including awful singers like myself—that is part of how we relate to being in community with God.

I enjoy playing the fiddle on my own, but I enjoy it way more during the times I am playing with others and we play as a group. When a banjo or guitar is playing with me, the music sounds fuller and more complete and makes more sense. I also can't hear my mistakes as much. A good banjo player covers a multitude of fiddle sins.

At some point, when you are learning to play a new instrument, the sounds gradually change from a chaotic, scratchy noise (It's interesting the Bible equates chaotic clamor and noise to a lack of love.) to some semblance of a recognizable tune. I'm not sure when that transition takes place, but your family will let you know—when you play, they'll stop glaring at you and encouraging you to leave the room by suggesting you "Take that thing somewhere else!" Out of random, undisciplined notes, organization emerges. In a very real sense, music is a picture of a Creation designed from order and of structure rising out of chaos. After God told the Israelites to build the temple, He not only enabled them to obey by telling them *how* to do it, but He also pointed out that He was gifting certain men to be good carpenters, seamstresses, and stonemasons. He also gifted men with the skill to make and play instruments. It was as important a part of the temple as the roof and the altar itself.

I am not a worship leader. Maybe that's why I admire them so much, not only for their skillfulness in the area of music, but also for the heat they take no matter what style of worship music they invite their congregations into. Music has a way of uniting us (like it does when we sing the national anthem), but it's also split a few churches over the years. I guess most of the problems arise over the notion of personal preference. Some people like a certain type of music and others don't. Such divisions come from a misunderstanding of what worship really is and what it is actually meant for in the first place.

William Temple, the Archbishop of Canterbury, once defined worship in this way: "Worship is the submission of all of our nature to God. It is the quickening of the conscience by His holiness, the nourishment of the mind by His truth, the purifying of imagination by His beauty; the opening of the heart to His love, the surrender of the will to His purpose—all this gathered up in adoration, the most selfless emotion of which our nature is capable."

Two things become clear: First, worship is an act of submission. Secondly, submission is a hard thing for us in the midst of so many temptations in the world.

I remember hearing a young college student at Georgia Tech ask a well-known Christian speaker how he was able to keep his thought life in check during his frequent travels away from his wife. He said he worships. There is something about the discipline of worship that draws our affections away from the pressing needs of the moment and captivates our attention in such a way as to center our affections on God. We are told that we are made in His image and—although we cannot create in the way that He uniquely creates things out of nothing—we can, however, be re-creators who use our imaginations, designed to imitate beauty, to express beauty and truth in very individualistic ways. Even a mathematician is an artist who is captivated by the order and rhythm of mathematics, and conversely, studies have shown that listening to music actually improves math scores.

But even though music can connect us to truth in an emotional, meaningful way during worship, it's important to point out that meaning and truth are not the same things. There are a lot of things that, though very meaningful to me, probably aren't true. There are other things, though true, I couldn't care less about. No matter how meaningful a narrative or a fact might be to me, if it's not true, its value plummets. There are a lot of a psychiatric hospitals filled with folks anchored in a meaningful reality known only to themselves and divorced from the stark reality of truth. I also know folks who are anchored in the truth. But they don't always act on the truth they know, because it simply isn't meaningful to them.

That's why knowing truth is not the same as leading a meaningful life. It's only when something we know to be true also becomes *meaningful* to us that our destiny is impacted in significant and redemptive ways.

Although I really like to play the fiddle song "Bonaparte's Retreat" (it's meaningful to me), I don't play it much because it's in a weird tuning of *D-A-D-D*—and is such a pain in the butt (truth) to get the thing tuned right. Even the normal violin tuning of *E-A-D-G* (and the one most fiddle tunes are played in) is hard to do, because unlike a guitar or banjo, a violin's tuning pegs are simply jammed into the wood on the neck. They are slippery buggers, and it's sometimes difficult to get them to stay the way I want them. Even when I do get the fiddle tuned, I generally have to relearn the song before I can play it well enough to not drive my wife out of the room. But I really like "Bonaparte's Retreat," and although I don't play it perfectly, I can still enjoy working on it, and if another fiddle player came into the room, I think he'd say, "Hey, that sounds like 'Bonaparte's Retreat'!" No matter how much I have tried to play that tune in the standard *E-A-D-G* tuning, I can't do it and it probably can't be done. I can play something that vaguely sounds *sorta* like it, but it *ain't* it at all—no matter what I *want* to call it. All that twisted analogy to say, meaning and truth are both needed to impact our world.

The eighteenth century Scottish patriot, Andrew Fletcher, once commented, "Let me make the songs of a Nation, I care not who makes its Laws." Although this quote might have originated as far back as Plato, the meaning behind this statement is as accurate as it is ancient: Our emotions are not the caboose at the end of the train of intellect, but one of the engines actually driving it. As John Piper once said, when we are called to give, it is a true thing that we *should* give. But the matter is not settled yet, because God loves a *cheerful* giver. Emotions are essential to meaning and truth. We are called to *weep with those who weep* and *rejoice with those who rejoice* because we actually feel concern, and understand the truth of God's purpose, working through us. As Stephen Foster wrote, there is something important about *sharing in the sorrows of the poor* that draws us closer, not just to the poor, but also to Jesus. Those are His people and He shares in their sorrows. We serve a weeping God who would have us weep too. He created us to be like Himself. *It is enough for a servant to be as His Master*, Jesus said.

I have been told by more than one person whose loved ones were struck with Alzheimer's or dementia, that though they would forget the names of their families, they would remember songs. In Alzheimer's cases, there are many reported cases of music even triggering some memory awakenings. The heart remembers things the mind can't recall.

During World War II, four young army chaplains from different denominations—a Methodist, a Catholic, a rabbi, and one from the reformed tradition—were on the troop ship, *Dorchester,* when it was sunk by the German U-boat, *U-223*, in the North Atlantic. There were more men on board than there were life jackets, and as the ship went down into those dark, cold waters, these four men of faith gave away their life preservers to others who had none, so those men could live. Instead of trying to flee the ship, these four men of faith went on helping the crew into the life boats to the very end. These four chaplains were last seen by the men in the water joining arms in unity as the ship went down praying . . . and *singing hymns.*

It is not unusual for soldiers, during their time of greatest despair, to join together in song to undergird the courage they need to face terrible danger or death. The martyred boys in Uganda did that too, singing and shouting encouragement to one another as they died in the flames for refusing to compromise their faith.

To stand firm in the face of adversity, I think maybe we, too, need music and sing spiritual songs. I believe that to be a *meaningful* thing for us.

CHAPTER 11

GEORGE WASHINGTON
MEMORIAL FOREST

"There is one rule, above all others, for being a man.
Whatever comes, face it on your feet."

—Robert Jordan

I was chatting up with Wally the other day about making a run to West Virginia to pick up some snake rail fence, and I was asking him about using his dump trailer. Wally has just about every tool, trailer, truck, and skid steer any man would need to . . . well . . . a man would just need. I wish I knew the secret of convincing my wife that we also *need* a dump trailer in our driveway. Maybe it was all my exposure to Tonka Toys when I was a lad, but I cannot pass an excavator or a bulldozer without checking it out and swerving a bit on the road when I am driving. I like the way he thinks. Like when I asked him why he bought a skid steer:

"I needed a skid steer to prep the pad for my shed to put the skid steer in." Brilliant.

I've known Wally almost thirty years now. And although I'm a little older than he is, even when Wally was in his early twenties, he sounded an awful lot like my dad.

"Hey, when is the last time you had the oil changed in that truck?" he'd ask.

Wally never went to college and is an average bell-curve guy like me. Wally doesn't try to impress anyone or pretend to be someone he's not, but in one area of life he's out on the fringe—Wally can fix anything mechanical. So he's the guy you want to call if you break down somewhere, or need help winterizing your boat, or need to bleed a diesel fuel line to get the air out when you've run it out of fuel . . .

"Jim, did you run this tractor out of fuel?! What were you thinking?!" He'd ask this in the *exact* tone of voice my dad would use.

The guy has a heart of gold and is generous to a fault, but like any mechanically gifted fella, he is very picky about maintaining his stuff and impatient with those who don't. So imagine this: one day, I borrowed his pristine, dual-axle, 4×4, recently waxed king cab truck and trailer to move a track hoe I was renting. I intended to use it to dig twenty-six cedar stumps out of a field I was planning to put into timothy hay later that spring. My friend, Peter (who was in his seventies and retired from a management-level sales job in New Jersey), was helping me. I thought he'd have fun running the hoe and digging the stumps up while I hauled them away with my tractor. We *did* have a blast digging stuff up and moving it around. Awesome guy stuff. But when we finished and went to load the hoe back onto the trailer, the arm of the hoe was positioned in such a way—as luck and providence would have it—that it was perfectly centered over the pristine, recently waxed tailgate. In a moment of confusion, and with the full *gazillion* pounds of hydraulic pressure behind it, we proceeded to crush the tailgate on Wally's immaculate truck like an aluminum coke can when you stomp on it. I was shocked at how easily it crumpled and then *re-shocked* when the realization hit me that it wasn't just *any* truck bumper we'd obliterated—but *Wally's*.

Although grown men in our fifties and seventies, we faced the crisis by immediately planning some evasive, cover-our-behind maneuvers to hide the screwup—asking ourselves the same questions any teenage boy would ask themselves when they're in a full blown damage control mode:

Will anyone find out?
Can we blame someone else?
Can we lie about it?

The bottom line was that I ended up driving my own poor abused truck to Wally's to tell him how we had crushed his truck. Although Wally took it well, it was the first time I ever saw him speechless. Even as I was spinning the story as best I could, he was eyeing my truck, and I just know he was dying to make a critical observation about its poor condition. Although I learned from my dad long ago that part of being a man is "fessing up to failure," it always takes me awhile to get there. I used to tell new American Airline captains, "It is never the accident that gets you fired, but generally what you do afterwards that matters. We all screw up from time to time, but how you handle it is almost as important." Just ask Nixon.

Of course, I've handled my own share of screwups poorly. Like we used to say in the military, one "Aw crap!" will cancel out a boat of a lot of "Atta boys!" Sometimes you can get away with pretending nothing's happened (If a tree falls in the forest and no one heard it, did it really fall?), but there's an audience of one who knows everything that happens. Plus, you'll know the truth of the matter even when others don't. (The Bible tells us we're surrounded by "a great cloud" of witnesses. That is pretty sobering.) Who you are is who you are when no one is watching.

The first time I went deer hunting with my dad, my sleeping bag caught on fire. That was another first on a trip of many memorable "firsts" for me. I was thirteen, and it was my first time deer hunting with my brand new 410 I had gotten for Christmas. It was the first time I had ever seen lightning and thunder in the middle of a snow storm, and it was my first exposure to alcohol (although I didn't know what it was at the time). We were planning on sleeping in the back of a 1968 Ford truck with a camper cap shell on it, and we'd parked at an old Virginia farm at the foot of the George Washington National Forest in the Shenandoah Valley. Since it was snowing, the farmer invited us up to his porch for some "apple cider." They let me have a small glass, and it sure helped me get to sleep when we settled down in the back of the truck a little later. The truck was equipped with a small heater that didn't put out much heat, but it was still hot enough (evidently) to catch my sleeping bag on fire as I slept. All I remember is waking up airborne as Dad picked me up and threw me (still inside the smoldering bag) out into a snow bank. Once the fire was out, Dad laughed a little chuckle in relief and said, "Well, Jimmy, Mom doesn't need to hear about this part of our little trip, right?"

He wasn't asking me to lie, just concluding we didn't need to let anyone else in on our little "fire in the bag" incident. It was a "need to know only" kind of thing. Like I said, guys hate to screw up and we'll do just about anything to make those screwups go away.

I always chuckle when I read the account of Aaron and his golden calf, which I am sure he thought was a good idea at the time. If you recall, Moses had climbed Mount Sinai because God had some serious business to discuss with him—business which obviously took some time. After he'd been gone awhile, folks got restless. How did Aaron respond to this lack of patience and direction? He went around and gathered all the gold in the camp, smelted it down, then spent time carefully etching and sculpting a golden calf so folks would have something to focus their attention on and worship. When Moses finally came down off the mountain and saw what was going on, he was royally pissed. Remember . . . this is the guy who, in a fit of temper, beat a soldier to death.

"Aaron! What did you do?" You can just picture the incredulous fury on Moses's face.

Of course, Aaron responded the way most guys do—in typical "damage control mode"—the same way guys like me do when they've just crushed a buddy's truck:

"They (these other people) gave all this stuff (the gold) to me, and when I threw it in the fire, a golden calf popped out!"

There you have it Moses—*"It" happens*. Not my fault.

I suppose the unexpected outcome always will happen. But my willingness to take responsibility for my part in those errors and mistakes isn't so certain. Fatherhood takes that problem to a new level since it brings the responsibility of setting an example for my own boys to follow.

Parenting Boys

About the time I had boys of my own, there were a host of parenting books to tell us how we should be *Bringing up Boys,* how to *Raise Modern Knights,* and how to teach them to be *Wild at Heart.* When I look back now, the most meaningful instruction—that which left the greatest imprint on my own sons, both good and bad—was the experience of my own upbringing by the man who was my father. I was fortunate to have a dad who took the role of fatherhood seriously.

My dad died a number of years ago. While sorting through their stuff in the basement, I came across some pictures of my parents and my grandparents. Those snapshots show a couple in their youth, first dating, then married, and a little later on, as young parents smiling out of old color photos with two little towheaded toddlers. I never remember my parents that way—being young. But I'm sure it's that way with *all* kids when they think about their folks. I never considered my dad as a *friend* or being *fun* either.

He was just my dad . . . and when "it" hit the fan, that's who was called.

It's a difficult thing to adequately sum up the very complex relationship between a son and his father. It's also hard to overstate its importance. It's *so* important, in fact, that back in the day, sons would compete for their father's blessing as Jacob and Esau did. When I was twelve or so, and helping my dad work on the family car, I remember asking my dad when I would become a man. (My dad didn't teach me much about how to fix a car,

Mom and Dad.

but I could fetch any tool in Dad's impressive arsenal of a toolbox.) He stopped and looked at me for a moment before replying.

"Jimmy, you'll be a man when a man is needed," he said, then turned back to his work.

Like many of his generation, my dad was forced to leave boyhood behind at an early age, and probably didn't spend much time agonizing over how to define what manhood meant in the context of work, marriage, and fatherhood. Seeking an understanding of that topic is just part of my own journey of self-examination, I guess. For my mom, it didn't seem a hard thing to submit herself to the kind of man my dad was—though in some quarters nowadays, that kind of willing submission isn't valued—and I think she found their marriage a pretty safe place. Maybe that's why I find it somewhat hard to separate my mother's life from the life she shared with my dad—because my dad, as a husband, gave her little cause to assert her autonomy. They clearly shared a mutual respect for each other.

When my dad died, my mother not only lost herself a husband . . . she lost herself *a man.* (I lost my mom too less than three weeks after her husband and my dad died, and only two days after Mother's Day.)

These days, manhood is a hotly debated topic that seems to have grown into its own marketing niche. The Marlboro man has morphed into the Dollar Shave Club. Podcasts devoted to the manly arts discuss manly grooming products and even provide a list of the top 100 best reasons to be a guy. Since the metrosexual detour at the turn of the century derailed the concept of manhood, guys have recently been investing big bucks in it. Lots of ink's been spilled on the topic as it's become a commercialized, high-dollar commodity. Despite all this marketing furor, I think much of what we are as men (both good and bad) simply comes from our fathers. Those who didn't have dads, or whose dads weren't around, sometimes found their ideas of manhood shaped by other kinds of icons; maybe it was an older brother or another man we looked up to, the military, a team sport, or an intentional mentor who knew the value of manhood and wanted to pass it on.

When King David was dying, he thought it was important to impart some essential truth to his son Solomon: "As David's time to die drew near, he charged Solomon his son, saying, 'I am going the way of all the earth. Be strong, therefore, and show yourself a man.'" (1 Kings 2:1–4 NASB)

We all know David himself didn't live out his manhood perfectly, but to his credit, he never changed his standards nor lowered that bar for his son. And David's life and legacy is not one defined by his failures, but by some pretty manly stuff—he killed lions and bears with a slingshot before going on to nail the giant who was picking on his people's army. He was a musician and a king who wasn't ashamed to dance with all his might before the Lord—choosing to please God instead of his wife, who was embarrassed by the spectacle. If anyone showed himself to be a man, it was David.

The fact that David was also a murderer and adulterer brings home to us men the uncomfortable biblical reminder that all men fail at some point. But even though David cratered morally in some really important ways, his throne and rule would still become the metaphor for all that would be great again for his people. The throne of David (i.e., the influence of his leadership on his society) was far greater than his personal failings as an individual. This reminds me of a conversation I had with one of my sons who was struggling in his first semester of college.

I remember telling him, *"The mark of a man,"* I told him, *"was not that a man fails, but what he does next—how he responds to those failures."*

Nothing is more humiliating than owning up to failure. But men are not called to engage in self-protecting damage control like a teenage boy. There is a difference between protecting yourself or your agenda, and legitimately protecting others from the consequences of your screwups. A man needs to be self-correcting when there's no one there to do it for him. Personally, I've learned a lot from my failures. Although painful, such lessons are powerful, teachable moments I don't readily forget. Failures force me to face the evidence of real actions and tangible consequences—they force me to ask the question, *"Is this who I really am?"*

I think God is waiting to meet us in those shameful, awful times of failure, because they speak to our identity and deepest sense of ourselves. It's part of being human, and it's also part of the growth process of maturing into manhood. A humble, broken man is what we are told is a man God finds useful.

A thousand years after King David, Paul would continue that theme and exhort the Corinthians in much the same way: "Be on the alert, stand firm in the faith, *act like men*, be strong" (1 Corinthians 16:13 NASB). My dad never gave me a charge like that *per se*—he simply lived the life I think he was expecting me to live, and he went about showing me what was worth imitating. My dad never *had the talk* with me or showed me how to shave. Instead, he took me tonging for oysters on Saturdays, and we'd hang out afterwards as he shucked oysters and drank beer. At other times, he'd let me tag along when he went hunting with some of his friends. But he never sat down and went through a "man book" like *Wild at Heart* or anything like that. I got more, I think, from just being around him. Over the years, I've found other men worth imitating as well. They've had their own collections of failures to be sure, and they weren't shy about sharing those when I asked. Mainly, they were men who leaned into the wind when it blew hard and who spent their energy actually doing the man dance rather than wasting energy simply talking about it. In fact, I noticed most of those guys rarely talked about it—they simply *lived* it.

A couple of guys I work with were having a cigar and a cold beer after work one day and the topic of another one of our colleagues (who happens to be an outspoken Christian believer) came up. His name is Larry. To look at him, you wouldn't think there was anything exceptional, nor would anyone mistake him for Jack Bauer, John Wayne, or Denzel Washington. He's just a compact, bald-headed guy with glasses who always seems to be in a good mood. But once you get to know him and spend time with him, and hear some of the stories folks tell about how Larry navigates through life, you get it. One of our colleagues at work was describing Larry to someone who'd never met him, and summed him up in this way:

"Larry is the guy we all wish we were."

Maybe my idea of the calling to manhood is outdated, uninformed, and provincial. That could be true. I'm in my sixties after all. But from the very beginning—when Adam tried to shift blame onto Eve in that infamous, disobedient moment in the garden—punting on responsibility and abdicating leadership has never sat well with me. Yet, it's the very thing I see myself doing in my worst moments.

A Temple

There is this weird arc of history that leads to things I never expected and find totally surprising. When I was growing up, for example, I never thought girls would be getting tattoos and men would be wearing earrings. Of course, Popeye, Marines, sailors, and bikers riding with the Hell's Angels had tattoos, but the body art I see nowadays is shocking in its utter normalcy on who is wearing it. Although there's nothing intrinsically wrong with that, those tattoos are like billboards showing just how much, and how quickly, times are changing. I now ask folks about their tattoos, because if someone has marked themselves up like that permanently, there is usually a good story behind it—or a sad story. But a story maybe worth hearing. At the end of the day, it's not the cover of the book that really matters anyway, but the story told in the pages that lay within that cover. My friend, Don, was in the habit of taking me and our friend, Jack, out for lunch for our birthdays since our birthdays were so close. Our waitress happened to have some numbers tattooed on her forearm, and as she was waiting for Don to figure out what he was going to order, which was not unusual for Don who is forever agonizing over food, I asked her about her tattoo. She said it was a date. In fact, it was the day when her sister died of a drug overdose and her little six-year-old niece was the one who found her. She now takes care of her niece and works two jobs to make ends meet for them both.

Not every tattoo is a work of art. All of them tell a story of something, though, even if it was "I woke up with a hangover and this tattoo."

I almost got a tattoo when I was overseas. I was thinking about getting the old "chicken, ball, and hook" (USMC eagle, globe, and anchor) when my sharp-witted wife told me that whatever tattoo I got, she would get in the same place. Somehow, I just couldn't visualize that on her.

Tattoos and jewelry are really just external fashion statements and maybe passing fads. But the recent confusion over gender identity is much more complicated and disturbing. This confusion has nothing to do with the outward appearance of a life, but speaks to a person's inner perception of themselves—a perception no longer rooted in objective biology, but subjective feelings of identity. Identity is a central component to meaning. Since science claims to deal in objective facts and evidence—rather than subjective feeling and emotion—this transition is odd to say the least. Yet here we are. Nowadays, you and I are asked to believe our objective biology no longer determines our gender. Instead, it's what we think or *wish* about ourselves that determines whether we are male or female. The obvious problem with this claim is the fact that there is a deeper existential problem that gets ignored. The fact is *most* people look at themselves in the mirror and wish they were someone, or something, else.

Manhood has now become a sexually defined thing when, in fact, it is so much more than that. I think there is a radical difference between being *male* and being a *man*. One *shows himself* to be a man by the way challenges are faced and overcome. In other words, there is a difference between rising above a circumstance and simply trying to change the circumstance itself. It is the same for a woman as well. The beauty of a woman is not simply anatomical. To believe that is to reduce a human being to a mere object. That is why Christians are so opposed to pornography. It debases the very essence of womanhood to merely a body. I have a certain level of sympathy for someone who might be confused about who they *want* to be, but ditching who you actually were created to be can't be something normal or healthy. As a case in point, I think the John Hopkins University Hospital stopped doing transgender operations because they were associated with high patient suicide rates.

No matter how cruelly we think nature has put us together, or how confused we are by our compulsions—be it gender dysphoria, illegitimate sexual impulses, unhealthy physical addictions, or simply low self-esteem—we must all strive to remember this one remarkable thing: We are each uniquely designed as a temple of the living God. Although outwardly mortal and perishing, we already bear the mark and design of divinity in our flesh as we await the resurrection of our present bodies. Sin has marred our physical forms to be sure, and the flesh is weak and easily corrupted, we know. But at the threshold of these living temples, our bodies, there is an incorruptible Spirit that waits to dwell within us. He offers an overcoming strength we have the privilege of tapping into at all times, saying, "Behold, I stand at the door and knock: if any man hear my voice and open the door, I will come in to him . . ." (Revelation 3:20 ASV).

Meaning is found not in the outer appearance of who or what we think we should be, but it is found in the life and habits of the inner man. The part of us that fellowships with the Divine.

We don't get to pick our physical traits or the circumstances we're born into. Even if we could, life itself is an uncomfortable and unpredictable experience much of the time, and a severe ordeal more often than not. But strangely enough, it's these very trials that form the stuff and foundation of our most epic stories. Trials give men the opportunity to step up and embrace their challenges and show themselves for who they are. It's not about income, ability, or biceps, but mostly about simply *showing up*. At the end of the day, when adversity comes, and when a man is needed—it doesn't matter how old you are or how confused you might be about your own desires and emotions—a man shows up. A man will emerge from the cocoon of his boyhood as he faces trials head on and learns to lean into the winds of adversity. The testing of his faith during such trials reveals who he really is and who he can become.

Average men become exceptional when they rise above the difficult circumstances we all face in times like these. But first . . . they simply have to *show up*.

Face it on your feet.

CHAPTER 12

ROMANIA

"How do you become an adult in a society
that doesn't ask for sacrifice?"

—Sebastian Junger

While walking through the basement of a brand new, nearly completed church in Lugoj, Romania, I noticed an older man working alone by himself. He was vigorously sanding what looked like some pews that he or someone else had recently made. As I passed by, he stopped what he was doing, bobbed his head, and smiled a toothy greeting. Sawdust covered his tattered overalls and his longish, unkempt gray hair and beard made him seem a pretty disheveled character. Amid the new construction smell of fresh paint and wood chips, he didn't look too out of place. A laborer.

Well, that's nice, I remember thinking. They're throwing some grunt work at one of the local down-and-outers leftover from the former communist state. That's a good thing for a church to do . . . get the old guy on his feet until he can function on his own.

Turns out the "old guy" was actually a world-class hydrophysicist and local university professor who just happened to be a very capable carpenter as well. I was told he'd even constructed an airplane around the engine of a downed WWII YAK (soviet fighter). After discovering the wreckage in a field near his house, he'd dragged the engine into his barn and built an airplane around it to escape Romania's repressive communist government. The only problem was he didn't actually know how to fly. When he tried to talk one of his Chinese students into flying him out, the student turned him in to the authorities instead. Such was life in a communist police state.

Despite his humble appearance, this man obviously had a great story to tell. It was an important reminder to me to avoid assuming things about the lives of the people I come across. Just as book covers can be deceiving, what a person looks like on the outside often disguises their hidden talents and amazing experiences. It is the pages of the story inside—woven from the years of a life—that matters.

Revolution

Romania is a beautiful country. In many ways, its topography and climate remind me of my own native Commonwealth of Virginia (circa pre-1940). Horse-drawn wagons are as prevalent there as they are in Amish country USA, but that's not by choice. I could see the country was very poor, and probably still is, despite its many natural wonders. In the Carpathian Mountains, for example, natural hot springs have been refreshing men and women since the days of Roman conquest as they plotted taking over the world.

Communist politicos enjoyed those same springs when they took *their own* turn at plotting to take over the world. But during the long decades of their atheistic oppression, Christian believers continued to come secretly at night to baptize new converts in those warm, spring-fed waters. When my wife, Terry, and I visited these hot springs ourselves, we saw women still doing their laundry in them as they have for millennia.

The soil of Romania is rich and fertile beneath a pleasant rolling landscape. Like a few other European countries, it's also a nation that has suffered the devastating consequences of two world wars. After the removal of their king sometime in the late 1940s, Romanians were forced to endure long, painful decades as a Soviet satellite state, and signs of change weren't seen until 1989. It was a time of revolution in Eastern Europe, and Romania was ripe for it along with the rest. As the Solidarity movement gained steam in Poland, the political climate in the region changed quickly.

In Romania, Hungarian Reformed Church pastor Laszlo Tokes spoke out honestly and boldly from his pulpit in the small college town of Timisoara. Pastor Tokes' fast-growing ministry and influence grew so exponentially over the next few years, he was seen as a threat to the ruling communist regime.

So what kind of threat does Christianity pose to a government or to a particular political party? Or to a community? Since the mandate from Jesus has always been to "love God—love people," it's initially hard to see from the middle of the bell curve how that presents a danger to anyone. But his-

Washing clothes in one of Romania's hot springs.

tory has repeatedly shown it does. Besides the politics and governmental control issues, Christianity is also viewed as a cultural menace in many places. Even in freedom-loving America, we see a growing antagonism toward the Christian community, and in my lifetime, it has become the one community it's okay to criticize and discriminate against. In some cases, that criticism is well deserved, I grant you, but in most cases, it is not. Moral issues have always been a primary concern of the church, but it has primarily been a concern for those *within* the church. The church is, and ought to be, concerned with the church. One would think there should be a lot to like about having a Christian church in a community. I hope your particular community appreciates yours.

People behaving badly should not be tolerated, regardless of who they are. But don't blame it on the Christian faith, just blame it on people's innate inclination to behave badly. As for Christ, He never condoned immoral behavior, be they priests or politicians. Nevertheless, antagonism toward Evangelicals is now part of a trendy, cultural narrative. Even in the United States—which is so tolerant of everything and everyone else— there seems to be an evangelical exception clause. Christianity's primary shortcoming (in the opinion of the culture police) is its "intolerant" stand on certain moral issues. Publicly proclaiming *anything* is morally wrong is now a moral crime itself in our *50 Shades of Gray* world. I wonder if those who criticize the church for labeling some things "morally wrong" believe there is anything anywhere that is ever wrong.

In Romania, Pastor Tokes was persecuted in ways Americans are starting to recognize here. At first, he was barred by his government from preaching biblical truth. Soon, he was denied the means to buy food and other stuff his family needed, and then was assaulted in his own home. Like Pastor Tokes, many other Romanian pastors were beaten and harassed for preaching the gospel inside their own country. In 1948, Richard Wurmbrand was imprisoned and then tortured for eight and a half years. His memoir, *Tortured for Christ,* describes this ordeal and relates how his wife was later imprisoned for continuing his work. This harrowing account is just one story among many detailing the atrocities believers and pastors endured in those dark years behind the Iron Curtain in the socialist satellite states of Eastern Europe. It is hard to imagine those who are clamoring for socialism in our own country understand exactly what they are asking for.

When the government tried to evict Tokes from his church, he refused and called upon his church to come bear witness to what would happen on the day the state authorities were to come for him. Of all the Eastern Bloc countries that transitioned away from communism during this period, Romania's revolution was maybe the only violent one. Children were gunned down on the church steps. I have seen the bullet holes on the sides of the church walls. I have met men who lost their children and loved ones.

When Terry and I first visited Romania in the fall of 1992, we took our thirteen-year-old daughter, Kate, along with us. The revolutionary events of a few years earlier were still pretty raw and fresh, and very much in evidence. We had come to visit a couple we'd never actually met in person: Dr. Titus and his wife, Nuta, with whom I had been corresponding. In those days, exchanging letters was a long and painful process, and it sometimes took six months for a letter to reach its destination—if it ever arrived at all. Even if it did, it may have been opened and its contents examined on the way. Of course, no email or Skype existed back then either, just old-school paper and pen. Snail mail. It was the first time I'd ever had to be careful with what I wrote.

What is interesting about our visit was that we were unsure if they even knew we were coming! Initially, we were to travel in January, but we changed our plans in the spring and decided to go in November. We sent the letter off in April, hoping they would be aware of our plans and meet us in Budapest where we would arrive at one of the two airports there. Not hearing from Titus, we launched off anyway (literally on a wing and a prayer). Landing in Eastern Europe during those days was not the family vacation spot it might be today. Taking Terry and a thirteen-year-old girl also added to the stress of not knowing who—if anyone—would be waiting for us when we got there.

Titus never got my letter. But this is the thing—he felt God was telling him that we were arriving that week in November, and thusly convinced, he sent two men from the church to drive the eight hours to Budapest to pick us up. Those men spent two nights in their van, travelling each day between the two airports with a sign that read, "Jim and Terry from Virginia." We later found my letter behind our piano where it slipped off.

I think it's hard for us in the West to comprehend just how awful communism and totalitarianism was for those who suffered under its tyranny. But as the days of our Romania visit unfolded, we began to get a sense of what it must have been like for its hapless citizens.

Some of history's most moving and inspiring examples recall the men and women who rose up in opposition to injustice or who simply and quietly endured hardship. The historical record is replete with heroic examples of this kind of steadfast endurance in response to persecution. To this day, people are still being victimized, dehumanized, and traumatized for simply believing and doing what we take for granted here in the West. Organizations like The Voice of the Martyrs have been established to shed light and give a voice to those who are, even now, undergoing unimaginable sufferings for their Christian faith.

What is interesting about the way many Eastern European countries transitioned away from communism is the primary role religion played in those transitions. In many of these communist countries, the impulse for freedom was a distinctly religious one—there was an intuitive understanding that any freedom without a moral center will always lead to a greater tyranny.

Pope John Paul II presides over history as a giant of the latter years of the past century for the role he played in challenging these communist and tyrannical regimes and for the moral vision he cast as a leader in the Catholic Church. I think the Catholic Church has not had a leader quite like him in this modern era and perhaps never will again. I say that as a Protestant Evangelical. He not only engaged the world's cultures with truth like no one else in our day, but he engaged the movers and shakers of those cultures as well. (His thoughtful lectures on the "Theology of the Human Body" was a remarkable gift to the Catholic Church as a whole.) He even invited Mother Theresa to open one of her orders—Missionaries of Charity—in Rome itself.

Think about that. *Rome.* How many Catholic organizations do you think there were in Rome already when he extended her that invitation?

Two Beatings Hurt, Not Two Meals

My friend, Titus, is a likable, somewhat intense man who hated communism and how it affected his people. He hated it so much that plans to escape Romania and come to the US captivated his thoughts from the time he was a very young man studying veterinary medicine at the University in Timisoara. In preparation for his escape, he began to teach himself English. He also started studying the Bible because he was under the impression that America was a Christian nation and anyone who showed up on our shores had better be prepared to answer questions about the Bible. He reminded me that even our currency says, "In God we trust." So Titus learned English mostly by sorting through the Scriptures, but as he did, Titus was introduced to a different kind of citizenship . . . and a different kind of a King. Titus was converted to Christian.

Many of our nights visiting him, we had the privilege of sitting at his table, listening to the stories of men and women who had paid a dear price for their faith—many suffering for worshipping in a country whose leaders saw Christians and their Christ as a threat. As I listened, I realized that communism takes Christianity far more seriously than most of us do here at home. And for my thirteen-year-old daughter, it was an unforgettable introduction into the broader reality of the Church beyond the youth groups and Sunday school she experienced in our small Shenandoah Valley town.

This introduction revealed a multilingual God who speaks Romanian as well as English and a people whose Christian faith was serious business.

With serious consequences. Titus and his fellow believers were willing to risk everything to flee Romania, and we were captivated to hear unbelievable stories of their daring escape attempts. In one instance, my friend, Titus, and two others tried to lead a group into Yugoslavia by crossing the Danube in a homemade submarine. How does one go about building a submarine? But they did it—and were on the bank of the river getting ready to cross when they were captured. The three guys who led the bold effort were subsequently beaten and imprisoned. Ironically, all of the folks (I think there were thirteen) who attempted the escape in that homemade sub, now live in the US. Only the three leaders who planned it and suffered for it stayed in Romania to help lead in a different way—as church elders.

Persecution

Persecution has always been a part of the Christian experience from the moment the first disciples were martyred for their faith. In many cases, persecution is a *key* part. It is something that Jesus promised for the Church, although I am not sure I really like and appreciate that promise very much. But the early Church saw persecution in a different light; many of those early Christians thought making the ultimate sacrifice of martyrdom a desirable thing to prove their affections toward their Lord. Although some Christians simply saw it as their duty, others actually saw it as a privilege. There are endless examples of these Christian martyrs since the time of Christ. Even now, in many places—whether in Muslim countries or in China, India, or Somalia—Christians endure incredible hardship for their faith. Only the Lord knows the full extent of their sacrifice since these modern martyrs are largely unknown, uncelebrated, and unmourned. Christians are suffering and dying for the things we so casually compromise on here as I had mentioned before. Living as we do in the West, I'm not sure we can really experience the intimacy of Jesus to the degree it is possible apart from the experience of persecution and suffering. Here in the West, that kind of thinking tends to be a hard thing to understand and appreciate.

But even here in the West, dark clouds of persecution are gathering in the distance. One senses a storm approaching, and the scent of religious persecution is in the air. In recent years, a new wave of young, media savvy atheists have attempted to go mainstream by staking their claims of evolutionary autonomy in the media arts. Their stated purpose is ridding the world of Christianity's influence, both in this country and abroad. Embedded in their reasoning is the premise that Christianity needs to be rooted out because it's been, and continues to be, an evil, intolerant influence that holds back the natural forward progress of man. An intolerant position to be sure—even as they level the accusation of intolerance at the church. These new atheists seem to have no problem with any other world view. Just the Christian worldview. In their minds, it is the root of all evil. But why? What is the essence of the antagonism atheists have toward Christianity? It's exclusivity. Yet many religions claim that same exclusivity. So why single out Christianity? It's impact. The truth of the gospel of Jesus Christ has shaped the world for the last two thousand years more dramatically than any other belief system. And yes, truth by its very nature *is* exclusive. "*True* truth," Francis Schaeffer called it.

Moreover, the new outspoken atheists seem to have little to offer in the arena of ethics and justice to take Christianity's place. In their brave new world of technological wonders and dazzling scientific progress, they have no basis for positing any specific ethic other than preference or opinion. Expediency rules all, and a desired result justifies any means used.

I think maybe it's a good thing these young atheists are challenging the Church. I really do. It forces us to examine our core beliefs, and it keeps Christians on their toes. To know what we believe and why we believe it is essential to faith. *Case for Christ* author, Lee Strobel, was a Pulitzer Prize-winning investigative journalist and atheist before he used his journalistic training to examine the massive amount of evidence supporting the claims of Christianity—and came to faith in Christ himself. There are many former atheists who have done the same, just as there are many atheists who don't bother to examine that body of evidence. Modern atheists who choose to deny the claims of Christ are not the first ones to predict the demise of an outmoded Christianity. Voltaire famously thought the Bible would be obsolete within 100 years, and yet a mere fifty years after his death, there was a printing press *in his own house* cranking out the Scriptures.

For this new generation of atheists, it is as if all of the good, self-sacrificial works to reach out and alleviate the suffering of humanity (like a Mother Theresa)—and all of the compassionate impulses to go and help do what others in their brave new world of progress cannot, and will not, do—have no worth or meaning. They are negated in their view by their own carefully constructed reductionist propositions they offer up as science, sprinkled with a few exceptions of historical Christian abuses. They do this while ignoring the natural and logical outworking of their own evolutionary propositions, and do not provide any sort of rationale for anyone in doing any sort of self-sacrificial things that the logical outworking of Christianity confesses before the world. Why should I give up my life for another, or make any sacrifices for anyone if this is all there is in life? In fact, any moral judgement an atheist offers really has no foundation other than personal preference, in which case it seems to me from my perch in the middle of the bell curve, any one preference is as good as another. (As I heard Christian apologist Dr. Zacharias observe, "In some cultures, they greet their neighbors, and in some cultures, they eat their neighbors—what would be your preference?") Or maybe the more simplistic bumper sticker I have seen on cars (well . . . mostly trucks) that reads, "My middle school student can beat up your middle school honor student up any day."

In Romania, Titus experienced firsthand the moral outworking of the atheistic philosophy governing his country. He was beaten, imprisoned, and for over a year and a half, endured solitary confinement—all for wanting to serve the God who says, "Render unto Caesar that which is Caesar's" (Matthew 22:21, author's paraphrase). The day before we arrived to visit, he had three teeth worked on without Novocain because there simply wasn't any to be had. In his veterinary practice, he often performed operations on animals using plum brandy as the only available anesthetic. Before one such procedure when he was preparing to perform a C-section on a cow, he gave the farmer some plum brandy for the cow to drink because he didn't have any anesthesia. But the cow kept jerking around anyway. He couldn't figure out why, and he just tried to finish the surgery as quickly as possible. At the end of the successful operation, the farmer insisted they celebrate with . . . plum brandy. Such are the benefits of socialism.

His jokes illustrated the terrible travesty of the life they'd known for so long: "It is illegal to leave your window open in the winter because someone passing by it outside might catch a cold." Or, "The president drove by a bakery with a two-block line waiting for bread that had run out, and was so enraged he demanded that they make more chairs for these people to sit on while they waited."

Even though Titus is a veterinarian and his wife, Nuta, is an engineer, they'd just gotten electricity in their home in Lugoj right before we came. We saw very few people smiling on the streets there. Food choices were limited, so it was a big deal when my daughter, Kate, was offered a piece of tropical fruit (a banana) while we were visiting. They still didn't have access to much fresh produce from outside the country then. But Titus always joked with us when we politely refused second helpings of food, "Two beatings hurt—not two meals!" he would say with a laugh.

On the eight-hour drive from Budapest, we had a chance to chat with the two men who picked us up. When I asked the men how the Church there was doing, I expected to hear good news. Communism was waning, and I knew those in the city were being allowed to build churches and worship openly without reprisal for the first time in over four decades. But I was surprised that our drivers both agreed spirituality in the Church had decreased as the building program increased—and that capitalism had brought new challenges.

One Sunday, we went to a Romanian church service in a small village—really just two rows of cottages on either side of a country dirt road. The service itself was being held in a one room house that looked like something straight out of a Grimm's fairy tale. When we filed in, I could see the place was constructed of wood and sparsely furnished, with benches lining the white plaster walls and rough wooden planks for a floor. A heated wood stove occupied the middle of the room, and as we sat down, its welcome warmth took the chill out of the brisk November morning. An earthy, smoky smell from years of heating with wood permeated the room. Like most of the cottages, it probably had about an acre or more of garden in the back, where they grew food needed to supplement the little they could afford to buy. And like Titus, they probably had a few hogs and some chickens running loose as well.

At the end of the service I recall all of us getting up from our benches and getting ready to leave, when a very old woman stood up and began to pray at which time we all immediately sat down again until she was finished. As we were leaving, I asked Titus who that old woman was and he said, "She was the woman who donated the house we were in to be the church. It was her home but she gave it up and now lives in a room with another family in the village." She gave away her home so they could have a church and now has nothing.

That sounds very much like a story Jesus would tell.

Titus and his wife have visited us several times here in the states at our home in Virginia. They would go into a Food Lion simply to look at all of the things on the shelf until the colors and volume and variety would give them a headache, and then they would have to leave. He would also take as many books home with them when they left as he could. I took them bowling one night, and I assumed that everyone kind of knew that the idea was to roll the ball down and knock these pins over. Everyone knows how to bowl right? These are university educated people after all. The first problem was they did not know how to grip the ball and began by shot-putting it down the lane. They graduated from there to heaving it sideways, swinging it like a golf club, and I swear I did not know there were so many ways to get that ball to roll down the lane. Folks bowling around us looked at us like we were from a special needs facility on a field trip. The arrogance of ignorance.

I find it hard to make significant sacrifices, and I struggle with even small ones. Compromise and rationalizing always are there at my fingertips to bail me out of the really hard things I push back from having to do. Suffering for me is when the air-conditioning goes out in the car or the dishwasher quits working. Even tithing can be difficult, and I generally excuse that away by righteously telling myself, *Well, we are not under the law are we?* The times I do reach down and cough up a good deed, nine times out of ten, I am casually looking around to see if anyone is noticing. I think I have more in common with the "rich young ruler" than the "widow and her two pennies." That is the dilemma and challenge of living in a world of freedom and choice.

That bothers me.

Like Titus, you, and everyone else, I am still a work in progress. Even at sixty. That's not an excuse, but we might underestimate the challenges that come with choice. When Moses led his people out of slavery into freedom, it was hard. They were hungry and fearful of all the unknown dangers that lay ahead. I am sure they missed the familiarity of their homes and all their stuff. It got to the point that they were grumbling so much, they were actually preferring to go back to a life of servitude and a life making bricks without straw than the life and freedom Moses offered them. So God did an interesting thing: He *tested* them by *blessing* them. He rained down bread on them from heaven. But they ended up grumbling about that too. It just wasn't the same as eating leeks and onions by the Nile. God made it perfectly clear He knew what and *whom* all the grumbling was *really* about. When the congregation grumbled against His chosen leaders and His provision, they were really grumbling against *Him.*

Grumbling

Grumbling *in* church and *about* church is not unusual in our Western culture, particularly here in the States. But most places around the world don't have that luxury. We have a lot of churches here, and if you don't like something and are tired of grumbling about it, well . . . folks, just leave and go grumble someplace else. We Americans are consumers after all. In fact, as I write this, I'm in Texas where the only things more prevalent than chain restaurants are churches. Some of them are as big as shopping malls. It reminds me of a joke I heard about a man who was rescued one day after years alone on a deserted island. As the boat scraped ashore, the bosun asked if there were any other castaways on the island.

"No," said the man, "I am the only one."

"Well, I saw three individual huts," the bosun replied, "so I thought there might be more of you. What are the other two for?"

"Oh," the man answered. "It's simple. The hut on the end is where I live."

"And that hut there?" the bosun asked, pointing to the one in the middle.

"That's where I go to church," the castaway said. "The third hut is where I used to go to church."

The last time we visited Romania, I went with my friend, Mark. As soon as we got there, we detoured to the northern part of Hungary to visit a couple who were pastoring a small Hungarian Reformed Church near the border of Russia (who also happened to be cousins of some folks in our church back home). What could possibly go wrong? We were a couple of young American guys on a pseudo road trip in an eastern bloc country. Our somewhat comical adventure started out well enough, as my friend, Mark (who grew up on a Nebraska farm), got excited when he saw some center-pivot irrigation machinery in a couple of the farm fields we passed. He even wanted a picture of them and the fields, although I didn't quite understand his interest. One farm field looks pretty much like any other field to me, regardless of what part of the world you're in—it's a flat expanse of brownish-black dirt with green stuff growing in it. So much for the fun part.

As evening approached, we arrived in the moderately sized town where the couple lived. But we soon discovered (*What do you mean, you don't have the address?*) we had absolutely no idea of where to go, how to find them, or what we ought to do next. We tried approaching folks on the sidewalks, but two Americans speaking English just earned us a cold shoulder. It also turned out the name of the couple we'd come to see was *Kovacs*, the Hungarian version of Smith or Jones. In frustration, we drove around until it started getting dark. We decided to find the biggest church in town in the hope someone there might know where the Kovacs lived. But the church was closed! At that point, we finally realized it was time to pray—the kind of "when all else *fails, it's time to loft up* a bail-us-out, Hail Mary kind of prayer." And do you know what? After we prayed, I was so encouraged I got out of the car and shouted out, "Kovacs! Anyone here know the Kovacs?" Right across the street, a door opened and a young guy peeked out. I could hear the note of incredulity in his voice, "Mark? Jim?" Obviously, prayer works just as well in northern Hungary as it does here.

We found the Eastern European churches had adopted a far more formal construct than those in America. Men sat on one side of the sanctuary and women on the other. And where American churches would typically offer worship music accompanied by guitars and drums, Romanian churches had trombones and French horns for worship—played by older folks mixed with younger ones. The church itself was very old, with a turret-like pulpit towering over the congregation. Sunday afternoons, we would go to a lunch after the service, and they would ask us questions. I was a curiosity. What is a pilot doing with a pastor talking about religious things? For them, church leadership was still a part of the credentialed class.

A young English-speaking woman went with us as we traveled around Hungary that week and acted as our interpreter for our short time there. Every now and then, she would stop chatting and offer up a little prayer in her native tongue. It took me some time before I figured out why. On the sides of the road, we'd seen young women standing by the highway like they were waiting for a bus. But they were really waiting for truck drivers to pull over to earn a little money. Our interpreter would pray for every single one of those poor girls we drove past. Each and every one of them. She could have judged them, but chose to pray for them instead.

When I asked her where she went to church, she told me she attended a small charismatic church near the border of Russia where she lived. She also explained she wasn't doctrinally affiliated with the church, and that they did some weird stuff she was a bit uncomfortable with. But it was the only church in the area, so she had no choice. As the saying goes, you learn to eat the fish and not choke on the bones when there is no other meal available. Like T in the days of communist oppression and scores of other believers today, so many live in a world where there are no choices. One common thread I've noticed running through all the stories of those I've met—whose lot it is to worship God in hard times and difficult places, where churches are scarce and often persecuted—is gratitude. Their spirits are marked more by gratefulness than by grumbling. These Christians are simply grateful they can worship freely, and that they have a place to do so.

Although brief, my few visits to Romania and Hungary offered many faith-building moments for me. I saw a church stripped bare of nonessential trappings and the peripheral "necessities" we find so essential in our own churches. I heard the stories of a church refined through suffering the flames of persecution—and which strengthened faith, in turn, helped bolster my own. There is a power in that exchange. If they could endure so much for their faith, maybe so could I.

It reminds me of something I read somewhere about an event in the life of Augustine:

When walking through a particularly affluent area of Rome, Augustine's companion said, "Isn't it nice that we Christians no longer have to say to the world, 'Gold and silver have we none?'"

To which Augustine replied, "And no longer can we say to the lame man, 'Arise and walk.'"

One of the many common road hazards—especially at night.

CHAPTER 13

ECUADOR

"There is something fascinating about science. One gets such whole-
sale returns of conjecture out of such a trifling investment of fact."

—Mark Twain

One of the most lasting memories I have from our Babbs Mountain Run house is one where I am coming down our basement steps and almost trip over these three prone bodies stretched out side by side on the floor. Two are Wauroni Indians from a remote part of the jungle, deep in the heart of Ecuador—one, an old grizzled killer; the other, the son of a killer—lying on either side of my twelve-year-old son, Andrew, as they watch *Jurassic Park* on TV and eat popcorn. They had just come in from wandering around our yard with these long, lethal, handmade blowguns looking for something to shoot at the behest of my son. These Amazonian gents were in the company of Steve Saint, part missionary, part inventor, part-time speaker, and full time adopted family member of the Stone Age visitors lying on my basement floor. How Steve became part of these guys' life is really his story and not mine to tell, but for those of you who are unfamiliar with it, I will briefly recap it for you.

Steve's dad, Nate, and four other young guys were missionaries in a small outpost on the edge of the jungle, trying to reach this tribe of vicious Stone Age killers in a very remote area of the Amazon in Ecuador in the late 1950s. The reason they were trying to reach them was because of the rash of killings by these same primitive tribal Indians of some Shell Oil employees and others encroaching into their area, the government decided to eradicate the problem. It was a race by these missionaries to hopefully beat this draconian governmental response to these killings in targeting and eliminating this tribe known then as the Aucas. The Aucas themselves were known and feared as vicious killers. They killed within even their own family groups. I remember asking at our dinner table one night what the word for "grandfather" was in their language, and after much deliberation, discovered that there was no such word. Men did not live that long before they were killed as to become grandfathers. No slight would go unavenged in the tribe. The spearing went back and forth among them, and even death by snake bite would have to be avenged with another spearing.

In order to rescue the lives of these remote indigenous folks, Steve's dad, Nate, and four other young men hatched a plan to try to reach them with the gospel, which was the one thing they believed could bring life and change to this vicious group of killers. After initially making contact with this tribe, and after only a few visits, they themselves were brutally and mercilessly speared. What happened afterwards is this remarkable story of redemption, and an extraordinary unfolding drama that saw two women—one whose husband and one whose brother were the victims of that spearing party—reach out and finish what those young men began. Elizabeth Elliot whose husband, Jim, was one of those young men speared that day, wrote her memoire of those events and the immediate aftermath in her classic book, *Through the Gates of Splendor*. Years later, Steve would be baptized by one of those men who had killed his father, men who now were elders in their own village church—and one of which was enjoying the movie, *Jurassic Park*, in my basement and eating my popcorn with my twelve-year-old son.

Less than a year after we had our twins, a mutual friend who taught at Rio Grande Bible Institute asked if we would be willing to take into our home a young Ecuadorian girl who was trying to learn English, and who needed a place to stay for the summer. He thought that she, in turn, could help us with our infant twin girls who were, even as infants, a handful. At the time, I was flying primarily the Caribbean and Latin America and was brushing up on my Spanish. I welcomed the chance to learn a little more Spanish to help me along, and it would be a win-win. It was. (Twenty years later, Debby is part of our family now, and even though she lives in Ecuador, she will spend a month with us every year or so.)

I first met Steve over the phone after hearing that Debby's boyfriend (and later, her husband), who wanted to be a missionary pilot, was staying with Steve in Ocala, Florida. Debby asked me if I would give Steve a call and sort out what was going on down there and so I did. Over the phone, I learned that this guy had a vision of training some of the young Ecuadorian guys to be pilots, and also training these same Stone Age villagers in the jungle to fly airplanes as well

Debby with the twins.

(sometimes the only way out for medical help in the jungle is by airplane). They saw the need to fend for themselves in an ever encircling world of technology without having to rely on Westerners to do it for them as they have had to in the past.

As an airline pilot, I was intrigued by this, so my friend, Mark Dreyer, and I went to visit Steve in Ocala where ITEC and his home was located. With the help of several medical/dental volunteers over the years, Steve already had these Indians doing rudimentary dental work and going about filling cavities with a bicycle powered drill. Although illiterate, they were very keen observers of how things worked and, only after seeing things once, could then repeat the process of whatever it was that was being done. On an earlier medical mission to the tribe, they had watched a dentist fill a cavity for example, and were able to imitate the steps in how to do that. One of the dentists then helped them properly apply the "thorn" to block the pain, and how to clean out and then fill a tooth.

I know what you dentists are now thinking, *He thinks dental work is so easy, even an illiterate Stone Age hunter-gatherer can do it.* I am not. But the fact is they actually are. As "luck" would have it, for example, Steve lost a filling while he was in the village and had to have one of the villagers who was trained in using his contraption fix his tooth. Wasn't the most polished or professional looking job, but it stopped the pain and prevented infection.

I am a professional pilot who has spent years refining my craft, yet these guys are flying themselves from one village to the next. Would I like them to be at the controls on a CAT III ILS approach into Kennedy on a snowy gusty night in IFR conditions? No. But the tribal pilot flies the tribal dentist to other villages and meets a need no one else can or will. Steve's workshop in Ocala was a hangar filled with all sorts of gadgets and gizmos, all designed for the purpose of aiding tribal believers in fending for themselves in the face of this advancing and encroaching world of technology. One of those things he was working on at the time when I was down there was a powered parachute. A powered parachute is this tricycle-looking go-cart with a big fan on the back, powered by a lawnmower engine that turns a prop that blows into the attached and very large parachute. This thing takes off in a very short distance and is steerable, carries two people, and is perfect for using in the jungle. I helped Steve carry this thing from Ocala, Florida to Quito, Ecuador . . . believe it or not, as carry-on luggage. (This was before 9/11.) His friend, Tementha, would be the pilot of this contraption. The irony in this is Tementha's dad was one of the men who was on the spearing party that killed Steve's father, the missionary pilot, on that fateful day of that killing so many years ago. So these tribal indigenous missionaries would load up the bicycle-driven dental operatory on their powered parachute, climb on, and fly from village to village sharing the gospel and filling teeth. Having did my time sitting in a dental chair with my mouth open getting drilled, this is a bit of genius; you have no choice but to listen to what is being said.

Others

Being sixty years old and living in these racially and politically divisive times, I am often encouraged to see how these men from different cultures and markedly different backgrounds can get along so well. The father whom Steve lost was in some ways befriended and replaced by a man who was responsible for that loss. In all of our Hollywood fantastical stories, who could have seen that one coming? In my own generation this story of sacrifice by these five young men was told and retold, and it was an inspiration for thousands of believers who drew faith and encouragement from their sacrifice. Particularly for a generation like mine that struggles with going *all in* on anything nowadays. I think this story is becoming lost in the dustbin of time and relevance, and few folks are probably aware of it anymore. It was a long time ago. But stories like these, I think, need to be retold and remembered. They are the stories of the church. Our church. The legacy of our people.

I will never forget these Amazonian tribesmen. Think of the courage it took for them just to get on an airplane. It reminds me that beneath the leathery colored skin canvased with homemade tattoos and piercings, it seems we are all made of pretty much the same stuff after all. They had a delightful sense of humor. There is a trap door, I think, we fall through when we treat ourselves to some sort of cultural high ground simply because we do things differently, or because we have a cable TV and Internet. I think there is a lot more to understanding what it means to be made in the image of God and being human than texting on the latest iPhone X with our opposing thumbs.

I was driving with some of my kids one day to one of their many activities and read this bumper sticker on the back of a Volvo station wagon just beneath a rainbow decal that read, "Racism is wrong." And so it is.

But sitting there in traffic, I got to thinking about how we as Christians are really the only ones who have any sort of a logical reason as to why racism is actually wrong. I say this because what the public schools teach, and our children grow up hearing, is that there is an evolutionary process where man has evolved in stages and so it is logical to assume therefore that there are some folks that are at a different developmental stage than maybe others. Perhaps a little higher on the developmental evolutionary ladder so to speak. That is what evolution implies.

It is the beginning of a subtle indoctrination into racial and ethnic discrimination. Hitler's book, *Mien Kampf* (My Struggle), for example, was a case study in what the logical outworking of evolution might easily lead to. His world was driven by the "survival of the fittest" philosophy of life. (Really, if we all came from slimy germs in some primordial bio soup, who should really care if the white germs or the black germs sit at the back of the bus?) Species adapt and change. We are no different in that regard. But there are no such things as the scientific community believed not so long ago as a *sub*human.

The Bible doesn't spend a lot of time going into detail on how the universe came into being. We are told that we were created in the last half of the last day, most likely so we would not think we had anything to do with it. There is plenty room there to wonder if it was over a long period of time or a short period of time, and there are those who have a definite idea about those things. All I know is that God's fingerprints are all over it. Even scientists will grudgingly admit that "out of nothing, nothing comes," and that there seems to be an intelligent design to things we see. We had a beginning. As a matter of fact, the Bible narrative opens up with this truth: *"In the beginning . . ."*

The Bible further most clearly states that we are *all* made in the image of God, even blowgun shooting Amazon tribesmen. Whether it is Steven Hawking or Holland, a precious, young Down's syndrome girl, both bear the stamp of the divine. Steve's dad and the other men who died were simply carrying out the logical outworking of their faith as they tried to reach out to these folks and literally save them. They did not do it to try to sell them anything, nor did they see them as any sort of "market" to exploit or a profit opportunity. They tried to reach out to them with a message that would take away the fear, take away the hate that leads to the impulse to kill, and deliver a message that would not only save their lives from what the government had planned for them but their very souls. These men didn't come as crusaders but came with a cross.

The Imago Dei

Whenever I am at work, or in a setting where the conversation drifts toward religion, rarely does tension ever arise over a disagreement about moral issues. (The Church is often at odds with itself over some of these issues.) Sometimes, though, I find myself having account for Christian abuses.

One of my coworkers told me, "You know, Jim, my mom left me and my two brothers to be raised alone by my dad as she followed Jim and Tammy Baker around in their 'ministry' while we had no mother. We do have a lifetime membership to some Christian resort though."

"You *bet* I have an axe to grind with the Christian faith!"

Unfortunately, as Christians, we must also carry these burdens of abuse, and for historical events like the crusades, the inquisition, and religious persecutions, that these things are in fact the illogical outworking and misrepresentation of what Christ taught. We all know of men and women who abuse others under the pretext of "ministry." The Church stands guilty of a lot of heinous things perpetrated in the name of Christ. Either by commission or omission. These are things that we should never forget and always be sensitive to. Every Christian at some point probably has shamed the gospel by what we have said, or what we have done at some juncture in our life. Opponents of our faith will take these abuses, normalize it as a rule, and then define Christianity and Christians by them. They do this while ignoring the logical outworking of their own evolutionary constructs. It is important to remember as one churchman observed, however, "*You never judge a philosophy by its abuses.*" Racism is one such abuse. If anything, the one great contribution the Church has given the world is the *Imago Dei*—the fact we are all made in the image of God.

The scientific community attempts to reduce all life to that of biomatter. And the stuff of biomatter—we are. That biology is one we share with all creation from cats to kangaroos. But though ants are incredible workers (in fact the Bible asks us to learn from their example), they have never built anything as majestically beautiful and lasting as an ant art museum, or as useful as an abacus in doing math. (In return, we as humans haven't ever been able to self-produce the majesty and grandeur of the Grand Canyon, Himalayas, or a simple green flash sunset over the Caribbean). Birds and whales sing, but they are eclipsed by the soul moving movements by Bach and others. Amoebas and paramecium are irreducibly complex creatures, but I cannot see how self-sacrificing love or justice or fairness or morality could have evolved from their cytoplasm. As they say, there is more to us than meets the eye.

Reducing things to mere biology has the unfortunate byproduct of dehumanization. Babies are now labeled as *fetuses,* in much of the same dehumanizing way as slaves and blacks who were once labeled *niggers,* and Jews were labeled *kikes,* and Southern white's as *crackers.* This dehumanization has now progressed to the point where Ivy League college professors are advocating terminating children up to a year old, and euthanasia for the elderly in some parts of Europe is done without the consent of the primary participants. I am not a sociologist, nor am I a scientist. I don't pretend to be and I have a lot of respect for their education and their discipline. But even I know that there is something wrong with this reductionist thinking. My niece was born with somewhat deformed legs that she had to have in braces until she was several years old, but went on to be a college all-American in track. What she was at year one is not what she is now.

Christianity asserts from the very beginning the fact that we are all created in the image of God. It is not where you live, how old you are, or the color of your skin that elevates a man or a woman in the hierarchy of humanity. We all have different capacities, and live on different parts of the bell curve. Our value, however, is in the One whose image we bear. It is puzzling to me how our culture on one hand decries the stigma of racism while at the same time teaches the moral philosophy of evolution, which is the foundation of racism and attempts to give it scientific legitimacy!

Mainstream academics do not even want theories like intelligent design mentioned in schools, let alone explored as a viable alternative theory in competition to the evolutionary "survival of the fittest" doctrine, now championed by most school systems. So when we hear of racially motivated violence, random shootings, and rampant sexual exploitation by the powerful, is as one poet observes, "It is just man worshipping his maker."

The families of the men who were killed those many years ago could have had a right to harbor some bitterness. Was this a fair trade? The lives of five men who had already contributed so much to society, families, and who had years of "productivity" left ahead of them? All for Amazonian tribesmen who were noted killers and of whom no one ever heard about anyway? They did not sacrifice their lives in order to share with them any sort of technological advances, nor was there any hope of remuneration. There was no investment with a bottomline return. There was nothing in it for those young men who were speared to death. For them, it was simply a call to obedience rooted in love—a very "unevolutionary-esc" virtue.

It was great having these tribal guys around our house and we got a huge chuckle out of their wonder and surprise over things we take for granted. Like automatic flushing toilets. I thought, one day, they would like to go fishing but they had never seen a fishing pole. Watching those guys fish was about as hilarious to me as it probably would be for them watching me climb a tree in the jungle to retrieve a dead monkey. What caught my attention was when they remarked on some of the "tribes" of young folks they saw here around town. I suppose tattoos, piercings, and body art have a cross-cultural flavor to them that they could immediately connect with. It was interesting that these Amazonian tribesmen were readily accepted in our church as "one of us." One of *our people*. I would hope our own pierced and tattooed young folks on the streets would receive the same kind of welcome. I don't know. Probably. Nowadays, it is more normal to see blue hair, plugged earlobes, and tattooed body art than it was in my day. To accept them *is* the logical outworking of what Christ taught. Love God—love people.

Seeing Steve and Mincaya joking around and sometimes laughing at the astonishment these Indians have at technology and vast cultural differences mostly created by these technologies, I see two men—both image bearers—partners on the journey set before them, united by the death of a father and of a son. It is a good reminder that it is a shared journey, and an all-inclusive one. We are all moving in the same direction. As are you. As am I. Pilgrims.

Jesus was a Jew of Middle Eastern ethnicity. He came from a particularly backwards place (*Can anything good ever come from Nazareth?*), and we infer from the Bible that He was not a very handsome man. He was dirt-poor. There was a stigma surrounding His birth. He was homeless, and His family was at one time homeless as well. His family were immigrants at one time, leaving a troubled region for safety.

That is the central figure of our faith and the One whom we worship and follow: a somewhat ugly, dark, complicated, homeless, dirt-poor, incarnate God who dictated the course of human history. I read the book *Same Kind of Different as Me,* and then saw the movie. When the homeless guy spoke at the end, he said something that has stuck with me: "You never know whose eyes God is looking at you through."

When I went to high school in the South, we were bussed to a black school in the late '60s, early '70s due to a governmental effort of integration. There were lots of issues including sit-ins and walkouts, all centered on racial issues. (Stuff like too many white girls on the drill team or cheerleaders.) Then we would take a few days off and then go back to school. Today, with the Black Lives Matter movement and the tearing down of statues, it seems like déjà vu all over again when it comes to racial issues.

Just like when I was in school. It doesn't seem to have gotten better. There is this cry of pain from the Black community that time has not healed, and that having a Black president has not fixed.

But Jesus also navigated through minefields of prejudice and tribalism. The world He lived in was a political, racial, and religious powder keg that would, in fact, explode not long after He was killed. Nationalism, tribalism, and rebellion was part of His social reality. His close group of followers consisted of a zealot and a tax collector. A Greek Sadducee and a Maccabean Pharisee. A prostitute and the wife of the governor. Religious leaders and outcasts. It is way too easy to underestimate the political and cultural currents simmering below the surface in just His twelve disciples alone. They were constantly fighting among themselves. In fact, the one thing that becomes clear as you read through the gospels is that these disciples were in competition to see who was the greatest.

All of the gospels give an account of the events in the upper room the night before Christ's betrayal. In every church, at some point, communion is celebrated as we remember the sacraments of the bread and the wine, and Jesus' proclamation of a new covenant. In the first three gospels, the synoptic gospels, this breaking of the bread and drinking of the wine is highlighted in the upper room. Not in the Gospel of John. John goes right to the foot washing. Something even slaves were not required to do then. I think the reason is this: In Luke, after Jesus gives this new covenant, we read that an argument then arises among the disciples as to—yep—who is the greatest. I think, Jesus, on hearing this, girds His loins and gives a demonstration of what that new covenant looks like. And then He says, "As I have done for you, now you do for one another."

In my circle of friends who are Christ followers, there is a Black felon and a White chairman of the Republican Party in my county. There is a guy who was in prison for tax rebellion and one of the Virginia State law enforcement investigators who helped bring him to justice. Victims and victimizers, some this and some that, all imperfect Christ followers. No one embodies this covenant perfectly, no one does that consistently, and all of us are growing up in what it means to follow Christ.

Peter would deny Jesus as He was being led away, yet Peter was the only one left who followed Him into the place where it was a dangerous place to be for a Jesus follower. All of the others ran away. Peter may have denied Jesus in that place, but he did it in a dangerous place at a dangerous time and he was all alone. He pursued Jesus into the lion's den. There are lots of ways to deny Jesus. One of them is simply pretending He does not have anything meaningful to offer us as we navigate the perils and pitfalls of life except on maybe Sundays and religious holidays. Pursuing Him in church is not the same as following after Him into the lion's den.

As Christ followers, we are taught that it is not ourselves and our circumstances that are primary—it is Christ and who He is that matters most, as well as the things and people He considers important. That leaves questions for Christian believers which beg asking:

What and who is it that is worth valuing?

Secondly, how does anyone even know that we value, whatever *that* or *who* is?

Who dictates who is "valuable" and who is not?

Heaven help us if we think that society can do that apart from any moral compass but our own.

And heaven has.

CHAPTER 14

CHARLOTTE, NORTH CAROLINA

"Mixed feelings like mixed drinks are a confusion to the soul."

—George Carman

When I was going through Aviation Indoctrination (AI) in Pensacola at the beginning of flight school, we Marines did some unusual stuff. We spent a week learning to box and at the end of the week, we were paired up with another guy of similar weight for a smoker (boxing match). Since we'd just spent six months trying to avoid getting our eyes poked out during night ambushes, or falling victim to other physical mishaps that would void our aviation contract, we weren't eager to get into the boxing ring and pummel each other onto the disability list. But on Friday, after a week of training, there we were. The stands filled up with onlookers who'd came to watch the show—because no matter how much boxing training you'd had, it always turned into a three-minute, undisciplined brawl. In some cases it was hilarious.

In another AI training exercise, we were strapped into parachutes, then attached to a 400-foot rope tied to the back of a pickup truck. After being jerked into the air like human kites (no kidding), we were supposed to release the line and float down to the ground in a successful "PLF."

During AI, we also did a bunch of water-dunker stuff, learned about VGVN diagrams, and how to use a Whizz (E6B) wheel.

We also learned about vertigo.

Vertigo is a killer. It tricks your body into telling you lies—even when you're absolutely convinced it's telling you the truth. You'll think you're doing one thing when in reality, you are doing just the opposite. You may think, for example, that you and your airplane are in a climbing left turn when in reality, you're spiraling downward in a death spiral. Our trainers demonstrated this by putting each one of us in a revolving chair and spinning us clockwise really fast. Afterwards, they'd stop the chair, then spun it more slowly in the same direction.

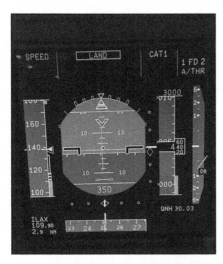

An attitude gyro among other devices.

When a trainer asked me which way I thought I was spinning—although I was still spinning clockwise—I could swear I was going counterclockwise instead. The point of the exercise was to demonstrate that relying on my subjective feelings could get me killed. The trainers were trying to get all of us to rely on our instruments instead of our feelings when we flew. There is more than one instrument in the cockpit of an airplane to verify what's actually happening, and we had to learn to trust what the objective data from those instruments was telling us. Developing such trust was hard when it conflicted with my senses, but I knew it could mean the difference between life and death. We didn't simply rely on one instrument, but on the story all of them were telling. But there was one central instrument that gave us our "attitude," the reflection of where we really were positioned in space, and that was the attitude gyro. All other instruments merely confirmed that what the attitude gyro was telling us was, in fact, the truth.

For Christians, the Bible has been used as that kind of attitude instrument for over 1700 years. We use it to understand objective truth as opposed to the subjective, ever-shifting truth claims of changing cultural norms and feelings.

Of course, I understand the Good Book is a collection of scriptures some religious traditions (Catholics for example) have added to. I also get the fact that there are ten different word-for-word translations of the Bible from the Hebrew, Greek, and Latin versions that are now transmitted to us in hundreds of languages. I'm also aware it's been looked at, studied, argued over, misused, and misinterpreted for thousands of years (especially the Old Testament portion) and that parts of it are very confusing. But I also believe that what the Scripture affirms and denies is the absolute truth, even though I fully recognize we do not have an absolute understanding of it at times. It is objective. The "other instruments" around it such as history, science, philosophy, and archeology have all indicated that what this instrument—this Bible—is telling us is true. Ironically, from what I can tell, any issues that critics seem to have with the Bible are generally tangential and not central to the main life-giving message of the Bible. The central orthodox truth claims are clear, understandable, and irrefutable. Even for a bell curve, average dude, C student like myself.

As much as we Americans like to live in a world where we can all do our own thing—where everybody and everything is tolerated and everyone is right about everything—truth, by its very nature, is exclusive. Though we might feel good about something, that doesn't mean it isn't dangerously wrong. That something we might be holding onto as true because it feels like it should be true, might in reality be part of our death spiral. There are many things I don't like about what the Bible tells me I should or should not do because it may not feel right to me at the time. But sometimes you just have to trust what the instruments (Bible) are telling you. Based on a lifetime of experience, I will say this about the Bible: It is logically consistent, empirically adequate, and experientially relevant. It is also the only religious book as far as I know that's been found to be true and asks us to test it to see for ourselves if it is indeed so.

I have often thought about how amazing and *magical* the written word is—that the innermost thoughts of one human being can be preserved in writing—then transmitted into the mind and heart of another person when they read them. I enjoy watching Ken Burn's documentaries on history, with the one on the Civil War being his most notable. What I find most riveting and moving in these documentaries are the moments when personal letters are read, laying bare all the emotions and thoughts of those in the midst of their joys and struggles. Such letters are an invitation into the intimate privacy of a person's soul. The New Testament is composed of many such letters of those who literally walked beside Jesus or met Him supernaturally, as did Paul on the road to Damascus. Many outside the faith still wonder if such writings can be trusted. It's a good question to ask, but it's also a question that needs to be answered logically.

Asking the Right Questions

Sometime back in 2000 or 2001, I was helping Steve Saint take a powered parachute down to Ecuador, so he could transport it to a more remote tribe in the Amazon. As I mentioned previously, a powered parachute is perfect for this kind of area. It's able to takeoff in a very short space and then land again in another small space (which is about all you get when hacking out a clearing in a jungle). What used to take over eight hours of hiking through jungle, scaling hills, and fording rivers would now take less than twenty minutes. The unique aspect of what Steve was doing was that he was training local tribesmen to fly the thing. Although I described meeting Steve and learning about his powered parachute, what I didn't mention was the conversation I had with a gentleman who was traveling along with Steve to help him haul the thing from Quito to Shell. (I left the next morning to go home.)

Making small talk on the flight from Miami to Quito, we had shared a bit about our families and discovered we both had eighteen-year-old daughters beginning their freshmen year at college. When I asked him how his daughter was doing, he shared an interesting experience she'd had defending her faith in class. Like most kids raised in an evangelical Christian home, she'd been taught the Bible was central to understanding, interpreting, and navigating a post-Christian culture rife with many competing truth claims and contradictory worldviews. At college, her biblical worldview was soon put to the test.

At the beginning of her first semester, she found herself in a large communication class where the professor was outlining all of the ways people communicate. At some point, this professor made the comment that some groups, like Christians, actually believe their Bible is a form of communication without error, and he wanted to know, "Is there anyone in this class who believes that?"

A dozen or so kids raised their hands. So he went on for another thirty to forty minutes explaining why it's not possible to have a document or book without error, and how the Bible is not divine or supernatural in any way.

Afterwards, he again asked, "Is there anyone here who still believes that the Bible is without error?"

My fellow traveler's eighteen-year-old daughter was the only one who still raised her hand. The professor nodded and said, "Good. Next time we meet, you can get up in front of the class and explain why you still believe that."

Now on the face of it, that seems a bit unfair, but I have to side with the professor on this. We should be able to articulate to others our perspective on things. My traveling companion offered to help his daughter when she called her parents and told them about what she had been asked to do, but she basically said, "I got this."

When her communication class met again, she walked to the front of the room and inquired, "How many here believe there is something else out there in the universe and that we are not alone?"

Almost everyone raised their hands. "Good," she nodded, "On that we are all agreed." (Fact is, almost everyone believes in either the supernatural, or aliens, or both.)

Then she set about asking the class a series of questions.

"If I want to pass along the raw, unfiltered thoughts and feelings from my heart and soul to my granddaughter's granddaughter, what is the best communication medium for doing that?" The consensus answer was by writing a letter or diary entries.

"In our system of jurisprudence and law, what is the legal means by which agreements are memorialized?" The group replied that it was done by signing a written agreement or contract.

And on and on she went. Through her patient questioning, she was able to lead the class to her own logical conclusion that if there was "Something" else out there, and if that "Someone" wanted to communicate and give direction, the best and most logical medium would be through the written word.

If we continue down her logic path, we can predict the likelihood such writings would be plentiful and reliable. And that's indeed the case. Our conclusion that the Bible is the inerrant Word of God is supported by a wealth of good evidence. In fact, there's a whole academic discipline called form criticism as well as a great volume of "Grade A" archaeological documents that support this conclusion. These documents confirm the Bible is remarkably consistent and that it has not been changed in any significant ways or revised over the centuries as many people allege.

In the Book of Exodus, we read that the Ten Commandments were written with the "Finger of God" and indeed, we see His fingerprints all over the Scriptures. Bible-believing Christians can be certain their faith in the Scripture is well founded. One other thing, the Bible doesn't cater to its readers.

There are some hard truths in there for sure.

Questions and Answers

What captivates me most, however, aren't the didactic explanations supporting a Christian's faith stance, but how questions can be used to help expose universal truth and lead others to a better understanding of why things are so.

God Himself does this repeatedly throughout the biblical narrative. He uses this approach, for example, when he famously asks Job some thirty-two questions to reveal His omnipotence and Jesus, too, revealed truth by asking questions like, "Why do you call me good?"; "Where is your husband?"; "What are you arguing about?"; and "Who do you say I am?" Asking good questions is an important part of establishing a meaningful dialogue. It takes the focus off the questioner and invites participation. It also establishes a point of agreement that can serve as a point of reference in moving forward with any significant subject. When Peter was sharing his faith with the Jews, his audience already knew about the Creation, Fall of Man, the Law of Moses, and he was able to reason from this common understanding forward. But when Paul shared the gospel to a mostly non-Jewish audience, he had to go all the way back to the Greek's belief in an unknown god and start from there. There needs to be a starting point of consensus where people can say, "On this, we all agree."

Some of my most meaningful conversations with others have been kick-started by a simple question from me. In one such conversation with a coworker, we were talking about our kids, and he shared a difficult story about an incident involving his seven-year-old daughter. She'd been invited to play at a friend's house and have cookies afterwards. Things unraveled when the hosting friend only wanted to play one thing that only she wanted to play. After her guest refused to do so, my coworker's daughter was asked to leave and she did so in tears. To comfort his little girl, my friend told her the other little girl was wrong to make her feel badly.

Curious about his moral "point of reference," I asked him, "Why did you tell your daughter it was wrong? If it made the other girl feel better, why was it wrong?" (Who gets to decide what's right and what's wrong in such a scenario, and based on what moral law or lawgiver?)

Instead of being offended, my questions led him to ask me about a shocking, recurring dream he'd been having and it gave me the opportunity to share some life-changing truths from my perspective with him. I was able to point out that whenever we use the words *"right and wrong," "fair or unfair," "just or unjust,"* we are using moral words that demand a point of reference. They appeal to an implicit understanding that there is some sort of moral law that enables us to differentiate between what is right and what is wrong, or what is moral or immoral. If there's a moral law, there has to be a moral Lawgiver.

Such conversations are vitally important because—on any given day, in any given conversation—there's bound to be disagreement over moral issues. These disagreements are often divisive and passionate because for some mysterious reason, moral issues are not like any other preference we might discuss. I think it's because we know in our heart of hearts there's something more at stake here than simply preferring red over green, or a Ford over a Chevy. The person most seemingly "tolerant" of every immoral act imaginable will always pause when you ask them, "Do you think there is *anything* that is *ever* wrong?" Theory will suddenly meet reality if you decide to punch them in the face and take their wallet. Moral issues are personal issues.

When German theologian Karl Barth testified that "Jesus loves me, this I know, for the Bible tells me so," he provided some pretty solid theology. But not everyone agrees with that Bible, and not everyone will concur with my beliefs about that Bible. In fact, many have gone to extraordinary lengths to disprove, minimize, or change the Bible. Back in the 1980s, for example, credentialed academics and other so-called "experts" were holding "Jesus seminars." During these gatherings, they'd assign colored marbles—each color corresponding to four different levels of reliability— to mark their assessment of Bible passages: *"This passage on what Jesus said is true"; "This passage may be true, He may have said or done this"; "I don't think this is true"; "This is not what Jesus said."* For a time, this passed as definitive scholarly work on the question of *"What did Jesus really say?"*

I get it when folks don't believe the Bible is either accurate or true. So I rarely cite the Bible when a conversation crops up that allows for meaningful dialogue over the big questions of life. Such questions always involve one or more of the four big topics of *origins, meaning, morality,* and *destiny.* Although I believe the Bible truly *is* "The Handbook" on how to live life well—providing the answers to those four big questions—I see it more as a personal handbook for me instead of a guide by which I expect others to live by, particularly nonbelievers.

So unless I'm asked, I generally make no mention of the Bible at all to those who do not share my Christian worldview. Sometimes I've found that if I do mention it, the conversation either shifts to disagreements over *"Is the Bible true?"* which is a rabbit trail I do not mind taking, but it is usually at the expense of a more personally meaningful road that we might have taken. Or it shuts down the conversation altogether. When that happens, the incredibly important questions of personal meaning, morality, and destiny are lost in an impersonal rabbit trail of opinion and debate. Frankly, you don't need to mention the Bible to share the gospel that lies within it. When Jesus sent out His disciples to all nations, no New Testament existed yet, and wouldn't for another 300 years.

I once remember hearing a speaker demonstrate this discussion tactic by asking two essential questions illustrated by a few emotionally relevant stories. First, she asked, "What is the highest thought or feeling one person can have toward another?"

If I were to ask you that question, you'd most likely answer, "Love," and you'd be in good company. When asked this same question internationally—across all races, genders, and socio-economic strata—the answer is always the same. *Love.* Even infants know whether they are loved or not. The primary desire of the heart is to be loved, no matter how young or how old a person might be.

Next she would ask, "What is the greatest expression of love one person can have toward another?"

Most likely, you're thinking, *When one gives up their life for another.* That, too, is a universally offered answer. (If we—with our finite ability to love—truly believe such sacrifice to be the supreme demonstration of love, why then would we not expect the One who created us and loves infinitely to be any different?)

On the flip side of love, certain obvious questions seem universal too:

Is it okay to rape you, torment you, or murder you?
Is it okay to torture and abuse children?
Can I steal from you and take anything or everything you have?

Most people would universally agree, "No, it's not okay to do these things. Such actions are wrong." But going back to my previous question, why are they wrong? Who gets to decide what's right and what's wrong, based on which moral code or lawgiver? If society is the final arbitrator for these things, then in the various places throughout the world where they have occurred, I guess holocausts are simply another form of acceptable social engineering.

Apologetics

About twenty years ago, Southern Evangelical Seminary located in Charlotte, North Carolina was offering a Master's in Apologetics. *Apologetics* is a word that basically means a verbal defense or reason for why you are doing or believing in something. Since I sometimes found myself believing something but unable to explain why, I thought such knowledge would be helpful. So I signed up, and for the next several years, toiled away writing papers with tightly reasoned, syllogistic arguments on why "this is that." Form criticism, logic, philosophy, and the ability to identify how language is used (univocal, equivocal, or analogical) were a few of the tools I added to my debating/reasoning toolbox.

I think studying such topics was good for me at the time, and I appreciated all that I learned. But at the end of the day, knowledge of those semi-esoteric things is really meant to bolster the faith of those who already believe and aren't very useful when engaging people who don't agree with your theological starting points or "givens." To be relevant to these folks, I've discovered I must first seek to be relational, rather than ideological, by first showing some concern for them as individuals. I believe the best way to do that is through good questions and very good listening. Permission to ask those questions is usually given when I demonstrate interest in them as people. As a human being and fellow traveler.

Otherwise, I simply end up answering questions that no one is asking in the first place.

One of the key verses used in any apologetics class is 1 Peter 3:15 NKJV, "*Always be ready to give a . . . reason for the hope that is in you.*" But that's only part of the verse. It goes on to tell us *how* to do it (with humility and respect) and *when* to give that reason—*when you are asked!* So why would someone ask you about your faith? It's what happens I believe, when a nonbeliever can relate to a disciple of Jesus Christ in the midst of normal, day-to-day interactions and sees they're different. We are not called to convert anyone to Christianity. We are only called to be disciples, i.e., Christ followers. A disciple embodies the reality of the gospel by following in the footsteps of Jesus as much as possible. Like St. Francis once said, "Preach the gospel at all times . . . if necessary use words." A disciple understands that the command to be "*in the world yet not of it*" is a two-part imperative. We are told to avoid what the Scripture calls sin and love our neighbor as ourselves. But who is my neighbor?

I was recently chatting with a friend of mine who was trying to connect with her son's mother-in-law. While discussing their children's marriage, the subject of the Scripture came up, and my friend said it was difficult to get this woman to believe the Bible was anything more than just a flawed piece of literature that had been changed and deliberately altered over time. In other words, my friend was trying to find common ground with someone for whom the Bible wasn't a reliable guide to morals or the teachings of Jesus. Basically, this woman thought a person could believe whatever they wanted and still call themselves a Christian—and that good people of all religions will one day find themselves in heaven.

Although this viewpoint may be distressing to Bible-believing Christians like my friend, the topic is really just a divisive debating point when there's no prior relationship. It's a case of *"I have my opinion, and you have yours."* Words like "form criticism" and "agape love" and other such Christian buzzwords will probably have little effect on changing this woman's viewpoint on either the Bible or Christianity. So I asked my friend if she loved this woman. Then I asked her, *"Does this woman know that?"* It is only when we really get to know one another that truth propositions turn personal and precious to someone, and abstract things become concrete realities with the power to change lives.

Disciples are called to love—not just God, but people too. I think Peter is saying that when someone who knows you well—through good times and bad—sees the joy, peace, and patience in you, there will come a time when they will want to know about that. Conveying God's truth is always conveyed best through love and concern for others, and it's often a slow laborious process. At some point—if the relationship is good enough and safe enough—my friend might get through to her son's mother-in-law through listening patiently to her views and concerns about the meaningful stuff of life.

When that finally happens in a relationship, I've learned from folks a lot smarter than me that there are four questions that can help us understand where a person is on their existential journey, and where we can find common ground to move from subjective opinions to the objective truth of the Scripture.

What exactly do you mean? All of us use words and phrases we assume are commonly understood. But just ask someone how they define the words "love," "God," "truth," and "science" and you'll find we understand words differently. It gets back again to finding a common starting place where "on *this*, we are all agreed."

Where did you get your information? From a radio show? Heard it somewhere? A credentialed source? A biased source? Your "gut"?

How do you know it is true? How do we know anything is true? Is truth knowable? When examining that question, I fall back on these "how to establish truth" questions: Is it logically consistent? Does it conform to the rules and discipline of logic and reason? Is it reasonable? Is it empirically adequate? Is there any evidence that supports an objective truth claim? Is it experientially relevant? Does it matter? How has this been evidenced in someone's life? What does that look like?

What difference does it make?

Can you, in fact, be in a death spiral, trusting your opinions and physical senses and not even know it? What if Hell is an actual place?

Death is real. You can believe that if you die, nothing happens except that you simply cease to exist like the gnat you just swatted. Or you may believe that everyone goes to heaven, or only the "good" souls do.

Like much of the world, you can believe that when you die, you get to come back as something, or someone, else. But a biblical Christian believes that after death comes a final judgement. All of these scenarios can be *wrong*, but one thing is for certain—they can't all be right.

Wouldn't you like to be right about this one?

CHAPTER 15

KENYA

"Be careful not to compromise what you
want most for what you want now."

—Zig Ziglar

When my mom was a young woman in the late 1940s, she worked as a proofreader for Doubleday publishing company. If there were any damaged copies of books they could not sell, she would take them home. Although I'm not sure, I think she got a discount, or more likely, they were free. And so it came to be that our house had shelves of books lining our very limited wall space. Some of these were even signed by the authors themselves who showed up at the publishing company from time to time.

One of my very first memories of my dad building something was watching him make a bookshelf for Mom's book collection. I kept that bookshelf for a long time after I was married myself. I didn't keep it because Dad made it, or because it was exquisitely crafted (it wasn't), but because I simply needed a place to put all of those wonderful, imperfect books. Truth be told, I still have most of them to this day, despite my wife's best efforts to cull a few because "they're dust collectors."

But those books are special to me. Mom and Dad didn't have a TV for many years while I was growing up, so reading was an important way to pass the time—especially when I was put on "restriction" and banished to my room for routine offenses. Persecuting my sister (who was a world-class tattler) was one such offense. Unfortunately, I was the one who always ended up on the short end of that stick and confined to "quarters." My parents weren't really strict, but I knew I'd "get the belt" when I was disrespectful to my mom or hit a girl (which unfortunately my sister qualified as). When either occurred, Dad sent me to my room to ruminate on my impending punishment. Later, he'd come in and somberly tell me, "This is going to hurt me more than it will you, son, but you need to start . . . (blah, blah, blah) . . . your sister."

Eventually, I grew out of the need for such measures, but I never grew out of my fondness for Mom's books. Between their covers, I lost myself on marvelous adventures to exotic places like India and Africa or explored the untamed early-American frontier. I shared the lives of courageous hunters, pioneers, sailors, and soldiers who took me with them to experience the unknown dangers of strange and hostile places. Even though I could risk it all from the safety and security of my own bedroom, deep down, I truly desired to be another Lord Jim or Daniel Morgan, or one of Kenneth Robert's frontiersman. Or Scott's *Ivanhoe*. Like Charlie Alnutt, I wanted to travel down the Congo River into the heart of darkness on a steamer like the *African Queen*. Africa was the stuff of true adventure and mystery with its prehistoric animals roaming the Serengeti and lost cities, riches, and civilizations waiting to be discovered.

The Heart of Darkness

It was in the late 1800s when missionary groups reached out to Africa with the Christian gospel. They weren't just going just to proselytize either. There was also an underlying motivation toward doing what they could to abolish the slave trade through the influence of Christianity—and with good reason. In our own country's history, it was Christian men and women who ran the Underground Railroad, funneling slaves to freedom at grave risk to themselves. In England, the eradication of slavery had already taken place through the efforts of the great Christian parliamentarian, Sir William Wilberforce, and countless others.

Although well-intentioned, the efforts to combat the barbarism of African slavery through Christian missions had the unfortunate side effect of also opening the door to unsavory opportunists. The missionaries themselves, however, worked hard to be difference-makers in the lives of the local population by assessing and meeting their most pressing needs in the name of Jesus Christ. They did this at great risk and personal cost to themselves. It is easy to assume these sacrificial servants in missions were extraordinary folks. Well, I've met a lot of missionaries, and on the whole, I've found they're simply average, middle-of-the bell-curve folks like you and me. Missions isn't reserved for the radically holy, but for normal Christians who are simply reaching out in a sacrificial way to share a bit of good news—much like one beggar telling another beggar where to find a loaf of bread.

It's also a useful reminder for us Westerners to realize the early church had a strong presence in Africa and that part of our spiritual and biblical heritage is rooted in places like Egypt, Ethiopia, Nubia, Canaan, and Nineveh. St. Augustine, who wrote *The City of God,* lived in North Africa as did Athanasius, Clement, Cyprian, and Cyril who all lived, wrote, and died in Africa too. In fact, one of the writings that most profoundly affected the early church—the account of Perpetua and Felicitas—took place in Carthage, North Africa somewhere around the year 202 AD.

The Passion of St. Perpetua, St. Felicitas, and their Companions is one of our earliest extra-biblical Christian texts, and I think there might be a few intact copies in existence. It is the prison diary of two young, pregnant women who were imprisoned for their faith and awaiting execution. One was a slave, the other a noblewoman. After their martyrdom, the diary was widely circulated among the churches and served to encourage early Christians facing persecution themselves. They would need such encouragement. A hundred years would pass before Constantine legalized Christianity.

During that time, believing the gospel came at a high cost for individuals whose faith in Jesus clashed with pagan cultures and traditions. There was no middle ground, and many early Christians paid with their lives. These were men and women who did not half step their faith. I remember reading somewhere that Perpetua's and Felicitas' accounts became so popular among the churches that believers were cautioned not to elevate it to the status of the Scripture. Their story of faith in the midst of suffering and impending death was *meaningful*.

Today, many Christians in Africa are being forced to choose either their faith or their safety—and even their lives. Countless narratives describe the suffering of African men, women, and children who endure persecution and martyrdom. It's hard to pick up a newspaper or read an online story without encountering descriptions of African Christians being targeted and tortured for their faith. The situation has all the makings of a modern-day holocaust. And for all of us in the land of supersized plenty, the suffering of believers in Africa should encourage us all to refuse to compromise so easily those things in our own country that they are dying for over in Africa.

As a matter of fact, large Episcopal churches in America (splitting over some important doctrinal issues) are turning to Anglican bishops in Africa for the strength of their leadership honed in persecution.

Musa from Nigeria

Sometime in the early '90s, I travelled to a BILD (Biblical Institute for Leadership Development) international mission conference in Ames, Iowa with my friend, Tim, who'd just taken charge of the missions program at our small, but growing, local church. Before Tim joined our program, we'd made the decision to lend what little support our small church could afford to help local, indigenous churches and he was all in with that. We wanted to focus on those churches that were already functioning in their own countries, but struggling to get established and viable. Earlier that year, we'd received a letter from an Anglican bishop in

Nigeria asking for help for five such struggling churches in that country. We were in the process of mulling over that request, wondering what we should do. I was at the BILD conference looking for someone from that part of the world I could chat with, and I figured a mission's conference like BILD, located in the Midwest, was a likely place to find one. When we arrived, I told Tim, "Keep your eyes peeled for Africans."

We got to the auditorium early to scout it out, but took our seats as the time came for the opening speaker to make his remarks. Not more than two minutes later, I kid you not, this Black dude in a colorful gown and cap came in and sat down right beside Tim.

It turned out the guy was Musa, one of the key speakers at the conference, and his story was a compelling one. After the introductory remarks, everyone scurried off to different "breakout sessions" and we made a beeline for Musa's room where he would be speaking. He began his presentation slideshow with slide after slide of grim statistics conveying how many churches had been burned, how many lives had been lost, and how many Christian pastors had been tortured or killed in Nigeria. But the most riveting of Musa's accounts was the personal and tragic story of his mentor's martyrdom. Musa explained how each and every day, this godly man had faithfully prayed in his home, in the same room, at the same time of day. Aware of this, a group of Islamic boys stormed into the house, and after binding him, they set him on fire. When his son tried to stop them, they cut his throat and killed him too. They were in the process of doing the same thing to this man's wife when Musa said he and some others fell upon them. As he was telling us this story, tears were streaming down his cheeks. Musa said he and his friends were so enraged by what had been done, they were about to kill those boys. But the wife whose husband and son lay dead at their feet prevented them, saying, "God did not give us a spirit of revenge . . . do not harm them."

As I share this account, it's tempting to make a comment or observation about this woman's response, but there are simply no words. What can one presume to say in the face of such grace and power at the moment of her greatest grief and injury? I can still see Musa in my mind, tearfully recounting that tragedy and describing how it has marked his life's story. How could it not? Yet such accounts make up the bloodstained foundation of the African church, from Perpetua and Felicitas in Carthage, to Musa in Nigeria.

The Carnivore

I had the chance to go to Kenya in December of 2001 with my son, Alex, his friend, Sam, and Sam's dad, Mike, as well as two other guys, Barry and another Mike. It was a short-term "missions trip" that (to me) felt more like a spring break excursion than any sort of sacrificial, religious trip. I figured it was one of those things that wouldn't really have much of an impact on much of anything, but I saw it as a great excuse to make a memory with my son. It was also an opportunity to travel to the place I had read about and yet had only ventured to in my imagination. Even though I hate traveling in the back of an airplane, I figured that it was worth the "sacrifice." It wasn't until we were there and experienced firsthand the stories and people who labor in the African orphanages and churches—trying to make a difference in a very hard place—that I came to appreciate the fact of how much just showing up there meant to them. I also discovered how much we have to learn about suffering.

During our layover in London, we rode one of city's famous double-decker buses in the blustery December cold, listening to the gossipy driver tell us whose head was spiked on what bridge and where Madonna and other celebrities lived. We were relieved to escape the chilly weather and board our BA 747 flight for the warmth of Nairobi. Many (card) hands of hearts later, we landed in that busy teeming city. Wrapped around the vast Nairobi National Park, it's the only urban area with a national park and game preserve lying within its city limits. I could see at first glance how commerce and poverty competed to dominate this sprawling setting.

Later that evening, we went to eat dinner at a restaurant called the Carnivore (one of the highlights of our stay in Nairobi). Built around a giant fire pit, it featured skewers of exotic meats roasting around an enormous bed of hot coals. It was all about the meat and not much else. But that was more than okay with the two high school guys we'd brought along. The waiters came around our table with skewers of roasted meat and asked a few simple questions: "*Croc? Tik-tik? Water buffalo? Zebra?*" Manly fare indeed! We tried it all in that smoky cathedral of charred meat. Of course, we assumed the chunks on those skewers were varied and "exotic" but no one knew for sure since charred meat all looks the same. After a while, it even tasted the same.

The next day, we drove back out to the airport, and some missionary pilots with African Inland Missions flew us to Kapenguria. Here, we were scheduled to participate in a Pokot youth conference in Kitale, a town located on the fringes of Pokot country. Our church has long partnered with Julius Murgor, a Pokot believer in Kitale, who's affiliated with the Harvesters Ministry. Harvesters' goal is to reach and encourage this very large tribe with close to 700,000 members living in the arid western region of Kenya and Uganda. I was told that in the mid-1900s, a British missionary lived with the Pokot people and tried to convert them to Christ for a number of years, but he finally gave up and left, believing and later writing that the Pokot tribe was unreachable with the gospel. Yet Julius was one of the first Pokot tribesmen to become a believer, and it was through the testimony of another Pokot who'd heard the gospel while working in Nairobi. I guess it takes a Pokot to reach a Pokot. Now, about twenty percent of Pokots claim to be evangelicals. We were there to take clothes and supplies to some of their orphanages and to encourage them (while staying out of their way) as we did so.

When the youth conference ended each evening, we returned to Kapenguria and stayed at what seemed to be an old British officer's club complete with mahogany walls and trim and a dart board in the bar area. (It might have been called the Kapenguria Hunt Club, but I can't remember now.) We had the place to ourselves and generally ordered the same thing to eat every night thinking, *Well . . . so far, so good.* Avoiding digestive problems was a priority since toilets at the conference consisted of a simple hole in the ground that saw a lot of traffic.

When the conference ended, Alex, Sam, Barry (a twenty-something guy who works with youth at my church), and I embarked on an epic cross-country trip into the far western reaches of Pokot country to deliver clothes we'd collected to one of the orphanages there. The journey turned out to be everything I'd imagined as a young lad reading about adventures in Africa. Most of the day was spent driving on a dirt track through vast open plains or through sparsely wooded areas where huge anthills, taller than our truck, poked out of the ground.

Alex and Sam rode standing in the back of the truck as we drove through the tribal lands of Pokot. Occasionally, we passed folks walking along the track. Sometimes it was a child of nine or ten carrying a chicken or a small bag of something, and at other times it was someone so poor they had no clothes. At one point, we ignored the protestations of our driver and insisted he stop to offer three young Pokot girls a five-mile ride to their village. They sang the whole way in the back of the truck, and when we got to their village, all the men and women came out and gathered around us to ask questions. We felt like celebrities, but we were really just average, bell-curve aliens passing through.

In another village we came to, a woman greeted us with a small girl at her side who was obviously very sick. The driver casually told us she had malaria and would probably die sometime very soon. Looking at that very sick young girl and the sad woman beside her, I could only think of my own two little girls back home. I desperately wished I was a doctor or a nurse at that moment, armed with medications that could easily have treated that poor child. In this part of Pokot territory, I knew medical teams wouldn't come around very often. I also knew death from malaria was common. But knowing that fact and talking with grieving parents was an entirely different thing.

Three Pokot girls and Sam.

One such couple overseeing an orphanage shared with tears and con-siderable difficulty how they'd recently lost a boy to the malaria fever and how hard it was for them. As we sat in their living room, the young hus-band told us how many of his kids had won national scholarship awards, and how they worked hard to make the orphanage a home for those kids. Toiling away in anonymity, this young Pokot couple were eager to share and model the love of God to those who really were the "least of these." Part of that was grieving for children no one else knew or cared about.

The trip into Pokot was a sobering one for us. After driving many dusty and eventful miles, the specific orphanage we were trying to reach finally came into view. Except for a few cinder block buildings with chil-dren running around them, there was nothing else there. It was a place ravaged by poverty, and the hand-me-downs and cast-off clothes we had brought with us were unimaginable treasures for these folks. There were no toys. But the kids were excited by our brief visit, and we took pictures of them to bring back to encourage those in our church who had given these few things as a way of encouragement.

When we left to travel back the way we'd come—back to our tempo-rary home at the Kapenguria Hunt Club and the chicken fried steak (or whatever it was) we ate night after night—we were far quieter and more aware of the huge disparity in our cultures. Our time in Pokot country was over, and we'd be heading to Migori, Kenya after we got a night's sleep.

The next morning, our pilot, Jim, showed up in a Cessna Caravan that belonged to Franklin Graham. It was being used by Graham's Samaritan's Purse Ministry to fly doctors, nurses, and other medical people to Somalia and other places (over 100 countries throughout the world, I think). Despite the effectiveness of this desperately needed ministry, Franklin Graham is generally a media target because he's Billy Graham's son. As the offspring of such a famous man, he's generally attacked in the press by those waiting in the wings to close in for the kill whenever they smell Christian blood in the water. But he's simply one man who is actually making this world a better place for folks no one knows about or cares about. Critics never think about the vast amount of energy and resources men like Franklin bring to bear on the very things Jesus would be interested in doing. That is the *logical outworking* of the Christian faith. Somehow, that always gets overlooked by the mainstream media in their neverending efforts to find hypocrisy in a saint.

The Cessna Caravan is a ministry workhorse.

But inspired by such saints, our five-man cohort was heading to Migori to meet up with Phillip Ocheing. Phillip was starting an orphanage for children whose parents had died in the AIDS epidemic there. Our church was giving him the money to begin construction on some land he'd been given, and we were there to encourage him and see how things were coming along.

On the way to Migori, our plane ride took us over the Serengeti where we flew above herds of elephants and other large grazing animals like zebras and antelopes. Listening to praise songs through our headsets, worship seemed the perfect response to our spectacular view of the majestic plains that unfurled below us. It was Africa as I had always imagined it to be. Our pilot, Jim, told us great stories of his time in Africa. He described hair-raising rescue missions to extract missionaries from some of the more dangerous jungle areas. And he also shared accounts of his adventures camping and riding his motorcycle across the Serengeti and how he'd seen a croc burst out of a river to grab a zebra, and a silverback tearing a Doberman in two.

Midway through our flight, we landed on a grass strip (it definitely did *not* deserve to be called a runway) so we could explore Maasai Mara—a game preserve planted in the middle of the Serengeti. We drove in an open lorry to check out all of the wildlife, and I was surprised the only animal that created any sort of anxiety in our driver was a river full of hippos. When we stopped nearby, he said they were very dangerous, and he would not let us get out of the vehicle. As a consolation, he pointed to the tree above us where we saw a white-spotted leopard sleeping on an outstretched limb. *That* was certainly more unnerving to me than a bunch of cruising overweight hippos in a muddy river. Sitting motionless, some of us eyed the docile-looking big boys in the river as the rest of us stared at the big cat sleeping over our heads. The cat was definitely within *easy* pouncing distance from his limb to my seat.

As we sat silently watching these animals, I realized I was hungry and remembered I still had a package of peanut butter crackers in my pocket. Great! But what happened next was just like a scene from a Mr. Bean movie. I slipped the crackers out of my pocket and stealthily began to unwrap them. Unfortunately, the moment I started to rip the cellophane off my snack, the loud crinkling noise woke the leopard from his snooze. In a flash, he stood up on the limb above us and looked down. Everyone in the lorry stared at *me* as I stared at the driver thinking, *What the heck are YOU waiting for? Let's get this rig moving to a minimum of 50 mph!* That was the speed I'd heard leopards could run (on a *Planet Earth* segment). But no one moved a muscle. The big cat simply jumped down and moved away from us. As we watched him go, I apologetically finished my crackers.

Phillip from Migori

When we got to Migori, we met Phillip Ocheing—a tall, thin, stately gentleman of indeterminate years—who, like many Kenyans, spoke with a clipped British accent. And like many of his countrymen, he was missing the central incisor from his lower jaw and spoke with a bit of a lisp. I was told the reason Kenyans have that tooth removed is so they can be fed if they get lockjaw (tetanus). Of all the pictures I have of Phillip, he isn't smiling in a single one of them.

Our church first met Phillip in India at the Asian Christian Academy. Someone from our church would go there periodically to teach or help out with the children at the orphanage they run there. In one of the classes, the teacher from our church noticed a tall, Black fellow in the classroom of brown faces who was at least a foot taller than everyone else sitting there. Curious, he asked about this guy's story—who he was and what in the world he was doing there. It turned out Philip was a school teacher from Kenya who was interested in getting a master's degree, and he had two choices: the United States or India. He decided on India because of the lower costs, and just a few days after stepping off the plane, he was confronted with the gospel and was converted to Christ. After finishing his MBA, he decided to go to seminary before going back home to Kenya because he felt God had called him to a mission—to go back home and start an orphanage for children whose parents had died of AIDS.

At the time, Kenya was the fourth largest country in the world suffering the tragic effects of the AIDS epidemic. Some of Phillip's own brothers and sisters and their spouses had died of AIDS, and his mom had assumed the responsibility of raising several of her own grandchildren. His family was just one of many so afflicted. It is estimated over 600,000 children are orphaned in Kenya alone as a result of this horrific epidemic. When our church learned Phillip wanted to start an orphanage, they gave him the money to begin construction on some land his Uncle Samson had donated to him in Kenya. Although blind from a botched eye operation, Samson was a delightful man who was also a school teacher and mentor to Phillip. As we spent time with Phillip, we prayed with him that he would find a wife who would also be a partner in this mission to children. After dinner on the night we were to leave—in a spontaneous moment before we parted—God led us into the privilege of washing Phillip's feet while this very reserved and stately Black Kenyan man wept silently. It

Terry and I with Phillip and his wife, Rose.

is an essential thing sometimes to know you are not alone in ministry . . . or simply not alone.

Phillip is now married to a wonderful woman named Rose, and they have children of their own. My son, Andrew, went to visit their orphanage some years ago with a group from our church youth group. When he returned, I heard numerous accounts of how they'd gotten their butts kicked in soccer matches with the kids there.

I also remember my son coming back and telling us, "You know, Dad, they had nothing. All they had was this one soccer ball, but they all seemed really, really happy." What an incredible testimony for our materialistic Western culture.

Visiting an orphanage in Kenya. Just showing up made a difference.

I'm somewhat embarrassed that I used to think these short-term mission trips were nothing more than a Christian version of spring break for adults. When I flew into Central and South America, I'd see Christian youth groups and church groups get off the jet with guitars, wearing tee shirts with some Bible verse on them, and I'd think, *What difference can a bunch of Americans make, blowing through a village for a few weeks?* The answer to that question is not found in any construction project or vacation Bible school craft, but in the moment one culturally diverse believer looks into the eyes of a fellow pilgrim and says, "I see you, and you matter." It is the affirmation that, together, we are all part of something bigger—the same kingdom, just different global neighborhoods. There is something connecting about sharing a meal or a work project with another life that God has impacted. Maybe it's a picture of what the Kingdom of God should, and one day will, look like.

In my own case, once I'd actually gone to Kenya and experienced firsthand the stories and people who labor in the Kenyan orphanages and churches, I came to understand how much our visit meant to them. I saw what it looks like to try and make a difference in a very hard place, and how much we have to learn about suffering. I also learned it's an encouragement to others when we just show up. That makes sense, since we so often ask God to do that very thing for *us*. To simply show up.

I also find it interesting that a few American churches are turning to Africa for leadership. Such was recently the case when some Episcopalian churches left the denominational fold over issues of homosexuality in the leadership and turned instead to submit themselves under the Anglican leadership in Africa. In a strange twist of historical irony, it was the King of Uganda who invited Anglican and Catholic missionaries into his country during the late 1800s to improve his country's moral culture.

Many years after the death of this king, his reprobate son, King Kabaka Mwanga, martyred some forty-five young page boys for not doing—because of their faith—what some of the more liberal Episcopalian churches now celebrate. They refused to submit themselves to sexual practices that the king demanded but that God had forbidden. As a result, they were forced to carry wood on their backs to fuel the fire that would eventually burn them alive. During the awful ordeal of immolation, they were heard to be singing and shouting encouragement to one another even as they were engulfed in the flames. This account is a compelling one that displays an important truth. Once planted, the seeds of the gospel always bear fruit as they did in Uganda. We are promised that God's Word never returns to Him void, but the cost of the harvest can be terrible. Those forty-five martyred boys of Uganda were one such harvest.

The interesting thing for me is how the African church—that initially gave so much to the building up of the church through the writings and ministry of the early church fathers—centuries later were themselves recipients of ministry and missionaries from a continent and country yet to be settled, like ours. Now they are pouring back into the modern church again with their persecution stories and leadership. In so many places there, it is an unsafe thing to practice the faith we are giving up here. These stories remind me of that. I take my freedom, as do we all, too much for granted.

Africa will always be a mysterious, wonderful place in my imagination and memory. A continent that affects the world's climate; its vast, untamed expanses call to the wild at heart to come marvel at the Eden-like diversity of creation in all of its natural beauty and complexity. But what is even more precious to me is that I also now have African faces and names attached to people I know there, whose hearts reflect the love of the Creator and the love for their own people and place. I think about their stories and the many accounts of sacrifice yet to be shared with us.

Meanwhile, I wonder if there will come a day, when like the king of Uganda, we here in the West will invite some African missionaries to help address the ills of our decaying moral climate and culture. For how much longer will that even be possible?

Our mission team visited Phillip and Rose Ocheing in Kenya where they care for children orphaned by the AIDs epidemic.

CHAPTER 16

MONTANA

"Any patch of sunlight in a wood will show you something about the
sun which you could never get from reading books on astronomy."
—C. S. Lewis

In 2006, my younger son, Andrew, and I traveled to South Central
Montana for a week of fly fishing and backpacking in the ruggedly
majestic Beartooth Mountains. It was an idea my friend, Don, and I
concocted as we worked our way through John Eldredge's book, *Wild at
Heart*, with our seventeen-year-old boys. We saw this manly adventure as
a perfectly fitting capstone to our weeks of getting together and talking
about important life questions: When is it okay for a man to fight? What
attracts women to men? What is the relationship between a man and his
work? What are the top ten things I wish I knew how to do as a man?
These manly how-to skills included knowing how to knot a tie, tune a car,
navigate with a map and compass, or make a fire without a match. Good
stuff. Guy stuff.

We fathers and sons usually talked about these things while staring
into an open fire, or after we'd blasted our way through about $100 worth
of ammunition. So it wasn't too long before we came to a logical conclusion: If we were really wild at heart, we ought to go somewhere with

wilderness and mountains and actually do some of the manly things we'd talked about doing or read about in the book. Don knew of a guy who was familiar with backpacking in Montana, and you don't get wilder at heart than Montana. We spent a lot of time preparing—going for short two-mile hikes with our packs strapped on our backs—to get used to carrying some weight and to break in our new boots. I felt a little silly traipsing around our small suburban neighborhood, dressed like a cross between a homeless guy and an L.L. Bean commercial. But I knew enough about backpacking to know cold-calling a mountain trail with fifty pounds on my back was a bad plan without first introducing my body to the idea. We packed and repacked, trying to decide what was necessary and what wasn't, always mulling over the weight-versus-comfort equation. I was fifty at the time and wasn't really looking forward to sleeping on the ground. To be honest, I wondered if I still had it in me to put one foot in front of the other on a grueling mountain trail. I started wondering about other things too.

Not long after we started our preparations, Don showed me a picture of a ranger in Montana holding up a bear paw from a twelve-foot grizzly. It dwarfed the man's chest. And he'd only been able to kill the huge creature by emptying his gun into it. After that, I was thinking a lot about grizzlies. There'd been nothing about grizzly bears in my *Wild at Heart* scenario. From then on—whenever I started thinking about our trip—I was picturing that scene from Jeremiah Johnson where Robert Redford was being chased into a cabin by a colossal grizzly bear.

Beartooth

It was early August by the time we took off down the Beartooth highway to a trailhead where we planned to begin our weeklong fishing trek. Not every guy who came along shared our vision of sleeping on the ground and swatting mosquitoes as a valuable life lesson for our sons, but to their credit, they showed up anyway. If I had to write a book on parenting for dads, that would probably be at the top of the list: Showing up. Had we lined up for a mug shot, that photo would have shown half a dozen out-of-shape, overweight, gimpy-kneed, overage men and their boys. Charley Bing and his son came along too. In addition to being an avid fisherman and outdoorsman, Charley was a noted author, speaker, and theologian. He led us in very short but very meaningful devotions before breakfast (trout) each morning and around dinner (more trout) each evening. Sometimes we sat perched beside riotous streams of clear mountain water in the pine-scented Montana woods. At other times, our devotions were held atop high mountain balconies, overlooking the jagged ridges of the Beartooth, stretching into a distance dotted by high mountain lakes—the clean, cold lakes we pulled our meals from (lots of trout).

When we first got to Montana and started our *Wild at Heart* trek, we stopped whenever we saw a stream pregnant with the possibility of hungry rainbow trout lurking beneath the surface. They seemed to be just waiting for us to pull them out. Some of us caught more than others, but we all caught fish. Before our first meal of trout, we would cut the heads and tails off the fish and carefully clean them. We even scraped their scales off with a toothbrush before tenderly frying them in a pan over an open fire. Then we'd all go and wash our hands and get cleaned up for dinner. By the end of the trip we were simply throwing the fish into the fire, then eating them with grubby hands that probably still had worm waste on them. We were living the *Wild at Heart* dream. In the mountains. In creation. In the company of men.

One of the men who went with us to Montana was my friend, Jack. Jack was a Southern boy from Memphis (a bell-curve baby like myself) who epitomized all of the manly traits you would want your son to have. Jack was a Navy pilot who knew what it was like to have the crap scared out of him behind the back end of a big gray boat—like most Navy pilots do at one time or another. An avid hunter and fisherman, Jack was a man who did the man dance really well. Most importantly, he was a devout man who embraced life seriously and uncompromisingly—a man who is now buried at Arlington Cemetery. When he died, there were no NPR specials on Jack or comments on his passing, no breaking news on CNN or headlines proclaiming the fact that "Tragedy struck recently . . . here was a man who finished well. A faithful man who was faithful to his wife, loyal to his friends, a patriot, a conscientious employee, and a sacrificial servant in his church. We will all be the poorer for this loss."

When Jack came with us to Montana, he not only brought his son who is a very fine young man himself—a former Marine, Naval Academy graduate, combat veteran, and now an FBI agent—and also another young man he had mentored and poured himself into as well. Jack was

Jack and I doing a high mountain devotional

also an environmentalist. We were over in WestPac about the same time in the early eighties and both flew for the same airline so I got to know Jack pretty well, and I miss him. He was a *Wild at Heart* brother and was the first guy Don and I asked to go with us. Here is a picture of Jack and I doing

devotions one evening after our great meal of . . . trout.

Jack's memory will always be engraved in my thoughts and memories of those glorious Beartooth mountain days and nights—a time when God spoke to us all so eloquently through His creation. There was something worshipful about that time, at least for me.

Far from manufactured things and the comforts of modern life, one feels more connected to creation and part of something powerful and beautiful. In the magnificence of the created world around us, we seemed to catch a glimpse of the Creator Himself, settling the question of *first cause* with a persuasive argument requiring no words at all. Like C. S Lewis once observed, we learned something of the Creator from His creation. At night, we looked up into dark skies, brilliant with stars, and saw evidence of the tremendous reservoirs of power that resides in the universe.

But you don't have to trek the Beartooth Mountains to know that. Anyone on earth can look around them and see the orderly nature of things. That's why I never get into the "young earth" versus "old earth" arguments you periodically hear in some Christian circles. I just see that His fingerprints are all over it—not only in the creation itself but also in our capacity to respond to Him and one another with reverence and love. Love is evident and even recognized as a reality among atheists and evolutionists as part of the reality of our being. Yet not one of them can explain how it happened to be instanced among humans and not the trout we enjoyed catching and eating. I've often wondered how sacrificial love fits in with the evolutionist's survival of the fittest model. It makes biological sense that parents will sacrifice to protect their genetic offspring, but how does evolutionary thinking explain the global dominance of Christianity when Christ Himself commanded us to love and forgive our enemies?

One of my daughters attended the University of North Dakota—a girl born and raised in Virginia who had never spent a winter above the Mason Dixon line in her life. My friend, Don, had spent a good number of years laboring in North Dakota and would smile every time I told

My daughter, Jenna.

him Jenna had called to let me know it was snowing sideways. During spring break, she went to stay at a friend's house in Montana and went fly fishing for the very first time. When she Snapchatted a picture holding a rainbow trout she had caught, the Montana memories came flooding back. I guess girls can be wild at heart too.

Don and I still talk about going back one day even though we are older, "gimpier," and more out of shape than before, and our boys—who carried most of the load back then—have embarked on their own journeys now as men and husbands. But we still think about going back out there anyway. A man's *Wild at Heart* nature does not diminish with age. So whenever thoughts of "out there" surface, I envision those mountain streams, colorful trout, and all the trappings of creation we experienced in that one glorious week.

Although I'm not a professional naturalist, a person doesn't have to be an expert to appreciate how different the Beartooth Mountains were from our own Blue Ridge Mountains or our carefully manicured suburbs here in the East. The scale and scope of those mountains in the Montana wilderness is on such a grand scale it (literally) takes your breath away. But where did all that grandeur come from? How did it develop, and what was it like in the beginning? Did it look back then (however long "back then" actually was) anything like it looks now? As a creationist, I can't help but wonder—when confronted by the irreducible complexity and the glorious magnificence of the majesty that is creation—how so many in the scientific community believe it simply just happened. But that's what I was taught so long ago by my science teachers when I was growing up. First there was nothing. Then there was something.

In a nutshell, evolution seems to be the scientific theory of "things happen."

Origins

Every now and then, I wonder about the origins of the earth and how it was formed. I understand how a stream erodes a bank, and how an avalanche will score a mountain face, but I have a hard time wrapping my mind around how it is that the diversity and complexity of life on earth could simply come from . . . nothing. Even an average guy like me gets the improbability of that. As far as I'm concerned, the fact that we even want to know about the earth's origins—and have curiosity about the world around us—is something contrary to evolutionary development. I'm sure a highly credentialed scientist can explain in technical, scientific terms how the universe exploded into being and how it is that life evolved over billions of years from nothing. But in the end, those explanations always end up sounding like my excuses I used to give to my teachers when I didn't have my homework to turn in. The more complicated the answer (my thinking went), the better chance I had of getting credit. Yet, the fact is created things are complicated—that much we know—so doesn't their creation have to be also? Even a single cell is too complex for us to replicate from scratch, applying all of our intelligence and scientific prowess. Just leaving a pile of raw materials in a laboratory for billions of years is no guarantee of success either. But suggesting intelligent design or an intentional Creator as the causation for life will get you thrown out of most academic circles.

Since I'm a pilot and half my life is spent testing the laws of gravity, the nature of flight holds some interest for me. It always has. Weather patterns, physics, and the laws of aerodynamics are all phenomena I find fascinating. Just consider the incredible complexity and usefulness of an avian wing's design. Even before I became a Christian, I had serious questions about how such a thing could have simply just happened. Science doesn't really have good answers that don't involve incredibly massive amounts of time and spontaneous, inexplicable mutations. Of course Darwinian theories of evolution can't be replicated or proven, but no one espousing this widely accepted premise really seems bothered by that lack of basic scientific proof. As in the children's tale "The Emperor's New Clothes," most pretend it's all very logical and don't dare suggest something's amiss.

But imagine for a moment some poor, prehistoric critter is about to be run down and devoured by a bigger and faster prehistoric monster which is more evolved. Critter "A" (the evolving aviator) is desperate to escape the hungry predator and is thinking, *I wish I could be invisible right now or fly the heck out of here!* Critter "B," on the other hand, isn't thinking about anything but making a meal of his wingless victim. This is "natural selection" at work, ensuring that only the strongest and best-adapted species survive. But wait, the story's not over yet. Critter "A" may not have gotten his wings, but his descendants do. The fossil record shows many creatures with wings, right? How do evolutionists explain this transformation? Believe it or not, one of their scientific solutions is that one day, Critter "A" laid an egg . . . and a baby Critter "A" with wings popped out! If that's true, the X-Men premise of spontaneous mutant evolution is science-based after all.

Okay, I'll concede that's a straw man oversimplification of a very complex scientific theory, but it is one a lot of the scientific community buys into. I know that. But sometimes the most logical explanation (i.e., intelligent design) is the one that turns out to be truest. It wasn't that long ago the bulk of the scientific community thought the world was flat, and you risked burning at the stake to say otherwise. (Disagreeing with popular scientific views these days just burns your hope of academic respectability and tenure.)

But seriously, how did baby Critter "A" learn to use those two very symmetrical and very complex appendages on either side of its body? It had no forbears to demonstrate winged flight, nor could the informational imprint of its DNA convey such expertise. Another logical problem with this "things happen and now I have wings" scenario is that the wing mutation had to have occurred in mammals, insects, and other very different species at the same time. What's more, the multiple wings of bees and hummingbirds are far more complicated than single wings—so complicated, in fact, they seem to defy the laws of physics. At what point did these creatures figure out one set of wings was not enough? How did they avoid getting eaten before their learning curve was finished? Lastly, there's simply no evidence in the fossil record showing the evolution of an avian wing. Fish scales are not feathers and fins aren't wings. But if you start with a preconceived bias, you end up with some very scientific sounding nonsense like the recapitulation theory and other shot-in-the-dark attempts to explain how something came from nothing. Of course, I'm just looking at the world from the middle of the bell curve—not the hallowed halls of academia—but even I know something can't come from nothing.

The alleged link between birds and reptiles is based on finding a bird fossil with teeth. Big deal. I know some people who have teeth and some who don't. If some future paleontologist found a toothless homo sapiens, could they claim all humans are toothless? The same goes for birds—despite what many evolutionists would have you believe. The modern Canada goose is just one example. They have black bills with lamellae or teeth. It all boils down to how the word tooth is defined, I guess. While watching birds come and go on our few acres, my lovely wife, Terry, and I have seen all sorts of birds. Their diversity is amazing. And much of that diversity is based, I'm sure, on having adapted within their species in response to earth's ever-changing environments.

As I mentioned before, I'm not a scientist but I understand scientists' fascination with the question of origins. Asking "Where did we come from?" isn't just a science question, but a philosophical and spiritual query about identity and meaning and one pondered by all of humanity. Although most highly educated scientists were probably born on the outer fringes of the bell curve for intellect (and not in the average, middle part of it like me), they are also very much divided over the theory of intelligent design. I find that fact weirdly comforting.

Intelligent design is a scientific proposition (biased detractors label it "pseudoscience") based on the premise that nature shows all the earmarks of having been intentionally designed. Since Christians also believe in a Divine Creator, most university professors and the scientific community as a whole automatically dismiss the theory. Some scientists like biochemist Dr. Michael Behe at Lehigh University, however, proposed the diversity of life on earth demonstrates it is "irreducibly complex." In other words, it's like a mousetrap in that all of its parts have to work together or it does not function. Nature itself is irreducibly complex, in the sense that if one thing is missing, nothing works. Creation had to show up complete. It is so finely tuned I read somewhere that if any of the physical properties that make life habitable on earth was missing, and we are taking fractions of a decimal place of a percentage, then life would not be possible.

I heard a parable once about two explorers trekking through a dense jungle full of undergrowth who came upon a beautiful garden. Surprised, they saw the garden was laid out in concentric rows of colorful, evenly spaced flowers. Blue and red flowers were neatly arranged between plants with light pink buds and white blossoms. Some varieties were tall and some were short, but the way they were placed set off the colors and shapes so well, the overall effect was very pleasing to the eye. It was obvious the ground had been recently tended, and it was so well cultivated there wasn't a single weed in the garden. Placed as it was in the midst of the tangled chaos of the jungle, the garden was a peaceful oasis of light and order.

One of the explorers exclaimed, "We have to meet this gardener and ask him how he made such a magnificent triumph of a garden in such dense jungle undergrowth!"

So they sat and waited for a long time. But no gardener appeared. Eager to get on with their journey, the other explorer said, "Look, there is no gardener or else we would have seen him come and tend to this garden."

"Maybe we can't see him," replied the other, "because he is invisible. Let's string some cans on a line, so when the gardener comes, we can hear the cans rattle!"

So they waited until morning . . . but they didn't see or hear the gardener arrive. The explorer who was anxious to continue their journey grew impatient.

"Let's just go! We're wasting our time—there is no gardener."

"Maybe," said the other one. "But maybe the gardener is so quiet, the only way we would know he is here is if we station ourselves in the garden, and when he brushes by us as he tries to move down these rows, we will feel him as he goes by!"

So they positioned themselves between the neat rows and waited all night, but by morning, neither had felt the gardener's presence.

Exasperated, the impatient explorer asked, "What's the difference between a gardener you can't see, can't hear, can't feel, and no gardener at all?"

Proponents of intelligent design give a short but irrefutable answer: The garden.

They'd say it's scientifically impossible that organized, neatly cultivated rows of flowers could randomly spring up in the midst of the jungle's vegetative chaos. The impatient explorer sees what isn't there while ignoring the ample evidence that's right in front of him. The other one moves from observing what is there to conclude what is logically probable. We cannot see, feel, or hear gravity but its tangible effects make all life on earth possible. Gravity is a reality we cannot touch, see, or feel, but its effects proclaim its dominion over matter and existence.

Unfortunately, such arguments won't help you if you are a scientist whose professional and reasoned inquiry and research has led you to conclude that what we see in nature is the result of intelligent design. Instead, you will undoubtedly be ostracized and blackballed from any state university job or teaching position. It doesn't matter how credentialed you are or how much of a leading scholar you are in your field of study. Why? Nowadays, acceptance or rejection of the intelligent design theory is more impacted by the social politics of academia than by any unbiased scientific evidence against it. I guess the good news for all the intelligent design people is that they get to know how Copernicus and Galileo felt when they tried to convince the scientific community of their time that the earth wasn't actually flat as most believed—and that this round globe we live on circles the sun and not the other way around.

To mainstream science acolytes, the intelligent design premise presupposes a designer who sounds an awful lot like the Creator in creationism.

Cultivating and Keeping

All of us Christians are (or at least should be) environmentalists due to the fact that God has given to us the responsibility of stewardship over the earth. If you are an evolutionist, on the other hand, it seems logical you'd have no problem with—or at least theoretically not have any opposition to—efforts to eliminate troublesome species of animals or insects that get in humanity's way or that we do not like or find irritating. From where I sit, this would seem the logical outworking of being the fittest species in a survival of the fittest worldview. But for Christians, it's different. We have been given a mandate by our Creator to steward, cultivate, and protect our environment and its inhabitants. All of them. Have we done a good job of that? No. But when you read about political hot-button issues like the oil pipeline in North Dakota, you should know there were Christians protesting the exploitation of that area alongside whoever else was there—and that our protest was not just a political response but one about stewardship. We worry about the impact on the environment.

Is there legitimacy to the theory of global warming? Probably. Maybe. So I'm going to err on the side of stewardship and conclude it should be taken seriously. I have flown too many instrument approaches on cloudless, weather-free days into cities where the pollution is so bad it obscures the visibility. I am all for breathing clean air I can't see.

There is something about nature that challenges us. In some instinctive way, I believe this harks back to that initial Genesis call to not only cultivate and keep, but also to subdue. I hear about mountaineers going after Everest or those foolhardy adrenaline junkies free-climbing El Capitan. I understand. I know what it's like to want to search for a 100-foot wave to ride and the urge to conquer bigger and "badder" surf. In such quests, there is something of a measuring that takes place. It's the desire to assume our place as part of nature, but it's also the need to master and subdue it. Many die trying because like the Creator Himself, the natural world He created isn't safe. Despite our modern technological wonders, His creation still has the power to awe, to instill fear, to surprise us, and to ultimately give us the means of life itself.

In answering the questions, "Where do we come from?" and "How did we get here?" I think it is imperative to think about the logical probability that we come from a Creator, and that we are as the Bible tells us, "Fearfully and wonderfully made." I think that it is by design. We are intelligently designed by an Intelligent Designer.

One day, we just might trek out to the Beartooth once again. It is perhaps the dream of old men to one day return to the joys of their past, but it is one that likely or not I still kind of yearn for and look forward to. But if we do not, we are promised that one day, that fallenness which has left its mark on us and on creation will be no more. In that day, not only will we be given new eyes unmarred by any imperfection, but we will behold a creation unmarred by the "thorns and thistles" of its own imperfections. A creation once defaced, but now returned to all of its original glory. As will we.

CHAPTER 17

LA TRANSCON

"The past is a foreign country, they do things differently there."

—L. P. Hartley

Identity. It's the one word that speaks directly to the "Who am I?" question. We all seem to want to identify with *something*, don't we? We want to be able to say, "This is my group and who I belong to." So we take ancestry DNA tests or join a political party, church denomination, gay community/ Black community/Hispanic community/biker community. Is it possible our longing for identity is really at the core of and a fundamental part of our search for meaning? Being a Republican, Democrat, or *whatever* will not necessarily bring meaning—only a party affiliation—to what might be an otherwise empty life. Neither will being a church member identifying with a particular denominational or nondenominational church. These are simply church affiliations. I think true meaning can only be discovered by understanding the intent of the One who created us in the first place.

Name Game

Some years ago, while on a transcontinental flight from Boston to Los Angeles, I introduced myself to the flight attendants and gave them their flight info as usual. Back in those days, we would give the flight attendants a slip of paper—with the pilot and copilots' names, flying time, and weather at the destination—and they would read that information over the PA (public address) system. After a quick glance, the "number 1 FA" (the first class flight attendant) commenced to grill me about what kind of name *Annable* was and asked how to pronounce it, which I appreciated. Some names were more complicated than others, and those names were regularly butchered beyond all recognition, or the FA would just make things up and wing it on the PA. We don't read those paper strips any more in this new electronic age.

First of all, I doubt anyone even cares if pilots have a name or not just so long as they're competent and "fit for duty," and are as interested as the passengers are in getting from point A to point B on time. Second of all, tech savvy passengers can sometimes know more about the destination weather than we do. Names do tell us something, though. If their pilot came from a military background for example, they probably might have had a "call sign," a kind of informal nickname used around the squadron and O Club during their active duty days. (Think Animal House.)

Sometimes these call signs were a play on your last name (John Picker or Bob Pickering would have the call sign "Cotton" or "Nose," and Bob Willows might be tagged as "Pussy" or "Weeping.") More times than not, though, pilots got harnessed with a call sign for something memorably unfortunate, usually because of some sort of self-inflicted mishap. A "Wheels" call sign might mean a pilot might have landed with their gear up, or "Splash" for ejecting out over the water because they'd ran out of gas and ended up having to give the jet back to the taxpayers. Maybe one poor chap would be tagged with the call sign "Vigit" because of acting like the village idiot whenever he got inebriated. Of course, all pilots came into their squadron wanting an awesome call sign like "Ace," "Mach," or "Maverick" as something cool to identify with. But in the end, most were forever known as "Goose," "Meat-gazer," or "Lurch." In my case, it was "Torch" because I inadvertently trashed an engine one memorable morning in flight school. Those kinds of identity names probably wouldn't go over well on the PA. "Well folks, this is 'Splash,' your CA today for our overwater flight to San Juan . . . ."

Growing up, my last name was always kind of a burden not because I come from a long line of notable horse thieves, but because it's commonly mispronounced *"Annabelle"* and regularly misspelled when someone has to write it down. As a kid, my name was always like a little blood in the water. Bullies tend to circle around like sharks when you have a girl's name for your last name. I wasn't quite a *"Boy Named Sue,"* but close enough. The truth of the matter? I'm not really sure how it's supposed to be pronounced since I've heard it said a number of ways. Sometimes I'd listen to flight attendants say it over the PA, so I could hear their delivery and what they made of it. But however it's pronounced . . . it is my name. It identifies my tribe and who my people are.

After we got to Los Angeles, we had a longish layover, so I decided to do something I've never done before: Google my last name. I found out there's a Hollywood actor with my surname who doesn't look at all like me. There's also a banker in Chicago with my same name. But in my searching the Internet, I discovered something really interesting. The first name on the pilgrim ship *Anne's* passenger manifest was my ancestor, Anthony Annable. Since both of us had grown up with the same last name—one that happens to begin with an "A"—I wondered if he, too, was always first to have to do stuff. The Marines, in particular, love to go in alphabetical order. *"Sit in the front row, candidate"* or . . . *"Attack that hill, candidate!"*

My Google expedition also led me to a cousin I'd never met before or even heard about, a woman named Audrey. It turns out she used to stay at my grandma's house in the summer. And she knew stuff about my dad I wish I'd known when he was alive, so I could have asked him about it. It was my great good fortune she'd done so much work chasing down the ghosts of our collective pasts—going all the way back to Pilgrim Anthony Annable. I was grateful I'd stumbled upon Audrey and her research when I answered a post asking if anyone knew of the offspring belonging to Orseamus Ebenezer Annable. Although I didn't know much about my dad's family (because Dad never talked about it), I *did* know that name. Dad would occasionally tell me he'd almost named me after his grandpa, Orseamus Ebenezer, then he and Mom would chuckle like it was an inside joke the two of them shared. I thought he was just making it up to tease me. Who in the world would name their kid Orseamus?

Think about the name Lazarus. It's interesting the only name Jesus ever mentions in His parables is that of Lazarus, the poor wretch at the gate of the rich man. Jesus honors him by sharing with us his name. Names are personal. Knowing another's name is a big step into relationship. I also find it interesting that God has a habit of renaming people. Abram, Sarah, Jacob, and Saul were a few. Likewise, Revelation tells us God will rename us too one day. A vital aspect of parenting, one supposes, is in the naming because they bestow identity. I'm sure this is why the writers of the Bible took such excruciating pains (albeit excruciating to read) to list the individual names of people throughout the generations. Of course, wading through lists of bizarre-sounding names may seem tedious and irrelevant to many. I find it interesting.

Names Are Important

Names are only just a part of our history and the past which shapes us. Our names are the organic link to that past and the history which has shaped our past and shapes our present. (The name that God might have for us is linked to our future.) We want to know our place in the world. We want to know where we came from, who we belong to, and what our tribe is. Christians believe that we all came from the same set of parents millennia ago. The scientific community now believes that also—having been able to trace mitochondrial DNA taken from over a hundred or so DNA samples from folks all over the world, concluding (whether you believe it or not) we all come from a common ancestor. We Christians were simply given the names of these first DNA donors in the very opening chapters of a book which title means *"beginning."*

My wife Terry's mom was Icelandic, so it's easy to trace her forbearers on that side of the family. A land with a small population of unpronounceable names, her ancestors were probably some Viking marauders. Terry's grandad's name was Solvi, and so her mom's name was Bjork Solvisdottir because her name identifies who she belongs to. The phone book might be a bit complicated, but it makes it easy to trace back who belonged to whom. I also admire the way the American Indians named their children. Some named their offspring after what they happened to see or experience at the time of birth: Sitting Bull, Running Bear, and Screaming Woman. Although impossible to trace back, such names live on in oral traditions carefully preserved to link their present with their tribal history, as do ours.

History is far more important than the Instagram culture might think it is today. Understanding the past is much like watching a movie. If you were to walk into the middle of any movie—say, *High Noon* with Gary Cooper (one of my favorites)—you'd have a lot of questions: What's so important about the train? Why is everyone so afraid, and why don't they want to help the sheriff? Who is the Mexican lady?

Understanding what happened at the beginning when we started watching the movie enables us to appreciate and prepare for what comes next in the story. History helps us make sense of the storyline, and so it is with our own life stories.

Knowing where we come from equips us to understand who we are and why events have unfolded in a certain way. If your life is a mess and you go see a therapist, they will go back into your history to find out why. That's why Christianity makes so much sense to me. It not only addresses the questions of origins and destiny, but explains why morality and ethics are so challenging for us and why meaning is so, well, meaningful to us. It makes sense of the blueprint on how we are to relate to the essential truth of our own existence and how we are to treat others. It solves the dilemma of why there is guilt, love, and sorrow. It also continuously proves itself by showing why and how history has taken the turns that it has.

If you read the Bible as a story (a true story), you'll find there are all kinds of ways to interpret and read it; but if you read it as a story and realize that this history is part of your *own* history, you'll begin to form a connection with those accounts and with the past. The German theologian Helmut Theilke once said that you really cannot understand the gospels until you insert yourself into that particular story. In reality, these stories are universal. I, too, have wept over the grave of a friend or passed by a "wounded" man on the fringes as I hurried off to do something "important." Think about it: How many times have we ignored the privilege of listening to another's pain and chosen to be a blessing to someone instead of rushing off to do something far less meaningful? Bonhoeffer once said that if you do not take the time to listen to the little things in a man's life, how then can you expect to earn the privilege of hearing the confession of their sin? I have seen myself in both the life of the prodigal son and his brother.

Glory Days

So we have all been in these conversations where we are on the cusp of diving into this great story about something that happened in our past, when (fill in the blank: wife/son/mom/daughter) pipes up and says, "No way, it didn't happen like that!" or, "I/you didn't say/do that!" and leaves you standing there feeling like a cheap politician trying to pad his resume. That sucks all the wind out of your "story sails," particularly if it is a really great story. It is almost as bad as someone blurting out the punch line in the middle of a great joke. That is probably because some recollections are like a multicar pileup on a freeway, everyone has a different narrative of what actually happened. Time has a way of coloring memory.

Then there is also a danger in living too much in the historical past. Like Bruce Springsteen's "Glory Days," you can live and relive that which is long gone at the expense of the here and now. (Those days probably weren't all that great anyhow most likely.)

My buddies, who are fellow vets, are now enjoying their past military service far more than when we were in the service, trust me. We sit around and tell stories about the "Old Corps," forgetting there was a reason we could not wait to get out in the first place. Time has a way of erasing all of those irritating and frustrating experiences that caused us to want to get out at the first opportunity. Like a buddy of mine said of his time at the Naval Academy, "It is a million dollar education shoved up your butt one nickel at a time." Terry keeps after me to get rid of all my old uniforms and flight suits, but I can't. I hang onto them and to the memories—even when time has faded them both. Past recollections as I mentioned are not necessarily accurate ones. Excepting of course for my wife. She has a keen sense of history when it comes to things having to do with our marriage.

To understand our future, I think it is imperative to understand our past. Our history.

In the Old Testament, the men of Issachar understood the sign of the times and what they should do about them. I think they only understood their present circumstances and came to a proper perspective, precisely because they understood their time in the historical context of the past. Jesus would point out the importance of evaluating the sign of the times and being discerning. In the larger evangelical context, this viewpoint is sometimes interpreted in the context of an "end times" scenario. I have a friend who lives in that world—where he meets regularly with other like-minded men who sort through current events, wondering when the world will end and when Jesus will have had enough of our nonsense and ride in to clean house. In the Second Vatican council, then Pope John XXIII thought that understanding the sign of the times meant paying attention to the world and its current circumstances, then sifting that through the grid of what the Church is called to do in light of those circumstances. Understanding our own culture is the first step to understanding how we, as a Church, can be faithful in our calling during the times in which we currently live. It's how we choose to act in the here and now that matters anyway. Jesus will come back, but I have no control over that. The only thing I can control is being discerning about the times I live in now and what I do about that. These days, forty-eight hours is my version of long-term planning anyway.

Like a lot of older people, my sister is really into the genealogy and ancestor discovery process. I say older folks, because I guess we have more time on our hands now than when we were working in the salt mines trying to pay our bills. She is seeking to verify a link in the pilgrim chain so as to solidify our family's place in the Mayflower Society, and that link is a guy named Prince Annable. She is putting together the documentation for the society even as I write this. (Prince is a way better name than Orseamus Ebenezer by the way. I could have shared it with the famous rock star, Prince.) I don't know what you get for belonging to the Mayflower Society, but if it's college scholarship help, that ship has already sailed for me and my kids. Maybe it's just encouraging to belong to a group of Christian believers, however far removed, who endured so much and risked everything for their faith and the freedom to exercise it.

History and its connection with our genealogy is also important because there are some sins the Bible tells us are generational sins, passed down from father to son, which is why we are commanded to teach God's truth to our children and our children's children, from one generation to the next. Don't ask me how that generational sin works, I just know that it is true. When you look at the genealogy in Matthew, for example, the very first book in the New Testament, there are some forty-two generations represented there. Buried in that genealogical narrative, there is a side comment about Bathsheba, the mother of King Solomon: "David was the father of Solomon by Bathsheba who had been the wife of Uriah" (Matthew 1:6 NASB). Uriah, the man David had killed so he could have his wife. I find it interesting God would stick that reminder in the narrative. We don't get to pick who our parents are, and ultimately, we are not responsible for who our children become. We are just called to parent them the best we can. In the final analysis, we are only responsible for who we choose to become. There is some freedom in that. We do get to decide who we are and first and foremost, we are the children of God. He has an eternal name picked out for each one of us. If you can't find meaning in that, you won't find it anywhere else that really matters.

It would be interesting, would it not, if we assigned folks in the church "call signs?" We would all want the ones like "Faithful," "Pew Warrior," "Hymn Singer," "Humble," "Donator," "Patient Listener," and "Name Locker." Kind of like a religious version of "Maverick" and "Ace" for pilots.

Ever wonder what your "call sign" would be among your church brothers? Whatever it is, unlike a pilot who is saddled with a misfortunate call sign because of some self-inflicted disaster, God gives us the grace to change the narrative and thus change the name. It is a grace worth extending to one another.

CHAPTER 18

GOOD SHIP PILGRIMAGE

"Only your real friends will tell you when your face is dirty."

—Sicilian Proverb

I n November, just a few short months after the tragedy of 9/11, I impulsively decided to buy a boat. Even though the airlines had slowly started to unravel, and it looked like my job was going to unravel right along with them—and despite the fact that we were approaching winter, long after boating season was over, and despite the fact that we knew absolutely nothing at all about boats—we signed the bank note assuming the debt on a 1983 Taiwanese trawler.

It seems all of my wounds are self-inflicted.

My lovely and vivacious wife, Terry, tries hard to prevent such wounding. Devoted to the art and science of "wifery," she always understood that part of her calling as a *helpmeet* was to stand at my side with a bucket of cold water—ready, willing, and able to dump it over my head—to douse any of the "great ideas" I might come up with for our family. Since I've had some really bad ideas over the years, she takes her role of cold water cowgirl very seriously. She carries it out with all the intensity and dedication of an Olympic athlete or Navy SEAL. My job is to come up with ideas, her job is to see they drown before they can draw a single life-giving breath.

So needless to say, I was more than a little surprised that she didn't immediately reject my idea of buying a boat when I first broached the subject. As I waited for the inevitable idea-killing dunking, she just stood there thinking (she told me later), *Maybe having a boat would be nice one day after we retire.* What *I* was thinking was, *Green light* and *anchors away!*

I was gratified she didn't kill my boat-buying idea despite the fact that our past boating adventures hadn't always been happy ones. When we were dating in college, I had a small open cockpit day sailer I'd trailer around Nebraska, looking for good sailing conditions: bodies of water big enough to sail (without having to tack every other minute), and a day when the wind was somewhere between a howling prairie gale and dead calm. When her little sisters would visit her at college, we sometimes took the girls sailing out on the lake. It seemed we always had enough of a breeze to get out to the middle of the lake but never quite enough to get back in. Inevitably, they'd bicker and fight as we all sat and sweated, waiting for any sort of breeze to move us along.

After reading anything by Willa Cather, you'd think the wind is always blowing across the Great Plains. Except, it seems, when you're becalmed on a lake in a sailboat and it was 100 degrees. Of course then, there was the time Terry and I went camping with my sailboat at one of the bigger lakes in western Nebraska (Sounds romantic, right?) only to end up spending the night in a park's cinder block outhouse of a "restroom" because of tornado warnings. Not just part of the night. All night. When she didn't stop dating me after that, I figured she *really* liked my sailboat, or she really liked me *in spite of* our boating misadventures.

So a month after Terry's surprising gift of a green light, I bought our Taiwanese trawler. It was the first (and only) really big purchase of our marriage that Terry didn't first test drive, walk through, or even take a look at. When we first got the boat, I bought the book *Chapman Piloting: Seamanship & Small Boat Handling,* thinking I didn't have that much to learn. Being an airplane pilot, I was sure there would be a lot of similarities to aviation in the areas of nautical terminology, navigation, dealing

with currents, and that sort of thing. In other words, I didn't think piloting a trawler looked that hard.

What an idiot.

On our very first foray into
the Chesapeake—before we even
got one hundred yards out of the
mouth of the river—we ran her
aground. Thus began our seafar-
ing days, months, and then years
with friends and family. We've had
that boat for going on eighteen
years now, and it's like a member
of the family. The first time we
took our young twin girls to see
Washington, DC, we travelled
there in our boat. Over the years,
we've hosted (literally) more than
a hundred guests on our boat, and
every one of those trips have been

*Jim and Vicky manning the decks
as regular crew.*

memorable for something. Mostly something good. We named our boat
the *Pilgrimage* because it's been a big part of the life journey we've travelled. A pilgrimage with family and friends over the course of many years
and many adventures. Lots of crabs and fish have been caught off that
boat. Lots of wines had been consumed, meals shared, cigars smoked,
sunsets appreciated, and sea disasters narrowly avoided—with friends.

Always with friends.

Friendship

Our friends, Jim and Vicky, are one couple we've had on the boat so
many times, I consider them part of our regular crew now. Like us, they're
Christian bell-curve baby boomers, and over the years, we've watched our
children grow up and venture out of the home together. When it came

time for their daughter, Tammy, to be married, we ferried the bride and her bridesmaids to her wedding ceremony on our boat. True to form, we ran aground before we even made it out of their small marina. All I had to do was to fetch them around the jetty into the Potomac and tie up at a dock where they would walk down the pier like a church aisle and get married. But the combined challenge of a dead low tide and a strong southeast breeze blowing the water out of the Potomac all conspired against us. To get to the wedding, we had to make it over the muddy sandbar at the entrance of their marina. We told ourselves we would *not* be the reason Tammy missed her wedding. So, like Captain Kirk of the Starship Enterprise, I resolved to *give it all she's got*—and after a running start, we powered through—sliding over the muddy bar to the raucous cheers of the bridesmaids below deck. I take pride in knowing that the first leg of Tammy's marriage pilgrimage began on the *Pilgrimage.*

Although typical middle-class Christian bell curvers, Jim and Vicky are actually a pretty unique couple. Jim is a union electrician, born and raised in Miami, Florida—the son of a WWII pilot and Baptist deacon—while Vicky is a gifted Montessori school teacher. They met in their church youth group and they've been a pair ever since. They had lots of good years in Miami when they were first married, but as their two kids approached middle school age, they decided Miami wasn't the place they wanted them to grow up. So they loaded up their station wagon and began driving north up I-81 until they got to Winchester, Virginia where—to our great good fortune—they stopped and went no further.

I've always admired Jim for leaving what was a comfortable life with a good income and take a risk for the sake of his family. And I'm grateful we met them when they visited our small church one Sunday. They just walked up to us and Jim stuck out his hand to shake mine as they introduced themselves. I think of Jim and Vicky when I hear folks complain that churches are cold and impersonal because no one greets or introduces themselves when they first come. If they would take the initiative like Jim and Vicky did, I bet their narrative would be a lot different.

My dad had two great friends in his life, and the first time I ever saw

GOOD SHIP PILGRIMAGE

my dad cry was when one of them died. That kind of friendship is rare anymore and I've discovered the church, and really the culture in general, shows a woeful dearth of genuine friendships. Especially among men. My friend, John, used to say men need three things: we need truth because men often lack it; we need encouragement because men often fail to act on the truth they already know; and lastly, we need friendship, because without it, men tend to pull away. I recently read that the millennial generation's lack of friendships is even more acute than the isolationism marking my own generation, and is statistically striking regardless of how many posts one collects on a Facebook page. If I had to hazard a guess, I'd say electronic media has a lot to do with that. Regardless of the cause, friendship is a gift and to not have that is to live an impoverished life.

The first time we read of Jesus weeping was when His friend, Lazarus, died. *"Jesus wept"* is the shortest verse in the Bible but it says all that's needed, and it is the most fitting of epitaphs one can give to a friend. I'm not sure Jesus *had* many friends besides that Jewish family comprised of Mary, Martha, and Lazarus. I recall it was really much later in Jesus' ministry when He told His disciples they were no longer His servants—but His friends. Friendship takes time and is steeped in shared sacrifices and experiences over the course of more than one fight.

I often wonder how much meaning that really has for folks who have never experienced the kind of friendships we were designed for and are invited to participate in. Friendship is cross generational, and the most noted of friendships in the Bible—David and Jonathan—allowed decades worth of distance in their ages. Thirty years ago, when we first came to the church we attend now, I was fortunate enough to meet an elder in the church named Bob. Because he was a retired Navy commander, we pretty much spoke the same language—which made it easy and comfortable to drop the masks of pretense and be honest in the way shipmates or squadron mates are. He was the first Christian man I'd met who I felt spoke honestly about life stuff, and in a language I could understand and appreciate. Honesty—it was an important first step into a meaningful friendship. Bob would jokingly remind me that the Marines were a department of the Navy and I would agree, reminding him we were the "*men's* department."

We'd talk about how we seemed to have experienced more sharing and more honesty in the military—at the bar in the Officer's Club during Friday night "happy hours"—than we did in the church. Bob was a real friend to me then. Even as he was dying and in his death, he modeled for me what it was like for a man to end well. He was not the only or the last friend of mine to end his life well.

I think a lot about that . . . about ending well. And I'm pretty sure friends are essential to that outcome.

One of my favorite stories about Jesus took place while He was preaching in someone's crowded house. Hearing there was a rabbi who was healing people, some boys tried to get their paralyzed buddy to Jesus. But there wasn't any way to get their friend close to this reputed healer, so they had to take some drastic action. I've always wondered why these guys were so motivated. It must have had something to do with their paralyzed friend—the guy on the stretcher. Of all the personalities we see come and go in the Scripture, this young man is the most mysterious. Who was he? What kind of things could a paralyzed person bring to the table of friendship? When and how did he get hurt? He obviously couldn't play, throw things, or fish, so why did the other boys like him so much? Unable to clean himself, he must have smelled pretty badly at times. So what *did* this young man have to offer these four guys that they were willing to make a hole in someone's roof, right in the middle of a rabbi's sermon? Who owned that house? Did they know how the homeowner would respond to his roof getting destroyed? Would the rabbi be pissed?

Picture this scene in your mind: Jesus is trying to speak important truths to an eager audience when a bunch of noise on the roof above Him starts getting louder and louder. Everyone looks up as bits and pieces of the roof start showering down. Suddenly, the noise stops and they see a man on a stretcher being lowered among a hail of straw and debris. I can only imagine the awkward silence and how everyone must have looked to the Rabbi Jesus, wondering what He'd say and do. What's interesting is that Jesus doesn't speak to this poor, damaged boy using his name, station, age, or by any other label except one—He calls him *friend* and reassures him, saying, "Your sins are forgiven."

It was the first time he'd addressed the young man on the pallet at all. **Friend.**

I think about this story and my own circumstances. Who would I be willing to go all *SEAL Team Six* for by ripping off a roof for their sake? Who would do it for me, and who is willing to take such risks for you? Who can you really count on, and who will weep over you when you're gone? Friendship is something highly prized by God. Moses was a prince and a prophet, but his highest honorific was being called a *"friend of God."*

When I was first introduced to Christ in Pensacola, Florida in 1980, my introduction was to a Savior offering to do something for me that I could not do for myself. And it scared me. I realized He was offering me something I *needed*. It was only later in my Christian journey that those needs changed and matured, and I became introduced to Him in a more complex and comprehensive way. I came to understand there was an offer on the table for something I actually *wanted*—a relationship. It is a vastly different thing to actually know someone rather than simply know things *about* them. It's when you spend time with people during dinner or during some therapy time on a boat, listening and telling stories, that you really get to know their heart and can take real pleasure in their company. You get a chance to see the things you have in common and what you appreciate in the other person. We are invited into their narrative and become intimate with their story. Those moments mark the beginning of a friendship that will germinate and take root.

You become friends.

Finally, when you get to know someone *really* well and when you are convinced of their goodness, only then will you really trust them—trust them enough to let them wound you in those places where sin festers and change is needed. There is a richness about a friend who encourages you toward that which God has built you to become. Such a friend makes the effort to fan the flames of goodness in other men and women by helping them deal with the hard and secret places where their sins lurk, avoiding the light of scrutiny. Faithful friends are willing to face the risk of rejection and conflict to help expose sin . . . because they love you. It may hurt a bit, but these are the wounds of a faithful friend. At sixty, I find those friendships are cherished and rare, and I appreciate them more with each passing year.

Boat Therapy

One of the best things about being with friends is the way they give you the courage to tackle stuff you would never think of doing on your own. In the middle of one of my many boat therapy sessions with Jim, for instance, I decided I wanted to get to the bottom of a nagging fuel leak in the bilge. Located at the very bottom of the boat, the bilge is generally a wet, smelly place where all fluids collect before they are (hopefully) ejected out of the boat via the bilge pump. There had been a slight odor of diesel and a slight slick in the water when I ran the bilge pump, so I figured it would be a good time to see if Jim and I could actually do something about it—and get something done besides killing a few bottles of beer.

The holy place (engine room) is located under the galley floor and all of our boat's primary power systems—from the Perkins six cylinder diesel engine, battery bank, and hot water heater and the heater hoses themselves—are spread about to allow some space to crawl around. Although it's difficult, there's just enough room to get to things that need fixing (wrench in hand) or when necessary, to lift a hatch allowing limited standing room. Jim and I quickly pinpointed the problem as an issue with what looked to be the fuel control thingy on the side of the engine, directly over the bilge, where all the nasty water collects from the crap leaking off this and that before being pumped overboard. All boats leak, I discovered.

Some leak more than others, but all bilges are pretty rank with leaky stuff.

After staring at the fuel control mechanism, I noticed it consisted of two pieces screwed together, so I said to Jim, "We can do this! We'll unscrew this, look at that, buy a new this, and then that will be that."

How hard can it be?

A lot of Jim's job description during such times—other than when I ran out of hands like "Hold the flashlight," "Hand me tools"—was point stuff out I needed to know because I'd missed something.

"Hey, Jimbo, before you ratchet the widget, you should loosen that sprocket . . . I wouldn't touch that . . . . Are you sure . . . ?"

On this occasion, we took the fuel control apart and two things happened: first, two small (and as we discovered later, very important) springs went *boing, boing* and flew into the murky waters of the bilge; second, Jim looked at me after a stunned silence and said, *"That wasn't good . . . . You ready for a beer now?"*

Undeterred, I was thinking a little threaded post sticking out of the fuel control device needed tightening, but the threads were stripped. So all we needed to do, my thinking went, was get it retapped and we would be in business. So we set off for an auto parts store . . . then a second one, and then a third one, before a parts guys finally said, "We can't tap anything that small, but if you go to Mike's garage, I'm sure he can fix you up."

So off we (eventually) went to an old, back-alley garage with a faded sign that read, "Mike's." As we went into the place, a hefty, bald-headed biker of a man who was all pierced and tattooed asked us what we wanted. So I told him, holding up my little post for dramatic effect, "This is the nail that goes into the shoe that goes onto the horse that the king rides. Unfortunately, it leaks diesel."

"Follow me," he said after a bit of confusion. And off we went into the back where there was a '69 Camaro and a late '60s Mustang on lifts amid an utter chaos of tools, car parts, a motorcycle or two, and more lifts, hoses, and noise.

He went right to a table, pulled out a tap, rethreaded it, replaced the rubber washers (which were the real problem) and handed it back. When

I asked him how much I owed him, he said, "Nothing." Mechanics like that are hard to find. So are friends like Jim.

Friendship gives a person the courage to tackle hard things on a boat or in life, and then helps you comb through all of the nasty bilges and problems that arise when life or boat repair doesn't turn out like you expect it should.

When Terry and I moved to Texas after we sold our house and the kids were gone, it was a good logical move for us. We had a house being built, my work was in Dallas, we'd pay no state income taxes in Texas, and four of my five kids lived within three hours from our apartment. But our friends were back in Virginia, and you can begin all sorts of new relationships wherever you move to but you cannot manufacture history. There is only one guy I really enjoy watching Nebraska football with and he doesn't live in Nebraska—he lives in Virginia—and we've been doing that for almost thirty years. I have another friend with Alzheimer's now and he needs my memory. All of my friends are getting older as I am. Life is getting harder now.

If you are searching for a meaningful life, it has to include a friend or two for the journey.

It would be unimaginably harder without my friends to pilgrimage with. I guess that's why our boat has been so important. It continues to forge ties that are more like actual lifelines on this journey we travel together. Over the years, the boat's been a great place to hang out with my buddies, smoking cigars, drinking a few beers, or having a glass of port during some iron-sharpens-iron discussions. It's also been a good place for Terry and I to visit with other couples—talking late into the night in dark, quiet anchorages, lit only by the blazing stars of the night sky, conversing to the music of gentle ripples lapping against the hull. We've pretty much solved all the problems of the world that we knew about and even some we didn't.

Sometimes, when it's just the hombres, we call it *boat therapy*. Every now and then over the years, I'd get a call from Jim, or maybe I would be the one to call him up—particularly after a difficult stretch or a rough

patch one of us was going through—and we'd say, "I need some therapy
. . ." So under the pretext of productivity, I'd tell Terry I needed to get
some chores done on the boat, and that Jim had volunteered to help me
out. Those chores still need doing sometimes. The good, honest labor of
friendship still strengthens us for what lies ahead. We dust off the fishing
poles, hit the cigar shop, grab some Pop-Tarts and a six pack, and meet
up on the *Pilgrimage.*

Sunset view from the Pilgrimage.

CHAPTER 19

TEXAS

"I am from Texas, and the reason I like Texas
is because there is no one in control."

—Willy Nelson

L et me begin this by saying that one of my best friends is from Texas
and is a lifelong, diehard University of Texas Longhorn. His wife is
too. Like most Texans, they're hardworking and optimistic folks. Texans
have to be since the geography and geology of the state they grew up in
doesn't give people much to work with. Texas is a big, harsh, and unfor-
giving place. The state braves the most tornados in the US and also claims
the dubious distinction of surviving the largest natural disaster in our
nation's history when a hurricane destroyed the city of Galveston. Texas
has no natural lakes—just man-made, snake-infested mudholes where
recreation is limited by wildly fluctuating temperatures. A balmy seven-
ty-degree day can spawn an ice storm and below freezing temperatures in
thirty minutes. I've been there when it's happened. And if you're *still* not
convinced, Texas also boasts the largest rattlesnake roundup in the world.
Let that fun fact sink in.

Despite these disquieting truths, my oldest son went to college
in Texas, and my aforementioned Texas buddy, John, got immense

satisfaction ribbing me about how many of my hard-earned dollars were going to support "The Great State of Texas" during those college years. Another son now actually lives there with his wife. Back in the day, I also went to advanced flight school in Texas (which was quite a while ago), so my comments aren't based on a few flimsy drive-by observations but on solid experience and bona fide encounters with the state: swatting mosquitoes the size of small fighter jets and watching the interior of my car slowly burn to death in the broiling sun of a Texas summer.

No doubt about it, Texas is a different kind of place. It is a state where it's still a hanging offense (literally) to plaster graffiti on your neighbor's cow or to expose yourself in front of a corpse. Driving the major highways are somewhat akin to *Mad Max Beyond Thunderdome* where you take your life into your hands by simply merging onto the free for all they call traffic patterns. In Texas, every school district is independent of the others and determines its own policies—a fact which precisely mirrors the personality of its citizens, myself excluded, of course. It is a state where folks want to be left alone so they can get on with it.

I say that because, as I write this, Terry and I are actually living in Texas. I'm waiting to pilot a flight out of Dallas and wishing the farmhouse we're building onto back home was finished so we could move back and start paying Virginia income taxes again. It's worth the money. Unfortunately for me, my employer is based in Texas, so I spend a lot of my time here. It's probably obvious by now, I have a lot of history here too.

It was in Texas where I first dipped my little toe in the murky, brown waters of politics. In 2000, I was elected to sit on our labor union's Pilot's Board of Directors. For two years, one out of every seven days was spent in Texas. It was a painful, two-year long lesson that taught me the simple truth that I am simply not cut out for the political life. My wife could have told me that . . . and she probably tried. My pastor and friends could have told me that too. They would all tell you the bottom line is that I do not have the right political stuff. Nowadays, I take that as a compliment. Back then, it was a frustrating lesson.

Union politics is really no different than municipal or national politics.

It's just another strongly opinionated group of people trying to impose their opinions on everyone else. In government, the financial stakes are greater and more than one representative has gotten caught with their hands in the cookie jar. But as in government, each side in union politics had their vision of utopia, an opinion on how to get there, and ideas about the various means they needed to use to achieve their goals. At some point in the political process—regardless of how well intentioned we all were—our ideological passions eventually turned personal and ultimately made compromise unreachable. The means (political process) became an end in itself. Or even worse, any means started to justify the desired outcomes. I was no different really. I got just as angry, and I was just as anchored in my own narrative as the other guys were in theirs. I remember we once spent an entire afternoon arguing late into the evening about whether we should adjourn early for the day long after the day was over. We were all just well-educated professionals passionately defending our turf. My takeaway? I think a person can have passion or wisdom, but it's rare to see them both instanced at the same time. (Unless maybe you are a parent.)

Sex, Politics, Religion

The advice to "never talk about sex, politics, and religion" looks good on paper, but our culture and media is captivated and awash in all three. You may wonder, *what's left to talk* if we avoid such topics, because we're all like alcoholics and we can't seem to help ourselves from wading into those supercharged minefields. Every titillating morsel is chewed up, spit out, and later reprocessed as news, partly because we live in a time when we want to be entertained 24/7. And boy, are we easily entertained. Try turning on a radio, picking up a newspaper, going to a movie, or clicking on a website and you'll probably be assaulted by at least one, or all three, of those enticingly divisive subjects. You simply can't get away from them.

Despite the fact that these polarizing topics inevitably cause controversy, they do generate an audience and profit. In other words, they help people sell stuff and it's a vicious cycle. We live in the information age with no shortage of information peddlers who profit from dispensing it. As a result of all this polemical discourse, the complexity of life has been reduced to an "us against them mentality," and with any middle ground absent, we now are forced to pick a political side in this self-destructive tug of war. For Americans, it's either the "Blue" side or the "Red" side.

Politics

Politics has long occupied the attention of philosophers as they explore what's required to live the good life. The "good life" is an ideal every commercial on TV uses in their quest to seduce and exploit you and me—the ever willing consumers reaching for our wallets—into buying anything from beer to blue jeans. For some, the good life might be defined by commercial-free TV or an all-you-can-eat buffet. But to the ancient philosophers like Aristotle, politics was a crucial component of the good life we all seek. Through politics, a society established the justice, ethics, and morality needed to create and maintain an ideal city -state in which its citizens could flourish and attain happiness. Politics is the means by which we all were to prosper.

Nowadays, morality is considered the language of religion, not politics. However, there is a new mood of amorality settling in and prevailing in popular culture, and a government that now seeks to exclude *every* religion and religious tenet from public affairs. Although the premise that "nature abhors a vacuum" is still considered to be true—meaning some kind of belief system will fill the space vacated by morals—religion and politics have never really enjoyed a happy "marriage" when these two have decided to hook up and cast a moral vision together.

Historically speaking, politics has always created tension between the moral good of an individual and the external political good of society. But without a *good* society according to those folks who think about these things, the good life for individuals isn't possible in the first place. Politics has always sought to balance the rights and responsibilities of individuals with the interests of the state and everyone else. These days, however, "politics" is just a word you use when you want to discredit somebody by saying something like, "They are just playing politics."

I find it interesting that the political forces at work in Israel during the time of Jesus Christ seemed to be very similar to those we are experiencing today. It was a time pregnant with rebellion and social unrest—unrest inflamed by religious persecution, ethnic discrimination, nationalism, tribute taxation, and tribalism. Jesus Himself was *seen* to be a political revolutionary during this period. (Jesus' exhortation to "pick up your cross and follow Me" was most likely a recruiting slogan of the zealots.) Ironically, it was the pagan Roman governor of Palestine (and not the Jewish religious leaders) who accepted Jesus' defense that "His kingdom was not of this world." However, in the end, Christ would die by the very means reserved for those who rise up against the state, with crucifixion being the punishment meted out for such criminals and insurrectionists. Religious blasphemers were supposed to be stoned to death, but political criminals were crucified. Anyone who has seen the movie *Spartacus* will tell you that. It was a horrific death, drawn out and very painful.

In the last several decades, I think we in the Evangelical Church have been captivated and, in turn, been held prisoner by the political impulses of our culture. It is hard to ignore the noisiness of the chattering voices who are incessantly beating one special interest drum or another. It's easy to get caught up in all this noise and find ourselves being influenced by the voices clamoring for this or that, because some of those tunes may, in fact, be music to our ears. We are citizens in this world after all. We still have a civic duty here in this place and in our community, and the Church *ought* to have a voice in the public square. A strong prophetic voice. The problem is in finding the *right* voice.

William Wilberforce is one of the greatest examples of such a Christian influencer. A member of the British Parliament in the late eighteenth and early nineteenth centuries, he used his moral vision to leave an indelible ethical imprint on his time by leading the charge to abolish slavery in the British Isles with his Slavery Abolition Act of 1834. Besides making a case for a just and moral center in society, the Church has always filled a prophetic function for the state, Alexis de Tocqueville would write this of a young America: "Liberty cannot be established without morality, nor morality without faith."

Kingdom of God

I really began my Christian journey in the early 1980s, a decade which saw churches springing up in shopping malls and coinciding with the rise of the Moral Majority, Focus on the Family, the pro-life movement, and the coming-of-age of the homeschool movement. It was also a time when we evangelicals were finding our voices in the public square. Those voices were more than welcomed by the Republican Party, and "Family Values" was the rallying cry. In the kingdom of this world, if you want to find an evangelical, chances are he or she will be a on the red team sporting an elephant logo.

But this world isn't the only kingdom we are told. Jesus talked about that fact a lot and He constantly drew our attention to this reality: We are in this world yet not to be of it, and we are ambassadors and citizens of the Kingdom of God. Somehow, it seems that we Christians still appear to be a bit confused about the nature of these two kingdoms. When Jesus was tempted in the wilderness, the devil took Him to a high mountain and showed Him all the kingdoms of the world and their glory. "All this I will give You," he said, "if You will fall down and worship me."

Jesus focused on something remarkably different altogether in saying, "Seek ye first the Kingdom of God and all else will be added unto you."

Jesus talked more about the reality of the Kingdom of God than of anything else, although admittedly, I'm no expert on such things. In the Gospel of Matthew alone, for example, Jesus refers to this Kingdom over fifty times, and many of these teachings were unique and central to the message of His Gospel. Luke mentions the Kingdom of God some thirty to forty times, and it's in Luke where Jesus reveals He was sent for this very purpose: *to preach the Kingdom of God.* This topic would be the very last thing the disciples would ask Jesus about, and the last thing Paul would be writing about in his prison apartments, as recorded in the last chapter and the last verse of the Book of Acts.

So what is this Kingdom? Is it an actual place, and if it is, is it recognizable? Is it "somewhere out there" or is it something spiritual? Is it something in the future, or is it breaking into the here and now? Does it have anything to do with the kingdoms we call home and the governments we pay taxes to? Does geography have anything to do with it?

Oddly enough, I think if you were to ask Jesus these questions, I'm not sure He would give you a straight yes or no answer. He would most likely tell you what this Kingdom was *like*. He might share a parable about it or tell you a story. When Jesus spoke about the Kingdom of God He spoke about a relationship between a King and His people, and about good news to the poor and for those who were outcast and oppressed. He would compare it to a child or growing things, like a mustard seed or grain. When He taught us to pray, it was to pray that the things we should be doing on earth are the things that are done in this Kingdom of His. In our kingdoms of the world, we classify and pigeonhole people based on their ethnicity, income, or capabilities. But in *His* Kingdom, every person is to be honored as an image bearer of the Creator who belongs in His family. In our kingdom of the world, we value the rich and the beautiful. Yet James reminds us that's not how it is to be in the Kingdom of God.

Maybe part of the confusion about these two kingdoms stems from thinking about a "kingdom" the way we think of borders and immigration issues. You can't build a wall around His Kingdom. I think when the Bible talks about the Kingdom of God, it is referring to a reign or sphere of influence, one that has no borders and one that is all about relationships. Influence is more important than geography in this Kingdom. It is about the relationship of a King to His people and the relationship of its citizens to one another. It is also about the mystery of relationship of God in Himself, and ultimately, an invitation into that inner sanctum of life with Him.

When the ancient Greek philosophers promoted the role of politics in a city state, it was to establish the happiness of its citizenry. But if you want to know what happiness in the Kingdom of God consists of, read the Sermon on the Mount. This world seeks political wholeness through its propositions and proposals—but in the Kingdom of God, it's found in a Person.

In the 1980s, during the heyday of the Moral Majority, Christians seemed to think that if we could just control the direction of our government, we Christian citizens could steer it in a happy, righteous direction. If we could just have that power and use it for good . . . .

The first problem with that line of thinking is the unfortunate fact that Christians themselves have never really been able to get along together. Christians abuse power just like everyone else. In fact, if you carefully read the Gospel accounts, one of the things you'll notice is that even Jesus' disciples couldn't get along with each other. And it never really got better. Church history is replete with the persecution of Christians at the hands of pagans . . . pagans at the hands of Christians . . . Christians at the hands of other Christians . . . and of wealthy, politically powerful churches.

Power and the Kingdom

As I mentioned before, while I was on a trip with a very long layover in California, a flight attendant asked me, "What kind of name is Annable?" Having been asked that question many times, I gave her my standard answer, "I have no idea—just a name I guess."

But I had lots of time on my hands and a computer handy, so I started digging into the question of my origins—a question I'd never tried to answer before: "What kind of name *is* Annable?" Regarding our family's ancestry, my dad used to say we were all probably descended from horse thieves, and he didn't really spend much time thinking about where he'd come from—just about where he was going. But after a long search, I was surprised to discover that my ancestors were among this nation's first illegal aliens, arriving on one of the pilgrim ships called the *Anne*. The very first name on the manifest was Anthony Annable. Fortunately, it turned

3

out that there's actually a lot of information about this Anthony, and one of the most interesting tidbits I found was that he and some other members of their church were driven away from their homestead because of some theological differences they had with other colonists concerning baptism. So here is a case of a group of Christians enduring all sorts of hardships and trials to make their way to a new world where they would not be persecuted for their religious convictions—who started persecuting each other.

When Jesus' disciples squabbled with one another, it was usually about prestige or future positions of power. Jesus tried to correct their ideas of power by getting on his knees and washing their feet. But they didn't really get it. Like us, they believed harnessing political power meant they could usher in some sort of "kingdom of the world" utopianism even though Jesus Himself did not pursue such a goal. He advocated just the opposite—calling us all to submit to authority—even when it was difficult and acted unrighteously. Jesus' last temptation in the wilderness was probably His most difficult, when the devil offered Him control over all of the political machinery of the "kingdoms of the world" that we evangelicals hanker after today. He turned down this offer only to be crucified by that same political machinery he'd rejected saying, "Surrender unto Caesar what is Caesar's" and "Suffer it to be so now."

His Kingdom was not about that kind of external power. Laws can provide a framework for right living, *but they cannot give anyone the power to do the right thing*, although you may know what that right thing is and actually wish to do it. *Even wisdom does not have that kind of power.* After amassing the unsurpassed wealth and power marking all such kingdoms of the world, Solomon's life ended badly even though we are told that his wisdom still remained with him. Human wisdom is not enough.

William Sangster once wrote, "The saints are the most convincing answer to atheism and agnosticism . . . . The world could not long ignore a holy church. The church is not despised because it is holy: it is despised because it is not holy enough. There is not enough difference between the people inside the church and those outside to be impressive. A church in

253

which the saints were as common as now they are rare would convict the world, if only by contrast."

I am not sure if the power we seek to establish the "good life" Jesus promised will be found embedded in a Christian positional plank in politics, but instead will be found in the power of a Holy Spirit-led church leaving its mark on the world. An imprint that is defined by justice, goodness, patience, faithfulness, and hope. The power of love.

The politics that I think Jesus would have us follow is "Kingdom politics" and a healthy understanding of what it means to be *in the world* yet *not of the world*.

CHAPTER 20

FLIGHT ACADEMY DFW

"I'm pissed! I'm . . . really pissed!"

—Unknown Pilot

Altitude gives one a unique but often distorted perspective of reality. From my climate-controlled cockpit environment, the world looks neat and clean from way up there at 39,000 feet. The snowcapped Rockies look majestic, white, and deceptively safe—almost like a living 3-D postcard—when they are actually an incredibly harsh, bitterly cold, and unforgivingly lethal environment. Distance can, in fact, distort reality. The principle of "moral altitude" is similar: the further you are away from the consequences of your actions, the more benign and excusable they seem. A bomber pilot raining death and destruction from unknown heights experiences a vastly different reality than that of the man trapped in hand-to-hand combat where they smell their enemy's breath and see the look of sweaty fear or hatred in their eyes. Justification is exponentially easier from a distance. The farther from the target you are, the easier it is to launch a nuke that will slaughter thousands of men, women, and children in a densely populated city far from any battlefield.

This is why proximity is an essential component to morality. When Peter denied Jesus, it wasn't until Jesus walked by and looked in His disciple's eyes that Peter broke down and wept. It was when He was close enough to look into the eyes of His friend. Peter showed us we can betray others with our words, and that it's an easy thing to betray someone from a distance. Gossip is like that too. When we launch damaging words from a distance—from a safe "moral altitude"—the scorched earth and radioactive fallout from slander is thus easily ignored or minimized. I think social media has really exacerbated this tendency. Hurtful, damaging words are easily lobbed from the safe distance of a keyboard. (Cyberbullying is a real and tragic issue.)

We all grew up hearing the ditty "sticks and stones will break my bones, but words will never hurt me." Except when they do. The words we choose to communicate to each other are an essential part of the moral calculus of a well-lived, meaningful life. So when I ask myself the question, *What does it mean to live well?* I think first of what we have to say to one another—and looking back—how it is the things I have said, or the things I have failed to say, that cause me the most regret.

When I used to train new captains for my airline, one of the many things I was sure to point out was, "The most dangerous button on this jet is the one attached to the PA (public address) system. Once you've said something to a captive audience of 160–280 passengers, whatever you've just said cannot be *unsaid*." I have to remind pilots of this fact, because part of how we pilots are wired is that we tend to think we are funnier and more amusing than we actually are. Or we think everyone else should find the things we deem humorous to be funny as well. We had one guy, for example, who conducted the whole pre-departure/take-off event like a passenger train leaving the station—complete with a train whistle, he would blow on the PA just prior to takeoff. Others have tried to channel their "inner Chuck Yeager" with long, folksy, Southern drawl monologues about "toad-strangling rain showers" or how we are "fixin' to cross the Red River." You might have heard some of those clueless goof-balls on one of your flights.

A perfect example of misguided pilot humor was when one of our Los Angeles flights had landed but couldn't pull up to the gate due to ongoing construction work around the terminal. When construction was going on anywhere in or around the taxiways, pilots were supposed to shut down their planes' engines so the construction guys didn't get blasted, then let the tug hook up and pull their planes into the gate. After one such landing, the captain told his first officer (FO), "Do me a favor and tell the folks to remain seated until we get to the gate, and then I will turn the seatbelt sign off."

The FO then picked up the PA mic and quipped, "Well, folks, we had just enough gas to get us here, but not quite enough to make it to the gate so if you could please remain seated . . ."

Needless to say, that bit of "humor" wasn't very well received by those particular members of the flying public.

The trouble is, sometimes, our own personalities leak into our PAs, and that can either be a good thing or a bad thing. When one of our salty New York captains was admiring the weather over the PA, he told his passengers, "It is so clear today you can see all the way to f___ Montauk!" He was from New York. So that's how he normally talked . . . but it's definitely *not* how you're supposed to talk on the PA. (Folks of my generation can relate to the unforgettable experience of getting their mouths washed out with soap for using words like that. That was the go-to consequence for having a "potty mouth.")

What you say on the PA can get you fired, fined, or furloughed because words have consequences.

Words

I was chatting with my editor, Cynthia, the other day and our conversation drifted into the shark-infested waters of thoughtless words and how we, in turn, have said things we regret. Everyone has. Words have the power to strike deep into the heart of a person's soul, and the stuff that comes out of our mouths can tear a person down or build them up. Life words and death words.

That's why the Bible has so much to say about our speech and how we are to use it. Over half a century after they are spoken, remembered words still have the power to make a grown man or woman weep, or they could be the catalyst to change the course of a life. Some things can never be unsaid—even after a lifetime. Such words may be all too easy to say when we're angry, hurt, scared, or insensitive. That's why one of the most difficult passages in the Bible to live up to for me is Ephesians 4:29: "Let no unwholesome word proceed from your mouth, but only that which edifies according to the need of the moment" (author's paraphrase). Every word. All the time. To every person. To a guy like me who speaks half a second faster than he thinks, that's a challenge. It always has been.

Part of that challenge is the fact that some words are just so perfectly descriptive but really inappropriate. Words like "*I'm f___!*" This phrase dispenses with wordy, emotionally descriptive narratives on why I'm distressed, and it conveys a pretty clear message on how things stand at the precise moment my life went haywire. In the military, we even abbreviated some of these commonly descriptive words into acronyms like FUBAR (*F___* Up Beyond All Recognition) and SNAFU (Situation Normal, All *F___* Up). "It was a real SNAFU," we would say. "BOHICA" (Bend Over, Here It Comes Again), we'd lament when the "you-know-what" was about to hit the fan. That's when you'd skip all attempts at eloquence and resignedly say to yourself, "I'm f___!"

When I upgraded to captain, the airline company I worked for brought my wife and I out to headquarters for what we call a "dog and pony show." It was three days of "charm school," during which the company attempted to give us a little more insight into how the airline worked from marketing to operations while at the same time marketing the company to us. While we were there, an aviation psychologist came to speak to attending couples about communication and I found his talk pretty informative. He would have us do things like listen to an aircraft accident and tell our wives what was happening as the crew made the fateful mistakes leading up to the crash. Another thing he did was talk about *how* we communicate and how men are dealing with a more stunted vocabulary than women.

Since Terry and I had never been to marriage counseling at that point, I was surprised to find out that we men have ten times fewer words to shoot out of our mouths—a fact that puts us at a distinct disadvantage. To illustrate this deficit, the psychologist asked the guys in the audience to come up with a word to describe being really mad and angry. We all picked the same word: *pissed*, as in *"I'm pissed!"*

Ever hopeful, the psychologist said, "Okay, give me more—give me a two-syllable word for when you are really angry." Our response? We offered, "pissed off," "f___ing pissed," and "really pissed." That was it. This was the entirety of our empty and impoverished word lockers as males. We males were trying to expand our vocabulary. The only tools we had to work with were the locker room variety we use to communicate with one another.

But all humor aside, I think such words by themselves are merely . . . *words.* Some are appropriate in some company and some aren't, and that is why it's important not to get in the reflexive habit of barking out some of these words thoughtlessly—like over an airline PA when you can see all the way to . . . *Montauk.*

Now I know Christians are instructed to "Let no unwholesome words proceed from your mouth," and I used to think those words were the ones on the list of "potty mouth" words my parents kept by the soap dish in the bathroom. But I've come to believe "unwholesome words" (the kind of words we will be accountable for one day) are the intentionally destructive words that mete out death in relationships and can damage your soul. Gossip words. Belittling words. The "You will never amount to much!" kind of words. I have more than my fair share of regrets in life, but the things I generally regret the most are having said things like that. Because words have power—particularly the written word. They are more than unwholesome. They are deadly.

Several decades ago as a somewhat new Christian, I decided to memorize a book of the Bible. Since my own name is James, I thought the Book of James seemed like a good place to start. It was a wonderful experience for me and surprisingly enriching. Like a lot of things in this Christian life that seem like chores on paper, I've found faith comes alive in the midst of completing such "chores." I hadn't gotten far into memorizing the epistle when I discovered the Book of James has a lot to say about words and how we use them, or rather, how we *misuse* them—how they can absolutely torch a relationship and burn it to the ground. In that same letter, James also wrote about the necessity of doing what we say we'll do by keeping our word.

If you could ask Jesus the question, "Jesus, what is the one thing that is the most important thing you would have me do?" I don't claim to be sure of the answer, but I know what his half-brother, James, wrote: "Above all things, let your yes be yes and your no be no." Obviously, what we say really matters. And whether we say *yes* or *no*, actually doing what we say we're going to do is vitally important. (Maybe because our own destinies rest on God's "yes.") In light of this, what's really crucial for Christians is that they keep the "yes" promises they make when they get married and don't bailout when they think their marriage is FUBAR. It dishonors the person they made those promises to, their own testimony as Christians, and ultimately, the cause of Christ.

On a much smaller scale, I get really "pissed" when someone agrees to meet me at a certain time and then they're late. All the time. There is something wrong with that. It's as if the person is telling me I don't really matter, and that my time and schedule are less important than theirs. It also means they aren't reliable, and I probably shouldn't trust them with anything important. Maybe that's a cultural thing, though, since "African time" is a real phenomenon that speaks to a society that doesn't operate by the clock as we do. But punctuality is a good way to practice doing what we say we're going to do and bless others too. The Scripture tells us a person who is faithful in small things can be trusted with larger things also. Our words are a good place to start.

Words and Truth

In *Mere Christianity*, C. S. Lewis wrote about how we can misuse words sometimes trying to sugarcoat serious things so as to be inoffensive. He was responding to the question of what qualified him (or any of us) to say who is a Christian and who is not:

"People ask, 'Who are you, to lay down who is, and who is not a Christian?', or 'May not many a man who cannot believe these doctrines be far more truly a Christian, far closer to the spirit of Christ, than some who do?' Now this objection is in one sense very right, very charitable, very spiritual, and very sensitive. It has every available quality except that of being useful. We simply cannot, without disaster, use language as these objectors want us to use it. I will try to make this clear by the history of another, and very much less important, word.

"The word gentleman originally meant something recognizable; one who had a coat of arms and some landed property. When you called someone 'a gentleman' you were not paying him a compliment, but merely stating a fact. If you said he was not 'a gentleman' you were not insulting him, but giving information. There was no contradiction in saying that John was a liar and a gentleman; any more than there now is in saying that James is a fool and an M.A. But then there came people who said—so rightly, charitably, spiritually, sensitively, so anything but usefully—'Ah but surely the important thing about a gentleman is not the coat of arms and the land, but the behavior? Surely he is the true gentleman who behaves as a gentleman should? Surely in that sense Edward is far more truly a gentleman than John?' They meant well. To be honorable and courteous and brave is of course a far better thing than to have a coat of arms. But it is not the same thing. Worse still, it is not a thing everyone will agree about."[2]

C. S. Lewis would go on and make the connection that the word "Christian" in a similar way has been somewhat hijacked from its objective meaning, and changed to a subjective idea of what we want it to

---

[2] Lewis, C. S. Mere Christianity. London: Geoffrey Bles, 1952.

mean. Lewis would go on and say, "In calling anyone a Christian they will mean that they think him a good man. But that way of using the word will be no enrichment of the language, for we already have the word good. Meanwhile, the word Christian will have been spoiled for any really useful purpose it might have served."[3]

With that in mind, whenever anyone makes a truth claim, or offers an opinion about something important, it is a good thing to first ask them exactly what they mean. As C. S. Lewis so eloquently explained, some words now have different meanings for different people. How do they define a thing? Do we both agree we each know what the other means when that particular word is being used? As C. S. Lewis pointed out, words mean things, particularly when the conversation drifts into the language of religion or philosophy. Jesus would ask that very question of a young, wealthy man when he called Jesus "good." "Why do you call me good?" Jesus would ask (Is our understanding of "goodness" compatible?)

Asking "What exactly do you mean?" is a good place to start. Whenever a conversation drifts into meaningful topics—even among fellow believers—it is a good idea to ask for clarification.

Personal opinions often masquerade as "truth" because those so-called "truths" may be personally believed by an individual who accepts their validity. The "make your own reality" movement of the 1960s initiated a new era in which "truth" varied depending on the viewpoint of the "believer." In other words, you and I are free to believe truth is whatever we decide it is . . . for *us*. Strangely enough, this system of thought coexists with a growing reverence for all things scientific—despite the fact that the scientific method itself requires objective tests before conclusions about what is actually true or false can be drawn.

The years have taught me several hard lessons about words and truth:

Opinion does not dictate what is true. I say that because there is no shortage of "opinionators" out there, especially on talk shows and social media. But if we're being honest with ourselves, that's probably where we

---

[3] Ibid.

get most of our information these days. The problem is that tendency obviously makes it difficult to separate the "wheat from the chaff" when trying to gather facts and get to the bottom of something. In politics, for example, truth often takes a back seat to a narrative that appeals to us. Still, I think most of us care about what is true and what is not. And more than what is *said*, a person's *actions* generally reflect what they believe to be true. Jesus always connected actions and belief, and the three synoptic Gospels bear that out. He modeled what the Kingdom of God was supposed to be like. Luke, who wrote more of the New Testament than anyone, began the Book of Acts with, "All He began to do and teach."

Truth is exclusive. Two opposing things cannot be true at the same time, in the same relationship. I can believe that eating all my vegetables and cleaning my plate will extend my years of life, and you, on the other hand, may believe that not eating anything at all no matter what you have on your plate will. Both beliefs may be wrong, but both cannot be right. Feelings aside, something cannot be true and untrue at the same time if it is dealing with the realm of empirical truth—defined as something verifiable or provable by means of observation or experiment.

Truth is absolute. We may not have an absolute understanding of it, but if something is true, it is true for all time, in all places, and for all people. It's really unfortunate that *opinion* is so often confused with what is *absolutely true.*

So at the end of Pilate's discussion with Jesus in the Gospel of John, Pilate will ask a curious thing. He will ask the question, "What is truth?" on the heels of Jesus' claim, "Anyone who is of the truth, hears my Voice." In the very first chapter of John, we are told that Jesus is "full of grace and truth" and that "grace and truth were realized in Christ Jesus."

So, what *is* truth?

Truth is that which is actually real, i.e. it *corresponds* to reality. It is not something I make up because it fits into an imaginary construct that makes me feel better or fits into my personal narrative or agenda. Jesus was a real person. Even secular historians know and admit that to be true, just as they acknowledge that Jesus was crucified and killed—facts that have been confirmed from numerous historical sources. He also appeared after His resurrection to over 500 people who included skeptics, family members, and strangers. Many well-researched books lay out the facts concerning the historical reliability of His life and its impact on humanity.

Jesus said it like this in John 3:19–21: "The Light has come into the world, but men loved the darkness rather than the Light, because their deeds were evil. Everyone who does evil hates the Light, and does not come into the Light for fear that his deeds will be exposed. But whoever practices the truth comes into the Light, so that it may be seen clearly that what he has done has been accomplished in God" (author's paraphrase).

I said earlier, a person's *actions* generally reflect what they believe to be true. If they think God's ways are good, their lives will reflect that as they seek to know and follow Jesus. They'll seek the light. What about you? If you haven't made up your mind—if you don't know what Jesus actually taught and, like Pilate, wonder *what is truth*—read what Jesus has to say about life, relationships, and religion and decide for yourself if what He says rings of truth and light.

In fact, the Bible is the only religious book that challenges us to test its veracity to see whether or not we find the Word of God reliable. If someone tries to tell you the New Testament isn't reliable and was changed over time, there are many scholarly resources that disprove that claim. We have more complete copies of the Greek New Testament in its entirety than any other ancient document accepted by secular experts—over 2,000, in fact. More copies, older copies than anything written in antiquity that are considered "grade A" historical documents.

There have been whole books written on this, it's called *Form Criticism* and it verifies how and why the Bible is a reliable source for truth. It corresponds to reality. Don't take my word for it. Read it for yourself.

This search for truth might just be the most important thing you'll ever do. If your own pilgrimage toward a meaningful life is based solely on opinion or speculation, you might be in for a rough ride.

And that is the truth of the matter.

CHAPTER 21

NORMANDY, FRANCE

"The enemy is within the gates; it is with our own luxury, our
own folly, our own criminality that we have to contend."

—Cicero

A s one stands in the cemetery of those buried but a small distance
from Omaha Beach in Normandy, you see clean white crosses that
stretch over the still green grass like a large Arkansas cotton field ready
for harvest. Over 10,000 of them. It is but one of many such cemeter-
ies of those American boys who now rest permanently on the soil of
France. There is an Army general officer resting beside a young corporal
from New York. A boy from Texas with the last name of Garcia and an
eighteen-year-old South Dakota lad who are now forever resting side by
side. As you walk through these neatly groomed rows—and yes this is a
respectfully well-maintained plot of ground given to the US by France—
one notices that there are entire aircrews buried together from bombers
shot down long ago alongside chaplains, sailors, and medics. I think every
state must be represented on this piece of hallowed ground. Crosses with
the Star of David mingle together with the others in this field, and it is a
place where rank has no privileges.

When you stand on the cliff of Pointe du Hoc and look down the cliff where 225 rangers scaled its face to silence the German guns savaging the American soldiers below, you are reminded that only ninety of these rangers would still be left standing when they were finally relieved. The hill itself is pockmarked with massive bomb craters where seventeen-, eighteen-, and nineteen-year-old German lads fought and died. Not far from the American cemetery, 23,000 of these German boys are now buried in their own final resting place. Such young boys, so far from home.

Terry and I visited this American cemetery near Omaha Beach in Normandy, France.

We made this trek to Normandy for no other reason than it seemed like an interesting place to see and visit on a vacation. The timing of our trip also fell on the week where the world was treated to a special Supreme Court nominee hearing, an embarrassing piece of kabuki theater that makes one wonder if we are evenly remotely related to those whom we now call the Greatest Generation.

Now, in a day and age when there is a felt need for crying and coloring rooms at many of our most "prestigious" universities for eighteen-, nineteen-, and twenty-year-olds who feel traumatized because someone they did not vote for is now president, we were reminded in this small patch of America in France of a different time when our youth were called out and went to war. I remember when one of my boys was in high school and was having some trouble taking it as seriously as we thought he should, I asked him if he knew how old the youngest Medal of Honor winner was in WWII. Turns out he was fifteen. (When he returned from the war do you know what he did? He went back and finished high school.)

We sat in the airport terminal to leave and watched these painful hearings on the airport TV monitor. A slow motion, national freak show. It made me wonder as we watched: *Who are we? At what point did the United States Senate become the Jerry Springer show?*

It was like watching an uninhibited display of public self-destruction, you want to look away but you can't take your eyes off of it.

As we stood on the Omaha beach itself, and we looked across that long flat sandy expanse at low tide, you feel the weight of history settling in over you like the wet, salty sea air blowing in from the channel. You are taken back to a time when America had a firm united sense of a calling, and a knowledge of who and what it was. When the nation felt a sense of common purpose. The folks back home sacrificed. The families of the men and women who were serving sacrificed. Of course, the over 200,000 men who were casualties during that three-month campaign that was the Normandy invasion suffered the ultimate sacrificial price. The local French citizenry paid their own dues as over 18,000 would die as well. Men, women, and children.

On Utah Beach, the invasion force would be led ashore by Gen. Teddy Roosevelt, the son of the former president of Rough Riders fame. He, too, would lose his life before the Normandy campaign would end. It was a time when leaders actually did what they were calling those whom they led to do, and they did it by leading by example. He would win the Medal of Honor.

Not everyone is as privileged as we were in being able to travel across to Europe for our weeklong vacation. That is unfortunate as this is a place for Americans to come see and to remember. In Israel, every new recruit is taken to the hilltop fortress of Masada as a reminder of the high stakes of nationhood. Our vacation became more of a pilgrimage for us as we walked these grounds reflectively and soberly.

Replica of a soldier hangs from the church steeple in Sainte-Mère-Église.

We also went to Sainte-Mère-Église, which is in one of the areas where the 89th and 101 airborne jumped in the dark early morning hours of June 6th. Almost half of these paratroopers would be casualties. In the town square, they still honor them by a replica model soldier hanging by his parachute, which was caught on the central church's steeple. He hung there for two hours before being captured. He would later escape and return to his unit. It hangs there as a perpetual reminder of the cost of towns liberation. It was costly and it was our kith and kin who footed the bill. Our people.

As I write this, the fate of a Supreme Court nominee hangs in the balance of gossipy, unsubstantiated allegations from decades ago, inflamed by a media struggling to find relevance in the info-entertainment world. When you read this, the matter will have been settled. Whatever happens, the divisive lines will be drawn deeper, and the faith in our institutions of government eroded just a little more. It is hard to take your eyes off of it.

The generation that saved a world at war have mostly passed on now, and there are few who remain. Many school districts I have discovered rarely dwell on WWII, they teach little about it, let alone think on its lessons. To our great loss, I think.

As a former Marine, and as the son of a veteran of a foreign war, and as the father-in-law of another veteran of a different foreign war, it pains me to say this: I think our finest hours are now behind us. We are a therapeutic nation in the process of being entertained to death and it is our most sacred institutions that are now the butt of the entertainment.

Turnings

William Strauss and Neil Howe, authors and generational historians, coauthored a book a number of years ago titled *The Fourth Turning: An American Prophecy—What the Cycles of the History Tell us. . . .* which looks at historical patterns in order to imagine what might be in store for our future. Any imaginative effort, of course, will have its critics and contrarians, particularly when it comes to interpreting history, but their conclusions have a canary-in-the-coal-mine quality about them. It is not my intention here to give a book report. Buy their book and draw your own conclusions.

But in a nutshell, they divide history according to generations, and they find that these roughly fall into four cycles defined by distinct moods and markers. The last two cycles, they call *"unraveling"* and *"crisis."* Crisis—or the "fourth" turning—is defined as a time of self-destruction or sometimes war and revolution when our institutions and institutional life is destroyed. This "turning" is preceded by what they call *unraveling* and as I write this, it surely describes how this time we live in feels. Like our nation is unraveling. This time of unraveling (they write), is characterized by an era in which our institutions are distrusted and weakened, while individualism flourishes instead. The *"I"* becomes sovereign over the *"we."*

Interestingly enough, the Bible speaks of time periods as well, and more often than, not it speaks generationally when it does. Significant periods of prophecy and time are defined by generations. *This generation will not pass away until . . . This is an evil and rebellious generation . . . .* The Bible sheds light on history by unfolding it in cycles—spiritual cycles. Israel, for example, *repeatedly* goes through such cycles, progressing through generational periods of *sin* ▶ *servitude* ▶ *supplication* ▶ *salvation.* A reading through the Book of Judges clearly illustrates this pattern.

When the secular historical exegesis of our own nation's history and the cyclical spiritual nature of God's people is considered, one can't help but see a *crisis* phase looming. Or at least, the potential for one. In many quarters, the Church itself has become an institution that seems to be struggling as it lurches from big-stage entertainment to edgy charismatic communicators in order to offer a saleable product to a nation of consumers. Consumers who see the gospel as a merely personal, self-defining, and ultimately self-serving reality. In some cases, the gospel is used to form individualistic enclaves where opinions rule the day to generate a self-interpreting spirituality. It is one that's often light, fun, and entertaining. If you do not like the message, the people, or the music, I guess you can always shop somewhere else. In some cases, it is the Church being impacted by the culture and not the other way around. As David Wells once observed, we sometimes forget that there is a specter of death that haunts and roams outside those church house doors.

Is there anything meaningful to be discovered in all this?

Follow Me

There was another great book written forty or so years ago by the late great Francis Schaeffer, *How Should We Then Live?* He, too, looks at historical movements after the fall of Rome and follows the scientific, theological, and philosophical trends that mark history. He concluded that any moral value system based on autonomy, and man as his own measure, would ultimately bring fragmentation, chaos, and *crisis*. But the question he titles his book with is an intriguing one.

How *shall* we then live in view of a coming crisis or a present societal unraveling? Or even a personal unraveling? Jesus would tell us to obey those who are in authority, and He would remind us that institutions were given to us by God to restrain evil. He never said either one of those would be perfect. He would also encourage us to actually *die* to self. To love others more than ourselves and that we are part of a body of believers and only function well when we are in community.

It is hard for us Christians to submit to things we disagree with and to people who are disagreeable. John Calvin would remark long ago that God could have put angels in charge of His Church, but instead chose men who are just like we are. He said that it teaches us humility to serve under those folks who are just like us. Can you imagine being a Roman nobleman, centurion, or a hereditary member of the Hebrew priesthood having to take instructions from fishermen and tax collectors? How about from an ugly, dirt-poor carpenter's son with a somewhat sketchy birth narrative?

During the Normandy invasion, the Omaha Beach was a disaster and was going nowhere. There was no plan anymore; many of the officers were killed or wounded. Men were literally piling high atop each other as they huddled behind around the limited protection afforded from the obstacles in the water and on the beach. They were disorganized, pinned down, ceasing to be effective anymore as a fighting unit. The leadership was decimated, units fragmented and destroyed, and it became every man for himself. There was no unity. Only self-preservation.

The key to success in the end was leadership. Small groups of men scratched together from other units who were finally cajoled, bullied, inspired, and encouraged to leave the safety at the water's edge and assault the enemy on the bluffs above. Rangers and engineers led by Brigadier General Norman "Dutch" Cota Sr. began a breakthrough that would ultimately open lanes for the assault troops to leave the water, and in doing so, ultimately save themselves. To stay on the beach would eventually have led to destruction. Leadership, sacrifice, and working together as a unit ultimately led to the victory. The self-preservation and autonomy the men enjoyed behind the limited protection at low tide seemed good for the moment. But it was not a lasting salvation.

I can't imagine what it must have been like that morning on June 6th 1944 to land in neck-deep water, heavily laden with gear amidst the debilitating noise and screams of a shocking, horrific, living nightmare. It would be hard to come out of a shelter no matter how limited to answer a call to "*follow me*" into a hail of what seems like sure death. It would take effort and falling back onto your training, and most of all, trust in the one who is calling you out. Trust in leadership.

Central to the gospel is, of course, Jesus. He was a historical figure in that His was a ministry and life rooted in history. He was also the Christ, Son of God, and a full member of the Trinity. Fully God—fully man. It is hard to wrap your mind around that concept isn't it? But that is what we are told is the case. As I have tried to navigate my own way through this theological and conceptual tangle, I have found that there are gutters on each side of that road. On one side, there are those who see Jesus as simply a good man to follow in His social justice footsteps. In the other gutter is the cosmic Jesus, a spiritualized entity that has no connection to the embodied life that we inhabit—a theology that rushes quickly from the birth narrative to the cross to get to the real lessons of the Bible—lessons found in the Epistles of Paul with a shout-out (maybe) to Peter or John. (James might be a bit too practical.)

Jesus was a human. A man. He was tempted as are we. He struggled emotionally too, at times angry and grief stricken. And He was disappointed in His followers and suffered many of the ailments we probably do. At the very least, He probably got blisters from walking, I would think. Maybe He couldn't carry a tune, which is why there are no great hymns or songs attributed to Him like there are for David. But He loved His mom, and even while suffering on the cross, made sure she would be well looked after.

By living a life of integrity, He demonstrated what that's actually like. A suffering servant, His ministry showed us what to value, what was important, and what it looks like to live well. He also gives us the power to live that way to and to do it *now* by showing us how to appropriate that power. Jesus is still fully God and fully man. Still.

Whatever battles we are in—some maybe even worse than being huddled on a beach with bullets flying around us—His call to us is "Follow Me!" Not just to salvation in the next life, but in this one as well.

I am not sure if our political and judicial institutions can survive the constant assault on their integrity. Maybe they will survive and perhaps one day thrive. Maybe not. Who knows? But whatever the outcome of the conflict, the challenge for the Church, and so for us, is to understand the call to live in the Kingdom of God while still citizens of this world, in this place, at this time.

So for us in the Church, the question remains: *How should we then live?*

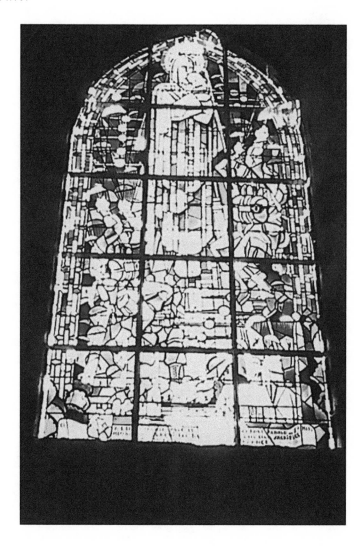

CHAPTER 22

TRANSFORMATION

"Now with God's help, I shall be myself."

—Søren Kierkegaard

Any businessman will tell you it's all about the bottom line, i.e. the outcome of your plan and purpose. My bottom line is that I've tried to fully experience this business of life as a gift, and I've worked hard to make sense of it over these many years—mostly as a professing Christian, but always as a human being. As I mentioned in the very beginning, the Christian life is **not** a fairy tale for grown-ups. Rather, it's a rugged journey based on the call of a Messiah that is rooted in history and marked by empirically verified evidence—one that is logically consistent and experientially relevant. The truth of this is reflected in the lives of those who have answered and embraced His call—an open invitation given by God Himself, and one that is open to all of us. Every single one of us.

Although the gospel's no fairy tale, fairy tales can be useful. They tell us a lot about the yearnings we have in our own life for something better and something extraordinary, which is why I think we are drawn to them so much as children. At the core of each of these fantastical stories lies the principle of transformation: A frog becomes a prince and a maid becomes a queen; the average, scullery maid stepdaughter becomes Cinderella; and the nobody boy, Arthur, ends up pulling a sword from a stone on his path to becoming the legendary King Arthur. In the end, even the witchy old hag is revealed for what she really and truly is (an archetype of evil using lies, deception, and trickery to achieve a greedy, self-driven agenda). Such evil represents the intentional opposition we all face reaching our God-given potential.

Likewise, all great movies reveal something in the life of the protagonist that challenges them to become a better person—one who embraces something outside of themselves. Often, this "becoming" results from experiencing the unexpected as the hero/heroine is taken from an average, mundane life and forced to confront the extraordinary. Their choice in that moment reveals who they really are, or what perhaps they will become. Our post (anti) Christian culture recognizes this, and we see it reflected in the commercial products and advertising slogans enticing us to change into something better than we are (albeit through the use of their products). The visual sleight of hand we've all come to expect in movies and ads baits us with the promise of an external quick fix, and many are eager to access this temporary transformation instead of seeking the internal, lasting change God wants to create within human hearts.

Most commercial products are intentionally advertised to convince us we'll be changed from someone who's simply average to someone who's amazing—if we'll just diet to lose weight with their program, use their makeup, wear their clothes, or drive their car. And it just might work . . . for a little while. We envision ourselves as the actors in these dazzling commercial stories, and see ourselves on that Harley or in that size four dress. All the money we have to spend is worth it if we can only look . . . and maybe be . . . just like *that*. All desired transformation has its sights set on something. We want to be accepted and admired for who we are— or what is more likely the case—who the culture thinks we *should* be. And most of us are convinced we need these external, commercialized things to help achieve cultural approval. As Oscar Wilde so delicately put it, "We live in an age where only the unnecessary things become our only necessities."

It's not that we really want to change into something different, so much as we have a latent need felt deep down in our souls, which whispers to us, "You were built for something better than this." Deep within us we long for acceptance and to be understood.

As children, we see who is popular and we imitate them in what they wear and how they act. I was no different. In the fall of 1969, when I was attending Plaza Junior High School in Virginia Beach, Virginia, discernibly cool teens were wearing Levi corduroys. Cuffed at the bottom and worn with a wide belt, they rode low at the waist advertising to everyone that here was a person with the right stuff. At the time, we weren't allowed to wear jeans to school, and the girls were not allowed to wear pants. (And yes, this was a public school where administrators decided what was appropriate to wear.) Of course, my goal was the same as every other kid in that school—to be accepted by looking like everyone else.

But every year in August, my mom would take my sister and me shopping on our yearly pilgrimage to buy school clothes at Roses Department Store. Once there, she would naturally gravitate to the *"We-can't-give-these-things-away"* discount-sales racks where all manner of hideous trousers and shirts hung like a polyester colony of lepers. It was the rack of clothes where dreams of fitting in at school went to die. Unfortunately, my mom quickly located a pair of brown, plaid bell bottoms and a green polyester pullover and was delighted at the price. My sister thought it was hilarious, but I was mortified. I envisioned looking like a cross between Elvis and Kermit the frog.

At the very outset of this Christian pilgrimage, transformation is communicated to us as something to be highly valued. And we all pretty much agree on what we should be transforming ourselves into. I think the Bible is crystal clear on that. But I've come to discover there is real disagreement in the Christian community over how one actually achieves that goal. Certainly, the Apostle Paul makes a great case in his multiple calls for imitation—exhorting us to imitate him as he imitates Christ. Likewise, in our churches and communities (be they local or global), we are to imitate people of faith who are imitating Jesus—people bearing the fruit of the Holy Spirit as evidence of authentic faith. But God is in the business of transformation. He loves us too much to leave us as we are.

Although the Bible is littered with transformational stories, they may seem distant and irrelevant to us even as we appreciate the vital message of such accounts. It is hard to connect to a 4,000-year-old shepherd with multiple wives even while we intellectually grasp the principle behind his story. And I have never seen a donkey speak. Fortunately, the modern world is rich with amazing stories of transformation, and it isn't hard to find them. There are thousands, probably millions of them, many unique and some riveting. In one, a Kenyan street boy and his world are radically changed after he finds Christ. In another, an Ivy League professor and noted theologian leaves the spotlight and finds his purpose caring for a young man who's severely handicapped. Others describe Islamic terrorists and mafia Dons coming to Christ and radically morphing into different people—people who are good and radically different.

These modern accounts are encouraging but may still seem remote because we don't see ourselves in their narrative. I am not a mafia Don. I am simply an average dude. Bell-curve babies live in the forgotten world of the average and mundane. There are no novels or great movies written about a man who faithfully goes to work every day to a job he does not enjoy, who stays faithful to his wife and sacrifices for his family, and whose "ministry" might be stacking chairs at the end of a Sunday morning service. But make no mistake, that man has been changed. We may live on the bell curve but God does not grade on one. This change that takes place within us marks the beginning of our expedition, not the end. It is a metamorphoses.

This is why I believe our own stories are so important to tell and celebrate with one another. We need the encouragement. The journey we are on is a shared one, and it is one that has repeated itself over and over again throughout the millennia. No one still living has yet to arrive at that place where the race has been finished, and the "*well done*" accolades have been meted out. We are all still running this race and fighting an ongoing battle with an implacable, invisible enemy. Like the pilgrim Christian on his journey to the Celestial City, we soldier on. Our personal faith stories help us motivate each other to stay the course, pursuing love and good deeds in the mundane, everyday world of the average bell-curve believer.

I've seen a forty-year-old felon change from a seriously unfaithful, hard drinking, irresponsible husband and father, who never once in ten years of marriage acknowledged it or her with a card, a bouquet of flowers, or a kind word. She didn't even have a wedding ring. Then they called us up one night to come over and pray with them because he had gotten her best friend pregnant, and they were in the middle of a mess and at the end of their rope. It's hard for a man who is African American and a felon to get a job. It's even harder for that man if he had no role model to help him rise above his history. Yet I have seen this guy stay with his wife even when they were separated (he was living in a car and she in a shelter) and even when he went to jail for a few years. I have seen this man slowly transform into a dad who prays for his family and himself on his way to work—one who is stepping up to do the man dance as best as he knows how—not perfectly, not all the time, but with a changed agenda that's transforming him. It makes me think about praying for my now grown-up kids more. His transformation fuels my own. It makes me want to examine my own agenda. He is a friend and a brother.

On the other end of the economic spectrum, I've seen friends and brothers who are very educated and mature professionals fail in their most intimate of relationships. But I've also seen some of those same men rise like the proverbial phoenix from the ashes of their failures by laying hold of biblical truths with the power to transform their lives into living testimonies of a loving, resurrected Christ. Those folks have become a tremendous encouragement to me.

In the midst of our Christian communities, transformations like these are occurring all around us. The change in people may happen in little stages, or it may happen in a dramatic all-of-a-sudden kind of way that leaves us astonished. Like some kind of spiritual alchemy, a leaden heart becomes gold. Faith and belief become embodied and relevant in the choices and priorities that shape a life. For many of us evangelicals, a lot of energy and time in church is spent making sure we believe the "right things." (As opposed to *that other church* where they apparently believe the wrong things.) But knowing is not the same as being. In fact, the Bible warns us that mere (head) knowledge can lead to a kind of intellectual arrogance. Acquiring information becomes an end in itself instead of the transformative means to a changed and repentant heart. Somewhere along the trajectory of this journey, belief must be turned into action, and it is in those critical moments that transformation takes place.

I, too, am being transformed day by day. I'm not the same man I was when I started this little memoir, and I won't be the same man when it is read.

But such is our faith that we are not allowed the luxury to continually march in place.

Semper Fi.

ACKNOWLEDGEMENTS

I want to thank Dr. Don Den Hartog and my shipmate, Jim Pool, for relentlessly encouraging me to write a book. Thanks also needs to go out to my editor, Cynthia Still, for her heroic efforts in editing a work by a guy who doesn't know the difference between a pickle and a participle. A very experienced editor, both in the technical field and literary, she was the invisible wind beneath the wings of many a published work, and I was thankful she agreed to do mine.

Since my wife, Terry, and I have five adult children and a growing cohort of grandchildren, this book started out as a memoir of sorts for my family. Like Solomon sharing his proverbs with his own offspring, my goal was for my amazing kids and grandkids to learn something about life from what I've experienced from my own pilgrim journey. The good, the bad, and the ugly. And to better understand the guy who is their father and grandfather.

Kate is married to a career Navy officer, and they have three beautiful daughters of their own: Sabrina, Sarah, and Simone. Kate is a Type 1 diabetic and she deals with that challenge with the same discipline and grace as she did my parenting. Our oldest son, Alex, is an American Airlines first officer on the 737–800 based out of DCA where I was also based for almost thirty years, and flies with the same guys and gals (now captains) whom I did years ago. Not to be outdone, our younger son is a captain on a 175 in DFW for Envoy, the American affiliate, and is married to an

American flight attendant. Our youngest two are twins, a set of remarkable young ladies who are both pilots as well. Jenna graduated cum laude from the University of North Dakota and is a pilot with Envoy. Meanwhile, her sister, Victoria, is a senior scholarship, dean's list student at the University of Oklahoma. She is not only a commercially rated pilot and flight instructor, but the wife of a former Navy man and mother of little June, our youngest granddaughter.

Although originally intended for family alone, I have elected to share my stories with a wider audience. Why? I realized my trajectory from youthful folly to relative wisdom is a universal one: the moral pitfalls and safety zones I learned to navigate through experience are really similar for all of us. My mistakes and successes are not so different from yours. Neither is my journey. Like you, I am forced to make choices as an individual soul while traveling alongside family, friends, and coworkers I am impacting with my choices—just as they are impacting me too.

I am particularly grateful for the impact of churches and organizations like RZIM, and the many faithful laborers who toil in the shadows of these ministries and churches.

Lastly, I want to thank God whom I have let down so many times, but yet has blessed me beyond measure. Sometimes distant, sometimes so close that I can snatch the echos of eternity in His voice, I know that He has never changed, nor has He ever moved, and has ever loved me. It is I, the pilgrim, moving ever so slowly and intentionally toward this one final destination.

There's no escaping this. We are all such *pilgrims*.

CPSIA information can be obtained
at www.ICGtesting.com
Printed in the USA
LVHW040747201219
641169LV00001B/2/P